MW00826931

BIG ISLAND
JOURNEY

*"Ua hala nā kūpuna,
a he ʻike kōliʻuliʻu wale nō kō keia lā,
i nā mea i ke au i hope lilo, iō kikilo."*

*"The ancestors have passed on;
today's people see but dimly times
long gone and far behind."*

—MARY KAWENA PUKUI

A Note on Names

Throughout the book, authentic Hawaiian names and spellings have been used except for the island of Hawai'i, which is universally referred to as "the Big Island." The Hawaiians did not speak of Moku Nui, which would have been their wording for "big island"; instead they spoke of Hawai'i. Today the entire state is called "Hawai'i." How this confusion happened is not quite clear. Historians think that when Kamehameha I united the islands under one rule while already reigning over Hawai'i Island, the expanded kingdom may simply have been considered as a part of his home base. Presently the name Hawai'i Island or Island of Hawai'i is gaining more usage and respect, a process which started with the Hawaiian Renaissance and is now backed by State agencies and departments. For simplicity, however, we have chosen mostly to use the common reference.

Copyright © 2009 by Mutual Publishing
No part of this book may be reproduced in any form or by any electronic or mechanical means, including information storage and retrieval devices or systems, without prior written permission from the publisher, except that brief passages may be quoted for reviews.

All photographs are owned and copyrighted by the photographer/illustrator/archives that appear in the credit at the end of the caption pertaining to the image or are otherwise stated elsewhere. No image may be used in any form or for any use without permission.
All rights reserved.

Design by Leo Gonzalez

ISBN-10: 1-56647-917-7
ISBN-13: 978-1-56647-917-2

First Printing, October 2009
Second Printing, October 2015

Library of Congress Cataloging-in-Publication Data
Schweitzer, Sophia V.
    Big Island journey : an illustrated narrative of the Island of Hawai'i / Sophia V. Schweitzer
        p. cm.
Includes bibliographical references and index.
ISBN-13: 978-1-56647-917-2 (alk. paper)
ISBN-10: 1-56647-917-7 (alk. paper)
1. Hawaii Island (Hawaii)—Pictorial works. 2. Hawaii Island (Hawaii)—History—Pictorial works. 3. Hawaii Island (Hawaii)—History, Local—Pictorial works. I. Title.
DU628.H28S39 2009
996.9—dc22
                                    2009034742

Mutual Publishing, LLC
1215 Center Street, Suite 210
Honolulu, Hawai'i 96816
Ph: 808-732-1709 / Fax: 808-734-4094
email: info@mutualpublishing.com
www.mutualpublishing.com

Printed in Taiwan

BIG ISLAND JOURNEY

AN ILLUSTRATED NARRATIVE OF
THE ISLAND OF HAWAI'I

Hawaii **Tribune**🔶**Herald**   **West Hawaii Today**

Hilo Bay, Hawaii

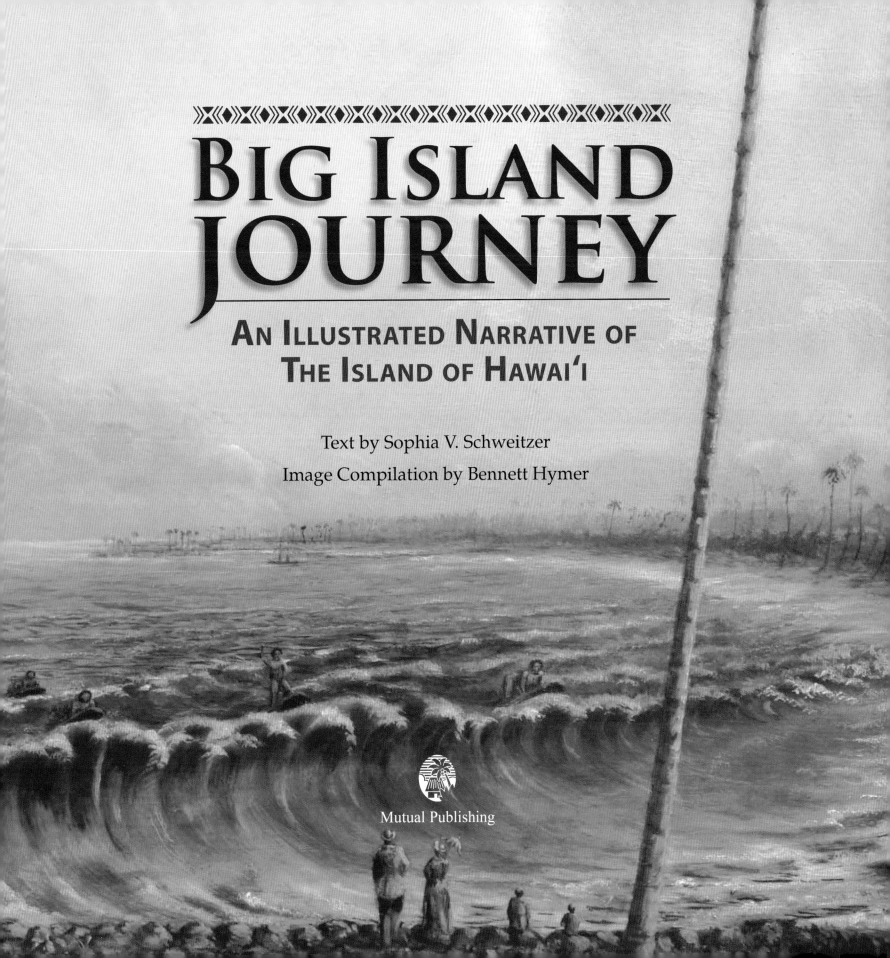

BIG ISLAND JOURNEY

AN ILLUSTRATED NARRATIVE OF THE ISLAND OF HAWAI'I

Text by Sophia V. Schweitzer

Image Compilation by Bennett Hymer

Mutual Publishing

Previous pages: Nineteenth-century missionaries did not approve of any water-related activity that exposed the flesh, but the Hawaiian love of he'e nalu, the sport of board surfing, was stronger than missionary remonstrances. It was a practice steeped in legend and practiced with fervor. Today, surfing remains a favorite activity. Fiberglass and other lightweight materials have replaced the

koa, breadfruit, and wiliwili wood traditionally used to make the boards. [Don Severson Collection]

Above: Noted photographer Ray Jerome Baker (leaning on car) always packed provisions as well as friends as he toured the Big Island. Circa 1920s. [Baker-Van Dyke Collection]

FOREWORD

When *Big Island Journey: An Illustrated Narrative of the Island of Hawai'i* first appeared in the fall of 2009, it quickly became a publishing icon. Its community photo album approach to the island's history immediately made the book a favorite to Big Islanders. Its vintage images included most of the island's major history—important events, per-

sonages—while the newer documentary stills from modern-day photographers captured disappearing ways of life.

With this release of a new edition differing only in fewer photo pages but including the entire narrative, Big Islanders can again enjoy their rich, diverse history.

Big Islanders are proud and conscious of their history. The island of Hawai'i holds it alive and dynamic, with many historical sites and museums record-ing and commemorat-

ing the Island's past: Volcano House, Pacific Tsunami Museum, Lyman House Memorial Museum, Laupa-hoehoe Train Museum, Ellison Onizuka Visitor Center, Kona Historical Society, Hulihe'e Palace, Pu'ukoholoa Honaunau National Historic Park, Mo'okini Heiau, Mokuaikaua Church, Keal-akekua Bay, Waipi'o Valley, historic Hilo town, and Parker Ranch.

We at the *Honolulu Star-Adver-tiser,* also publisher of *Hawai'i Tri-bune Herald* and *West Hawai'i Today,* the Big Island's two dailies, know how much people in Hawai'i value their past as a connection to their roots. Our daily coverage of island news becomes tomorrow's history and our archives of stories and photos become source material for historians and scholars.

Participating in the publishing of this new edition of *Big Island Journey* is our way of sharing in keeping Hawai'i's history alive and making it easily accessible and enjoyable so it can help guide us into the future.

—Dennis Francis, President
Hawaii Tribune Herald, West Hawaii Today

TABLE OF CONTENTS

⟩⟨◇⟩⟨◇⟩⟨◇⟩⟨◇⟩⟨◇⟩⟨

This early 1900s photo shows a steam engine being used to harvest koa lumber in Pāhoa. The flooring used in homes at the time was made from either koa or 'ōhia trees. [Richard Otaki Collection]

ACKNOWLEDGMENTS

So many helped. *Big Island Journey* could not have been completed without the support and assistance of numerous people, many of whom volunteered their time. A team effort involving many persons and institutions was indispensable to complete this book

We are indebted to the historians, translators, authors, artists, and photographers who recorded their observations and understandings of the Big Island in both text and imagery. Without their journals, drawings, log books, notes, travel accounts, and photos *Big Island Journey* could not have been researched or compiled. We are also indebted to the people who from ancient times through today have given the island its unique and colorful history.

Among the present sources who provided counsel and generous insights in preparing the text were Sheree Chase (Kona Historical Society), Agnes Conrad, John Cross, Suzanne Hill, Arnold Hiura, Robert McLaren, Maile Melrose, Barry Mizuno, Frank Morgan, Jan Morgan, Claude Onizuka, Bill Shontell, Walter Steiger, and Lynn Wolforth. Thanks are also due to the State of Hawai'i DBEDT Library for providing facts and statistics, the staff at the Bond Memorial Public Library in North Kohala, especially Dawn Shibano and Joleen Soares, for their patient assistance, and to longtime members of the Big Island's many communities, who provided information and assistance in small and large ways.

Without the dedicated staffs, past and present, who catalogue and document at Hawai'i's archives, there would be few photographs available for either enjoyment viewing or historical research. Hawai'i has been fortunate to have many excellent repositories whose missions include not only preserving but making visual collections accessible to the public.

A special mahalo to the following, who help maintain these photo collections and assist the people of Hawai'i to use them: Alice Clark at Pacific War Memorial Association; Judy Kearny at Hawaiian Mission Children's Society; Barbara Dunn at Hawaiian Historical Society; Pauline Sugino at Honolulu Academy of Arts; Desoto Brown, Leah Caldeira, Deanne Dupont, and Charlie Myers at Bishop Museum; the entire staff at Hawai'i State Archives; Libby Burke at Lyman House Museum; and Jill Olson and Pixie Navas at Kona Historical Society.

Those providing assistance in organizing the photos, preparing captions, integrating text with images, or helping to obtain photo permissions were Ernest Bouvet, Gavan Daws, George Engebretson, Wayne Levin, Karen Lofstrom, Kepa Maly, Ken Okimoto, James Raschick, Danny Simon, Gordon Bryson, longtime members of the Waimea community, and Kiyomi Yoshimatsu.

Appreciation is due to present and former staff of Mutual Publishing who provided the infrastructure support necessary for the completion of this large undertaking, particularly Jane Gillespie, Kyle Higa, Emily Lee, Lani Miyahara, Erika Roberts, Dawn Sueoka, Elisa Tsukayama, and Courtney Young.

And thanks to Hawai'i's photographers of both bygone eras and the present day, without whom there would not be the photographs with which to create illustrated narratives.

And finally a very special thanks to our significant others, Rick Gordon and Galyn Wong, for enduring and tolerating us while we worked on and finished the project. Your generous and loving spirit was much appreciated.

Needless to say, errors and omissions are entirely our doing.

This photo of Hilo Bay was taken before Hilo had grown into Hawai'i's second city and construction had altered the waterfront. A man in an outrigger canoe navigates Wailoa Pond. Around the bay, frame houses nestle in lush vegetation. Circa 1900s. [Baker-Van Dyke Collection]

Moʻokini Heiau ○   Kamehameha Statue
Hāwī ●   ○ ● **Kapaʻau**
Māhukona ●

KOHALA

Waipiʻo ●   **Honokaʻa**
●
Paʻauilo ●
Kawaihae ●   **Waimea** ●   Laupāhoehoe   ● **Papaʻaloa**
Puʻukoholā Heiau ○
Puakō ●   **HĀMĀKUA**
Puakō Petroglyphs ○   **HAWAIʻI**

ʻANAEHOʻOMALU BAY   ● **Honomū**
Waikoloa ●   Pepeʻekeo ●
●   ● **Onomea**
Puʻuanahulu ●
MAUNA KEA
KEĀHOLE   **HILO**
POINT   **KONA**   ● **Hilo**

Honokōhau ●
Ahuʻena Heiau ○ ● **Kailua-Kona**   Keaʻau ●
Huliheʻe Palace ○ ●
● **Keauhou**
PUNA
● **Pāhoa** ● **Kapoho**
KEALAKEKUA BAY   Volcano
Puʻuhonua o Hōnaunau ○   House ● **Volcano**
MAUNA LOA
● **Hoʻokena**   **Kalapana** ●
KAʻŪ

● **Miloliʻi**   **Pāhala** ●

● **Honuʻapo**
Nāʻālehu ●

KA LAE
(South Point)

Hawaiian
Islands

PREFACE

Big Island Journey was originally intended as an illustrated history or narrative. While there have been many illustrated books about Big Island life and history, most focused on a specific subject or geographical area. An earlier Mutual book, *Hawai'i Looking Back,* had been well received, and we wanted to follow up with a similar Big Island volume.

When we began our photo search, we quickly discovered that the Big Island is rich not only in history but also in visual images that record its past. Archives, including the Bishop Museum and Hawai'i State Archives on O'ahu, and the Lyman House Museum and Kona Historical Society on the Big Island, have maintained large collections of photographs pertaining to the Big Island. The availability of so many images made us reconsider our focus and produce less an informal illustrative history and more a community photo album.

The shift in emphasis made even more sense when private contemporary collections became accessible from Franco Salmoiraghi, Mary Ann Lynch, and Boone Morrison, who had all been, or still are, residents of the Big Island. Their work visually recorded places, people, and lifestyles of the 1970s and 1980s that had changed dramatically. Richard Otaki, the proprietor of the former Ace Photo Studio, had in his collection some unusual images of the second half of the twentieth century. The Pacific War Memorial Association's collection of Camp Tarawa images was a priceless resource for coverage of the war years, particularly of the Marine divisions who had trained at Waimea and fought at Iwo Jima and other places in the Pacific. For the present day, the photographs of Doug Peebles, Kucera Design and Ski Kwiatkowski was invaluable. And our visual coverage of pre-Western contact Hawai'i would not have been possible without the art of Big Island resident and native, artist Herb Kawanui Kāne, who very generously allowed his work to be used. Unfortunately, we had limited access to family photos that could have provided visual recollections of work, recreation and family life in days gone by.

Even aiming at creating a community photo album had its share of difficulties. Not every event or person could be integrated without losing cohesiveness in the chapters we had designated according to large periods of time. In general, what was never photographed or illustrated had to be left out, along with what didn't fit into convenient subject groupings within a chapter. There are thus omissions and gaps of subjects that belong in a Big Island history.

We took poetic license in arranging material by using photos of a later period to illustrate an earlier era, particularly for nineteenth-century Hawaiian life and the sugar industry, including immigrant life. Until the late 1880s, photos were scarce or limited, as photography was just getting started. Also, where a subject was significant in more than one time period we sometimes were able to cover it only once.

Compiling a book like *Big Island Journey* makes one appreciate what a unique place the island is. While the island has changed over the past two centuries, there is still a sense of historic place here, much more so than on any of the other islands. Reminders of the past are everywhere—architectural ruins, old battlefields, remnants of rock walls and heiau, petroglyphs, old buildings, abandoned sugar mills, churches, ethnic pageants and celebrations.

One wonders what will appear in a similar picture book or a later edition fifty years from now of *Big Island Journey.* Certainly there will be much material for the chapter "Towns and Places" as villages become towns, towns become cities, the suburbs become the city, and new developments take place. A "Then and Now" chapter of aerials will probably be needed to show the dramatic effects of population and economic growth. (Hopefully pristine areas will not have been obliterated by the works of man.) A section on "Hawaiian Ways" should show more cultural traditions being practiced and more social and political gains for the descendants of Hawai'i's original settlers. Hopefully there will be no need to expand the coverage of natural forces and their devastation by updating coverage of nature's fury. The "On the Road" section should be the most interesting—what new lifestyles have emerged, and which of the present ones will have dramatically changed or vanished. And finally, there should still be the familiar images of what makes the island so special—paniolo, ethnic celebrations, gatherings, small-town charm and ambience, and Island families going about Island life.

Note: Our usage of the term "Big Island" is explained on page ii. Also, current population figures are from State of Hawai'i sources.

INTRODUCTION

The sugar industry created a new class of wage-earners among the dislocated Hawaiian community, who, instead of tending their taro farms or fishponds, now earned an hourly salary on the plantations or as manual laborers, such as these roadworkers at ʻOlaʻa in 1921. [Hawaiian Historical Society]

Of all the islands, the Big Island is the largest, the most varied, and home to the most dramatic contrasts in terrain and climate. It was the first island settled and is at the root of all Hawaiian history. During pre-contact times, it was the most populous island, and its chiefs were among the most powerful.

In 1779, the island was "discovered" by the British explorer Captain Cook; his visit was followed by a tumultuous time of overwhelming changes. Other ships from the West arrived. New diseases devastated the population. Eventually, cash-based values replaced the traditional economy, and much of Hawaiʻi's culture was lost or survived only tenuously.

One of the largest initial changes was the unification of the islands. With the aid of Western guns and ships, and Western sailors to help him manage them, the Big Island chief later known as Kamehameha I united the islands under one rule, in the year 1810.

At first, the Big Island remained the seat of government for the new kingdom. But in 1819, shortly after the death of Kamehameha I, Kamehameha's son and successor, Liholiho, moved the court to Honolulu, where commercial enterprise was rapidly growing. Once one of the most populated islands, the Big Island became a rural outpost, where, in remote areas, Hawaiians were able to preserve many of the old traditions.

Christian missionaries arrived in the islands in the 1820s, bringing schools, literacy, Western medicine, and intolerant disapproval of the old ways.

Cattle, a gift from British captain George Vancouver to Kamehameha I in 1793 and 1794, multiplied on Big Island slopes so rapidly that wild herds ravaged forests and Hawaiian agriculture. These herds eventually gave rise to the island's thriving ranching industry and a new breed of cowboys, the paniolo, who would later earn recognition for their skill and daring.

Land reforms in the late 1840s introduced private ownership of real estate, ushering in the age of sugar plantations, which thrived, selling sugar to the United States. Tens of thousands of immigrant workers were imported from China, the Portuguese Atlantic Islands, the South Seas, Puerto Rico, Japan, Scandinavia, Korea, and the Philippines. Immigrant cultures and traditions combined to form an interracial, multi-ethnic population.

World War II interrupted sleepy plantation life, as thousands of troops came to train on ranch and forest lands. The Big Island's isolation made it an ideal location for well-concealed military training grounds. At the same time, hundreds of local men left the island, joining the American armed forces to fight overseas.

The war shifted Hawaiʻi's economy. Sugar laborers signed union contracts that improved work and living conditions but also affected the industry's ability to compete internationally. With Hawaiʻi sugar's demise in the latter part of the twentieth century, plantation fields lay fallow, and the Big Island was forced to search for new industries.

Tourism proved ideal. Mauna Loa and Kīlauea volcanoes had been drawing visitors since the 1900s, while the white sand beaches of the Kona and Kohala coasts lent themselves to superior luxury resort development. The Big Island also became the cradle for a new diversified agricultural economy. The resurgence was led by Kona's coffee industry, which started in the 1830s, experienced a number of booms and busts, and revived as a source of gourmet coffee in the 1980s. The seemingly inaccessible summit of Mauna Kea also became a focal point for astronomy, attracting scientific communities and investment.

Natural forces have always ruled the Big Island. Volcanic eruptions killed hundreds in 1790. A history-making tsunami was recorded in Hilo in 1837. A massive earthquake in 1869 split the earth. In 1946, and again in 1960, two tsunamis destroyed Hilo's downtown. Kīlauea, arguably the most active volcano on earth, has swallowed villages and forests with her lava flows.

Social changes and economic development have threatened the Big Island's unique environment, home to some of the last remaining pristine Hawaiian rain- and dry forests, and habitats for endangered species. They have also threatened Native Hawaiian culture, which the early missionaries suppressed and tourism later commercialized. However, the Hawaiian Renaissance of the 1970s fanned the smoldering embers of the old culture. The Hawaiian language, arts, and traditions are stronger than they have been in generations. The Big Island has been in the forefront of this revival.

Estimates of the Big Island's population at the time of Western contact in 1779 range from 106,000 (a widely accepted figure) to as high as 300,000. Continued archaeological work may illuminate this acrimonious debate. Westerners inadvertently introduced new diseases, against which Hawaiians had no natural immunities. Native communities were ravaged by frightful epidemics. By 1853, only 24,450 Hawaiians were left on the Big Island.

Today the island has a population of 185,079 as well as many part-time residents with second homes. Ethnicity is widely varied; many people are *hapa*, belonging to two or more ethnic groups. Caucasian (33 percent) and Hawaiian/part-Hawaiian (31 percent) are the two largest ethnic groups in the total population. The Japanese account for 11 percent, Filipinos 7 percent, and mixed race 18 percent (excluding Hawaiian). Other groups represented are African-Americans, Chinese, Koreans, and Pacific Islanders.

The last two centuries of Big Island history have indeed been tumultuous. There have been vast changes in culture, language, government, economy, and population. Reminders of this past can be found all over the island. We hope that this volume will give readers a greater appreciation for Big Island history and strengthen efforts to preserve the island's historic monuments, lively local culture, and unique environment.

THE KING KAMEHAMEHA STATUE

In 1883, an eight-and-a-half-foot bronze statue of Kamehameha I was installed in Kapaʻau, in the Kohala region where the monarch had been born and raised. A new railroad running along the North Kohala coast had just been finished, so the railroad was ceremonially opened and the statue was unveiled at the same time. The honors were performed by the then current Hawaiian king, Kalākaua. It was a grand spectacle.

The statue had been commissioned by the kingdom's legislature five years earlier, to beautify Honolulu—not Kohala. The sculptor chosen for the project lived in Italy; he sent the statue to Oʻahu on the ship *G.F. Haendel*. When the *Haendel* sank off the shores of the Falkland Islands, the Legislature ordered a replica made. What they did not know was that divers had salvaged the original statue, which turned out to have suffered only minor damage. A ship captain purchased the statue and brought it to the Islands, where he resold it to Kalākaua for a handsome profit. The replica arrived while the original was being repaired. There were now two statues. What was to be done?

The Big Island's governess, Princess Kekaulike, suggested that the repaired original go to Kohala and the pristine replica remain in Honolulu. The original was duly shipped to Kohala, where it arrived on May 1, 1883. Kalākaua followed five days later, aboard a Russian warship. The ship fired a crashing royal gun salute when it sailed into the North Kohala port of Māhukona. The King's entourage—Russian officers, more than one hundred guardsmen, government officials, royalty, and the Royal Hawaiian Band—filled all six coaches of Kohala's new train. Several days of festivities culminated in the statue's unveiling on May 8, 1883. King Kalākaua opted to return to Māhukona by horseback. However, the teak passenger wagons from London in which he had traveled would go into history as "the Kalākaua cars." When the railroad closed in 1955, the cars were shipped to California to be restored. Only one car remained, on Maui. [Bishop Museum]

PEOPLE OF OLD

The Hawaiian archipelago was discovered
and settled by oceangoing Polynesian navigators
from the South Pacific.
The ancient Hawaiians lived on the most isolated
islands in the biggest ocean on the face of the earth.
Separate from the rest of humankind for more than a
thousand years, Hawaiian culture evolved in its own way.
Hawaiians had their own explanations of the
creation of the world, and of the laws of nature,
from the mountains to the sea.
They had their own rich language to chant
the story of how the islands were born from fire,
and how the gods commanded their people to live—
permitting this, prohibiting that, demanding
obedience and sacrifices in order to keep
the universe in balance.
The prayers of Hawaiians were always that
life should not change. Then, late in the eighteenth
century, the isolation of the Islands was broken.
The big world came to Hawaiʻi by way of Western
explorers' ships, and life was irreversibly transformed.

VOLCANIC LANDSCAPES

Previous pages: Ki'i pōhaku, or petro-glyphs, are found all over the Big Island, most commonly on pāhoehoe lava, whose smooth and porous rock makes for an ideal carving surface. They were often carved near or at trail junctions, or in areas considered to have mana, or divine power. Most likely the practice of making petroglyphs was brought by the first Polynesian settlers. With no form of writing as we know it, the ancient Hawaiians used petroglyphs as forms of religious communication with the gods, spirits and other obser-vances, or to commemorate important events, to indicate places of concentra-ted mana, and in some instances, even for mundane purposes. Whatever their purpose, ki'i pōhaku hold a certain ancient and inexplicable power over the beholder. [P.F. Kwiatkowski]

Right: Approaching the Islands, the early Polynesian voyagers saw snow-capped mountains on one side and fiery volca-noes on the other, sights they had never witnessed before. [**The Discovery of Hawai'i**/Herb Kawainui Kāne]

About 70 million years ago, a massive rupture deep within the earth's mantle below the North Pacific, a plume of magma, or molten rock, to rise toward the surface of the earth. As the earth's crust moved above the plume, the plume punched through the crust, pushing up mountains of solid lava rock. These stupendous mountains rose from the ocean floor, broke the surface of the water, and formed a chain of islands: the 1,500-mile-long Hawaiian archi-pelago. The Big Island, the youngest island, about one million years old, is still growing. Twenty miles to the southeast is an underwater volcano, Lō'ihi, spewing lava—an estimated 60,000 years from surfacing.

Seven volcanoes contributed to the formation of the 4,028-square-mile Big Island, the largest in the Hawaiian chain. Nīnole and Kūlani volcanoes were absorbed by massive Mauna Loa early on. Hualālai last erupted in 1801, and Mauna Loa, the largest moun-tain on earth, last erupted in 1984. Kīlauea volcano has been erupting continuously since January 3, 1983, and is the most active volcano on earth. Both Kohala, the oldest volcano, and Mauna Kea, the tallest moun-tain on earth when measured from the ocean floor, are dormant. Rain and wind have heavily eroded the dormant volcanoes of the northern part of the island, producing steep cliffs, dramatic deep valleys, and rich volcanic soil. The southern part of the island has only pockets of good soil and great stretches of lava-rock wasteland.

Hawai'i's prevailing tradewinds gather in clouds on the northeastern slopes of the island's mountains, where they drop their moisture in abundant rains. The Big Island is divided into ko'olau, a wet, windward side, and kona, a dry, leeward side. Ko'olau and kona can be further subdivided into climate zones defined by altitude and prevailing trade winds. The whole island is divided into eleven different climate zones, each with its characteristic flora and fauna.

Over the millennia, spores, seeds, insects, and snails were carried to the islands by wind, wings, and waves, colonizing Hawai'i at a rate of roughly one spe-cies every 70,000 years. Each species adapted to local conditions. Far away from predators, they lost their defense mechanisms. Mint no longer needed its scent, nettles lost their sting, and birds became flightless. The nēnē, the Hawaiian goose, a probable descendant of the Canadian goose, developed feet that could walk on Mauna Loa's lava flows. Yellow- and red-feathered honeycreepers adapted to foraging in the rain forests around Kīlauea. Wolf spiders developed camouflage that let them hide in lava cracks.

From each original ancestor, dozens of subspecies evolved. Great biodiversity flourished on Hawai'i's once-barren lava—a unique illustration of evolution and the power of life. By the time the first settlers arrived, nearly two millennia ago, much of the Big Island was an oasis of fertile volcanic soil and teeming with life. Today, over 90 percent of its native plants and animals are endemic—found nowhere else on Earth.

Pele, Poli'ahu and Kamapua'a

The ancestors of the Hawaiians were oceangoing voyagers from the Marquesas Islands in the South Pacific. They brought with them a religion and mythology that they shared, in large part, with their cousins in the rest of Polynesia. They believed in the Polynesian gods—Kāne, Kanaloa, Lono, and Kū. Kāne was the giver of water, sunlight, and forests. Kanaloa ruled the ocean and an abundance of fish. Lono brought peace, clouds, winds, agriculture, and fertility, and Kū was the god of war. But the Hawaiians also recognized new gods, unique to Hawai'i, and they told new stories. The Big Island became the place for legends of gods, demi-gods, and tricksters as well as stories about the chiefs of old.

Hawaiians explained the volcanic landscape of the Big Island as the result of the activities of the gods. Three of these gods were native to the Big Island: Poli'ahu, 'Aila'au, and Kamapua'a. The goddess Poli'ahu lived on the summit of Mauna Kea, where she spread her white mantle and wrapped herself in the rays of the sun. Hawaiians climbed to her home to fill their gourds with her snow. Poli'ahu extinguished the fires ignited by 'Aila'au, the lava god and forest eater who roamed Mauna Loa and Kīlauea. In windward, rainy Kohala, the pig god Kamapua'a made his home, drawn to the deep black mud that nurtured his taro plants.

So matters stood when the volcano goddess Pele arrived. She and her family had left their faraway home and sailed for the islands in voyaging canoes. Pele first landed on Ni'ihau, at the northern end of the island chain, but it was not the volcanic home she wanted. She traveled down the islands, looking for a crater to call home. Finally she arrived on the Big Island and found Kīlauea completely to her taste. She fought with 'Aila'au, driving him into underground caverns, and took up residence in Halema'uma'u, Kīlauea's crater. Pele detested gentle Poli'ahu, and the two engaged in battles of earthquakes and eruptions. The saddle between Mauna Loa and Mauna Kea was created to keep the two goddesses forever apart.

Drawn to Pele's legendary beauty, Kamapua'a became her lover. Kamapua'a could shift form at will, from an ugly hog to a handsome youth. The couple agreed that Pele would rule leeward Puna, Kona, and Ka'ū, while Kamapua'a could have all of windward Hilo, Hāmākua, and Kohala. Then the couple fought. Pele chased Kamapua'a, hurling lava after him. Kamapua'a plunged into the ocean to escape her burning wrath; there he took the form of the humuhumunukunukuāpua'a, in modern times, Hawai'i's state fish.

The ancient Hawaiian religion, with its heiau, or shrines, priests, and chiefly support, died out after the breaking of the kapu, or taboo, in 1819 and the subsequent arrival of the missionaries. But the gods and spirits that were close to the heart survived, particularly away from Western and missionary eyes. Fishermen still left offerings at fishing shrines. Families still told stories of their 'aumākua, or ancestral spirits, who show themselves as animals such as sharks or owls. People still worshipped Pele and left offerings at Halema'uma'u crater. Pele was reported to show herself from time to time, appearing as an old woman walking on the side of the road, or a young and beautiful woman glimpsed in passing. Still today there are stories of encounters with Pele. [Pele/Herb Kawainui Kāne]

THE PEOPLE OF OLD: A NEW CULTURE

⊠◇⊠◇⊠◇⊠◇⊠◇⊠◇⊠

Opposite: "Sailing was the primary power mode for the ancient voyaging canoes, the distances being too great to travel by paddling. The classical Hawaiian canoe evolved later as a design more suited for paddling. Dangerous political waters made it prudent to take numerous bodyguards on inter-island voyages—men who could also serve as paddlers, enabling chiefs to travel in any direction without waiting for favorable winds. The arched crossbeams connecting the hulls are uniquely Hawaiian, attributed to the seventeenth century designer Kanuha. This painting conforms to measurements recorded by the Cook expedition of a canoe of the [great chief], Kalaniopu'u: length 70', overall beam 12', hull depth 3'5"." Voyagers [A Wa'a Kaulua of Hawai'i/ Herb Kawainui Kāne]

Below: When in 1779 John Webber, an artist with Captain Cook, drew "A Chief of the Sandwich Islands" and "A Chiefess of the Sandwich Islands," the elaborate feather lei, cape and helmet of the ali'i were considered some of the finest featherwork found anywhere. [Hawai'i State Archives]

Voyagers from the Marquesas in the South Pacific came to settle the Hawaiian Islands, possibly as early as 300 A.D. Their double-hulled canoes featured lashings made of natural fibers and sails of woven pandanus leaves. Master navigators, they traveled for thousands of miles guided only by stellar constellations, wave patterns, changing winds, and the flight of birds. They brought with them a selection of plants and seeds to ensure food, medicine, and materials for mats, dye, kapa or bark cloth, ropes, and shelter. Archaeologists believe that they may have brought twenty-four to thirty species, including kalo or taro root, wauke or paper mulberry, niu or coconut, 'ulu or breadfruit, and uhi or sweet potato. Pigs, chickens, and dogs also journeyed in the canoes. The ubiquitous rat was a stowaway.

On the Big Island, small hamlets developed on the green windward side, where the land was suitable for agriculture. There were thriving villages in the valleys of Waipi'o and Waimanu, along the gulches of North Kohala, and on the wet plateaus around Hilo Bay. The starchy taro corm was the favorite wetland crop.

The Hawaiians also discovered rich fishing grounds, both inshore and offshore. The richest offshore fishery was at the southern end of the island, in Ka Lae, in the district of Ka'ū. There, archaeologists have excavated hundreds of fish hooks, from earliest times to the present, as well as campsites and a fishing shrine.

Over time, the population grew. Some Hawaiians moved to the dry leeward areas where they grew dryland taro and sweet potatoes. They shared with their coastal kin, or traded their upland products for coastal harvests, such as fish and coconuts. Both coastal and upland populations used products of the upland forests or the inland stone quarries.

Political divisions reflected this interdependence. Each chiefdom, or moku, was divided into ahupua'a, running from the mountain peaks through valleys to the shoreline. Most of the necessities of life could be obtained within each ahupua'a.

Archaeologist Ross Cordy estimates that in 1779, when Captain James Cook anchored in Kealakekua Bay, there were approximately 106,000 Hawaiians living on the island. The land was divided into six large moku; each moku was divided into dozens of ahupua'a. The ahupua'a were divided into 'ili, or small farming or fishing communities, each with its designated boundaries. Each ahupua'a had a konohiki, or land agent, who administered the land on behalf of the ruling chief. The maka'āinana, or commoners, overseen by the konohiki, fished or tended the kuleana 'āina, their farm lots. Bird catchers roamed the high forests, collecting feathers for high chiefs' cloaks and helmets. At the bottom of the social scale were the kauwā, the outcasts, possibly law breakers or prisoners of war, working as slaves.

The chiefs were advised by their kālaimoku, or prime ministers, and their kahuna, or priests. Some kahuna were specialists, expert in medicine, others in building houses and canoes, others in hula or genealogies. To support themselves and their courts, the chiefs collected taxes from the maka'āinana in the form of taro, hogs, vegetables, fish hooks, feathers, kapa cloth, mats, and other resources. In return, the commoners expected protection from rival chiefs, and direction of common efforts such as the construction of irrigation systems and heiau, or temples. Chiefs and their priests led religious ceremonies and ensured that mana, divine energy, was channeled into social harmony and bounteous harvests.

Warriors of chiefly rank fought each other for control of moku, sometimes controlling several at a time. With each conquest, lands were redistributed and hierarchies rearranged. Victorious chiefs made advantageous marriages with women of high rank, ensuring exalted rank for the children of such unions.

Over time, chiefdoms grew larger and more stratified, and the demands of the chiefs upon the commoners became ever more stringent.

To solicit the favor of the gods and avert their wrath, chiefs and priests enforced the kapu system, an intricate protocol of prohibitions and religious observances. The kapu system influenced all decisions and activities. Only with the death of a chief was a brief period of sanctioned chaos allowed, after which the

chief's successor would reinstate the kapu.

In Hawaiian belief, the gods appointed the ali'i as their worldly representatives and imbued them with mana. A chief of high social rank carried so much mana that it was believed that its power could destroy a commoner. Ordinary chiefs might mingle with the people, but some high chiefs had such strict kapu that they could only leave their houses at night. Commoners who crossed their paths fell flat on the ground, hiding their faces.

In deference to the gods, men and women could not eat together, nor could their food be cooked in the same ovens. Women were not allowed to eat certain foods such as pork, bananas, coconuts, fowl, and turtles, which were reserved for gods and men.

Aware that natural resources were not limitless, the chiefs regulated fishing by means of kapu. Certain fish and shellfish might be kapu, forbidden, at certain

This engraving of a heiau near Kealakekua was drawn by ship artist Robert Dampier in 1824. It is a simple affair: a thatch house surrounded by a fence and sacred images. Not all heiau were imposing stone structures. After the kapu was abolished in 1819 and Christianity arrived in 1820, the old religion was abandoned and heiau, modest or massive, were no longer attended to or maintained (at least publicly), serving only as reminders of the past. Today there are nearly 150 heiau sites on the Big Island, most of which are only stone mound remnants of once-imposing structures that have endured natural forces, animal contact, and unwitting human theft. [Hawai'i State Archives]

times of year, or kapu to commoners. Chiefs also laid kapu on their favorite fishing ponds and surfing spots.

To an outsider's eye, the kapu system might seem arbitrary and overly strict. For Hawaiians of traditional times, these rules were a divinely ordained way to keep life organized, orderly, decent, and clean.

Big Island chiefs of the time of Captain Cook believed that they were descended from a common ancestor named Pili. It was said that the chief Pili, his priest Pa'ao, and their kin and followers arrived at the Big Island in their long canoes, having journeyed from Kahiki (Tahiti). Because Pili was of pure descent, uncontaminated by intermarriage with commoners, he was immediately accepted as high chief by the existing Big Island chiefs. His high priest Pa'ao introduced new religious customs, such as human sacrifice and prostrating kapu.

These stories were collected in the nineteenth century and for a long time were accepted as historical fact. It was believed that after the first migration from the Marquesas, there was a second migration from Kahiki sometime in the 1300s. However, archaeologists have not been able to find any physical evidence of such a migration. Most historians now believe that the story of Pili and Pa'ao is a myth that served to legitimate Big Island chiefs (who traced their ancestry to Pili) and an order of priests (who traced their ancestry to Pa'ao). It explained the Hawaiian social order as it existed when Westerners first came to the islands, an order in which a small stratum of chiefs ruled over commoners with whom they recognized no kinship. However, there are still many Hawaiians and some historians who believe that there was a second migration, and that Pili and Pa'ao may have been historical figures.

At the time of Captain Cook's arrival in 1779, the Hawaiian year was divided into eight months of war and four months of agriculture, play, and games. Peace started at the onset of the Makahiki harvest festival in October when an around-the-island procession signaled the ascendancy of the god Lono. Kū, the war god, was in eclipse. At each stop on the procession's route, the chiefs collected tribute at ahupua'a boundaries—tools, kapa, and mats along with animals and produce. This was the time to celebrate agriculture, crafts, peace, and prosperity.

▷◁▷◁▷◁▷◁▷◁▷◁▷◁▷◁

Left: "A View in Owhyee with one of the Priest's Houses." This quaintly titled engraving shows a Hawaiian village still untouched by the influence of the outside world. The word "Owhyee" is one of several attempts to spell "Hawai'i" in English, made before the Hawaiian language was put in written form by a committee of early missionaries. There were no true cities or towns in old Hawai'i. People gathered in small coastal villages (kauhale) near good fishing grounds or beside fertile land, where they grew taro and sweet potatoes, two main staples of their diet. The better Hawaiian house (hale) was raised on a stone foundation platform and the floor was covered with small smooth pebbles. The homes of commoners had earthen floors covered with dry grasses and lauhala mats. [Hawai'i State Archives]

Below left: The woman is beating wauke bark to make kapa, which was used for clothing and blankets. Kapa, known also as tapa, can best be described as a kind of soft, pliable paper. Kapa was decorated in various colors using natural plant and shellfish dyes, with geometric designs applied by block-printing. Hawaiians carried the art of kapa decoration to a high state, using more colors and designs than any other Polynesian people. Mats, blankets, and a huge old-style wooden surfboard lie about the compound. What appears to be a metal bucket may be a sign of encroaching Western influence. Note also the wooden table and the doorways of the houses. However, the picture may not be completely accurate, as Western artists of the day sometimes took considerable liberties with the facts. [Hawai'i State Archives]

✕◊✕◊✕◊✕◊✕◊✕

Below: At the time of Western contact the closely cropped hair bleached white at the front of the hairline was considered very fashionable for adult women, while long hair was reserved for girls. [Hawai'i State Archives]

Kamakahonu, one of Hawai'i's most important historic sites, was a chiefly compound in the ahupua'a of Lanihau, in what is today Kailua-Kona. Kamehameha I lived his last years on this land, dying there in 1819. In the same year, Kamehameha's widow Ka'ahumanu convinced the young Kamehameha II to eat with her, breaking one of the strongest tenets of the kapu system. Kamehameha II (Liholiho) subsequently ordered the destruction of heiau and carved images of gods. Here also, in 1820, the first company of American missionaries sought official permission from Kamehameha II to land and begin the Christianization of the islands.

The Ahu'ena heiau was a great raised stonework platform built on a point at the western end of Kamakahonu. Louis Choris, an artist who accompanied Otto von Rotzebue's voyage to the islands in 1816, made many sketches and watercolors such as this drawing (above) which shows that the temple house built on top was the most imposing structure in the Kamakahonu complex. It was thatched with bundled of dried kī leaves and stood within a fenced enclosure. The heiau was of ancient origin, and was rebuilt and rededicated by Kamehameha I. John I'i, who was part of Kamehameha's court at the time this drawing was made, described the building and complex in considerable detail:

Ahu'ena was enclosed with a fence of lama wood and within this fence, toward the front on the west and facing inland, there was an 'anu'u, or tower. A row of images stood along its front, as befitted a Hale o Lono (House of Lono, god of peace and agriculture). Images stood at the northwest corner of the house, with a stone pavement in front. On the west side of the outer entrance was a large image named Koleamoku, on whose helmet perched the figure of a plover.

The carved figures that stood watch before the temple were probably 'aumākua, or ancestral gods. Choris wrote that the image with the bird perched on top was a war god, but this identification is disputed.

Beyond the heiau and the towers were two guardian figures with uplifted arms, and behind them were two small thatched houses, which were part of the royal complex. Although the scene is unusually barren of plant life, the lithograph published in Choris' account shows the groves of palms and other plants that existed at the time.

*[**Temple on the Island of Hawaii, 1816**/ LOUIS CHORIS, Honolulu Academy of Arts]*

THE HULA OF OLD

Dancing skirts varied widely. Here the dancers appear to be wearing tapa-cloth wraparounds with complicated knots and bows. Grass skirts are not authentically Hawaiian; they were introduced after the Hawaiians came by Gilbert Islanders in the late 1870s. [Hawai'i State Archives]

Many of the original sketches made by the early European ship artists were later retouched by copyists who changed the body and facial appearance of the Hawaiians to conform to Western ideas of beauty. But in this engraving by Choris (above left), the Hawaiian male dancers are fairly accurately depicted. The dancers carry elaborately decorated leather-embellished gourd rattles and wear dog-tooth anklets, which make distinctive rattling sounds as they perform. Bracelets of large boar tusks decorate their wrists, contributing to the visual impact of the arm movements. The dancers do not wear the customary malo or loin cloths but seem to be wearing intricately wrapped tapa cloth or even imported cotton cloth from a trading ship. The music was often combined with the chanting of a mele, that the dance depicted.

Behind the dancers (above right), sat the musicians and singers and chanters. Hawaiian musical instruments used for hula included gourd drums, bamboo nose flutes, wooden drums with sharkskin heads, feather-decorated gourd rattles, smooth stones used as castanets, bamboo rattles, and sticks used for beating time. There were also small gourd whistles, which were unique to the Islands. Conch shell trumpets, used extensively on occasions of high ceremony, made a very distinctive sound that could be heard at great distances.

THE DISTRICTS AND THEIR RULING CHIEFS

The Hawaiian ali'i, or chiefly class, made a marked impression on early Westerners, who wrote about their royal bearing, magnificent feather capes and helmets, beautiful accoutrements of rank, and the pageantry of their processions. This tattooed chief, drawn by French ship artist Jacques Arago in August 1819, wears symbols of chiefly rank, including the mahiole, or feather helmet, and 'ahu'ula, or feather cape. The traditional tattoos, including squares on the chest and triangles on the left thigh and lower leg, were spiritual motifs indicating the rank and genealogy of the bearer.
"Hawaiian tattoo designs were generally not as bold as those of the South Pacific. At their first glimpse of Polynesians, some early Europeans in the Pacific mistook Polynesian tattooing for tight-fitting clothing. Sailors who admired the art returned to Europe sporting Polynesian tattoos. 'Tattoo' comes from the Tahitian tatau (Hawaiian kakau)."—Herb Kāne, Ancient Hawaii. [Hawai'i State Archives]

Natural Land Divisions

The Big Island was traditionally divided into six districts, or moku: Kohala, Kona, Ka'ū, Puna, Hilo, and Hāmākua. In the centuries just before the arrival of the Westerners, the moku chiefs contended to bring several moku, or even the whole island, under their control. Some succeeded, but the districts frequently split apart again. In 1791, Kamehameha I finally unified all six districts under his sole authority.

Kohala district, at the northwestern tip, reached west from the high plateaus of the Kohala Mountains and the foothills of Mauna Kea to embrace the windward, fertile valleys of an isolated peninsula. It included ahupua'a that ran from Waimea's green upcountry lands down to dry, leeward, lava-strewn shores, and the fishponds of 'Anaeho'omalu and Kalāhuipua'a

The district of Kona, entirely in leeward lands, comprised the ahupua'a around Hualālai and the west flanks of Mauna Loa. It encompassed the 64-mile coast down from 'Anaeho'omalu in the north to Manukā in the south, and faced calm waters. The protected bays of Central Kona, including Kailua and Kealakekua, were safe harbors for the first Western ships. North of the rapidly growing village of Kailua, in the arid lands of Kekaha, were the fishponds of Kaloko, Kīholo, and Ka'ūpūlehu. Mauna Loa's lava flows frequently altered the landscape, especially in the south.

The isolated district of Ka'ū, also on the leeward side, bordered Kona at Manukā, encompassed the crater and southern slopes of Mauna Loa, then ended at Wood Valley and Kīlauea crater. With about 64 miles of lava-strewn shores, it was the home of Pele, the volano goddess. The district included many kīpuka, "islands" of forest surrounded by old lava flows, green places where koa and 'ōhi'a trees thrived. It also included Ka Lae, the island's southern most point, where strong winds and currents often swept canoes away.

Puna covered the area east of Ka'ū, where windward conditions should have allowed rich rain forests and agriculture, had it not been for Kīlauea's active lava flows. Kīlauea's southeast rift zone, highly eruptive, cinder-cone-dotted, ran right through Puna, east of Ka'ū to windward. Active lava flows meant that rain forests and agriculture did not develop. The reefs were rich in shellfish, but otherwise Puna was chronically short of food, which made it a hard place for ambitious chiefs to develop power, because not enough food could be grown to raise young warriors. At the same time, the striking coastline and rough seas made invasion difficult.

Fertile, windward, and wet, the district of Hilo lay on the east side of the island north of Puna controlled the ahupua'a that ran down the eastern flanks of Mauna Kea. At sea level, rainfall was 100 inches a year, rising to 250 at the summit of the volcano. The ahupua'a included weathered cliffs and inaccessible, forested gulches, as well as the agricultural lands that surrounded Wailoa River. Inside Hilo Bay, the ocean's strong currents were calm, later making it the site of a major port for Western ships.

Hāmākua in the north extended inland from coastal Laupāhoehoe and the northeastern slopes of Mauna Kea, across the volcano's summit, and up the slopes of Hualālai and Mauna Loa. The wide, eroded, stream-rich, fertile valleys of Kohala Mountain, Waipi'o, and Wainamu opened to gentle bays, and supported large populations with an abundance of crops. Strategically, Hāmākua was perhaps the most advantageous base for ambitious chiefs to raise armies.

Connecting the six districts was a network of intersecting long-distance trails, ala loa, made from ocean-worn stones, running inland, and, where possible, circumnavigating the island. Along the trails and in caves that provided shelter for travelers were petroglyphs carved in the lava rock.

Līloa and 'Umi

The story of Līloa and 'Umi stands at the border of legend and history. Some accept the story as factual; others say that it is a mixture of fact and myth.

It is said that sometime in the late 1500s, a great chief named Līloa, a descendent of Pili, ruled over the whole island of Hawai'i. While he was touring the district of Hāmākua, he had an affair with a commoner. When she told him that she was pregnant, he gave her certain items by which he could recognize his child if ever they were to meet. After several years, the mother sent the child, a boy named 'Umi, to his father in Waipi'o Valley. Legends say that the boy showed no fear when he broke a severe kapu by entering the royal residence. He leapt on his father's lap, saying: "I am 'Umi a Līloa," showing Līloa the tokens. Līloa accepted the boy as his legitimate child.

"A council of chiefs discusses tactics before leading their commoners into battle. In the foreground, the man at left holds a weapon inset with sharks teeth (lei o mano). Around his waist is a belly protector of strong matting decorated with feathers. His companion holds a throwing spear (ihe) and a stone headed club (newa). Throwing spears, long lances (pololu) and wooden daggers (pahoa) are seen among the men in the background. As Captain Cook's men learned from personal experience, the feathered capes and helmets were '... battle apparel. The cape might be worn over the shoulders, but in battle it was pulled around the left side of the body and held forward with the left hand to snag a thrust from a dagger or the point of a thrown spear. In this position the right arm was exposed and free to wield a weapon. Feathers were black, white, red, yellow, green and the long rust-red and black feathers of the fighting cock. These were tied over a light netting of cord in a great variety of designs.' In battle, the brilliant capes helped warriors identify and rally to their chiefs. Helmet made of a strong, lightweight basketry protected the head from the impact of stones shot from slings..."
Ancient Hawai'i [**Warrior Chiefs**/Herb Kawainui Kāne]

Above: Olopana, a chief of Waipi'o Valley, led a voyage to "Tahiti of the Golden Haze," the first in a saga of ancient voyages spanning three generations. Ancient Hawai'i [*Olopana*/Herb Kawainui Kāne]

Legend says that 'Umi ruled with justice and kindness, having known what it was like to be a commoner. He is said to have built Ahu a 'Umi Heiau, in Kona, which stood at the intersection of several major trails. 'Umi's last resting place is reputed to be a cave in Waipi'o.

Alapa'inui and Kalani'ōpu'u

In the early 1700s, the Kona chief Keawe, of the line of Pili and 'Umi, united Hawai'i's eastern Hilo and western Kona districts. After his death, Kohala chief Alapa'inui seized the power from Keawe's heir, conquered the ruler of the Hilo district, and established his sway over all of the Big Island. To stifle revolt, Alapa'inui took under his wing Keawe's grandsons, the half-brothers Kalani'ōpu'u and Keōuakalani, who were also his own nephews, and named them his generals. The island remained relatively subdued until around 1758, when a Maui chief, Kekaulike, raided the Big Island. Alapa'inui assembled his canoes and his warriors, including his general Keōuakalani. He sailed to Maui to attack Kekaulike. There, he found that Kekaulike had just died. Alapa'i made peace with the new ruler, then sailed to Moloka'i and O'ahu for further battles and conquests. The era of inter-island warfare was well under way.

It is said that the night before Keōua (Keōuakalani) sailed to Maui with Alapa'i, one of his wives gave birth. The child was sent off to be fostered by Nae'ole, in Kohala. Later, the child was returned to Alapa'i's court, where one of Alapa'i's wives raised him as her own. This child was later given the name Kamehameha, the lonely one, who eventually became the ruler of all the islands.

Some years after Kamehameha's birth, his father Keōua died. Keōua's brother claimed that Keōua had been poisoned and declared his independence from his old uncle's court. He tried to remove Kamehameha from Alapa'inui's control, but failed.

When Alapa'inui died, around 1760, his eldest son succeeded him. Kalani'ōpu'u overthrew him and seized power, becoming the mo'i, the ruler of a whole island. He adopted his brother Keōua's child, Kamehameha. However, Kalani'ōpu'u already had a son, Kīwala'ō, and Kamehameha was not raised as an heir.

When Līloa died, Hākau, his oldest son and 'Umi's half-brother, succeeded as ruler. 'Umi, Līloa had decreed, would tend to Waipi'o's luakini heiau, Paka'alana, and the war god Kū. (Such a split between religious and secular rule was not uncommon, though it often led to war.) When Hākau, a cruel leader, forced 'Umi into exile, his own priests deserted him and helped 'Umi to reassert himself. After sacrificing Hākau at Paka'alana, 'Umi succeeded him as ruler.

"Along the ancient trail that passes 'Anaeho'omalu (now Waikoloa Beach Resort), thousands of petroglyphs tell of those who stopped to record their passage over the centuries. Much speculation has been offered, but little is really known about the meaning of these rock carvings. Some may have been clan emblems; others may have commemorated events. They are treasured today as evidence of the original culture of Hawai'i, irreplaceable and priceless." Voyagers [*The Petroglyph Maker/* Herb Kawainui Kāne]

Below left and below: Ki'i pōhaku, or petroglyphs, were carved in the rocks of Hawai'i as silent, beautiful images of a great civilization that flourished for nearly two thousand years on the most remote islands in the world. These depict a surfer (left, from Lāna'i) and two human figures (below), possibly representing a mother and son (at Puakō, Hawai'i). [P.F. Kwiatkowski]

Just one of several ancient fishing settlements close to anchialine ponds and springs, Puakō, on the leeward coast in the district of Kohala, shelters one of the largest, most unusual, and most detailed petroglyph fields in the islands. It consists of groups totaling more than 3,000 figures carved into lava. Some say that they tell of events of village life. An image of twenty-nine stick men, possibly warriors, is known as "The Marchers."

*Pu'ukoholā Heiau was built by Kamehameha as a gift for his war god Kuka'ilimoku. [**Kamehameha Building Pu'ukoholā Heiau**/Herb Kawainui Kāne]*

Pu'ukoholā Heiau

Pu'ukoholā Heiau, is located on the bluff of a 130-foot hill in Kawaihae, and has splendid views of the ocean 200 yards below. The current structure (which replaced an older, smaller heiau) was built by Kamehameha I, the chief who unified the Islands, at a time when he was still struggling to establish his control over the whole of the Big Island. He believed that the heiau would win divine favor and eventual victory. Accounts tell of the large numbers of human victims sacrificed in construction rituals. They talk of the thousands of laborers and chiefs encamped nearby. Kamehameha participated in the work. The heiau was finished in the summer of 1791 and consisted of three walls and two sloping terraces. It measured 224 by 100 feet. The walls in some places were twenty feet thick and twenty feet high.

Pu'ukoholā Heiau became a National Historic Site in 1972. Today it is a U.S. National Park and has been partially restored.

❈❈❈❈❈❈❈❈❈❈

Above: The completed Pu'ukoholā Heiau served as the home of Kamehameha's powerful war god Kūkā'ilimoku, honored by innumerable human sacrifices. In return, Kamehameha was blessed with military strength and dominance. [**A Ceremony at Pu'ukoholā**/Herb Kawainui Kāne]

Left: One of the last heiau to be built on the Big Island was Pu'ukoholā. It was abandoned after the overthrow of the kapu in 1819. The men in the foreground stand near a simple fishing hut of a much later date. 1890. [Hawai'i State Archives]

Below: Ahu'ena Heiau at Kailua-Kona was an important religious and political site during the early reign of Kamehameha I. Located next to the king's residence at Kamakahonu, the temple was restored by Kamehameha after his unification of the islands in 1812, and dedicated to Lono, a god of peace, agriculture and prosperity. The ancient edifice has been restored by the King Kamehameha Hotel, showing replicas of the structures, religious images, and grass-thatched houses that once stood on this sacred ground. [Douglas Peebles]

Pu'uhonua o Hōnaunau

Pu'uhonua o Hōnaunau, a place of refuge in South Kona, was the largest of ten pu'uhonua on the island. The pu'uhonua stood as sanctuaries in a society ruled by the kapu. Kapu-breakers who reached them escaped the death penalty. In times of war, women, children, and those who were not fighters could also find safety in pu'uhonua. Enemy warriors could retreat here.

Adjacent to the ocean, Pu'uhonua o Hōnaunau was secluded by an L-shaped wall, built in the 1500s. Once 1,000 feet long, 10 feet high, and 17 feet wide, the Great Wall is still standing today. Two heiau, possibly luakini, have been discovered within the pu'uhonua. A royal residence stood next to the pu'uhonua; its canoe landing was marked by a ki'i, an image of the gods. The great chief Keawe, who reigned in the early 1700s, often resided at Hōnaunau. Upon his death, his son repurposed Keawe's home as a mausoleum. The bones of Keawe and numerous successor chiefs rested here, wrapped in sacred kapa cloth and guarded by the feathered statues of the gods. Their mana, or spiritual power, increased the area's sacredness. Today, Pu'uhonua o Hōnaunau is a U.S. National Park. [Douglas Peebles]

One of the most impressive temples in the entire archipelago is Mo'okini Heiau, located in Kohala on the island of Hawai'i. Its massive walls were not destroyed with the overthrow of the kapu system in 1819, although the heiau was abandoned to lonely isolation on the rolling plains of Kohala. To this day, its guardianship has been passed down from generation to generation through the Mo'okini family. [Douglas Peebles]

Mo'okini Heiau

Some legends say that it was the priest Pa'ao himself who directed the construction of Mo'okini Heiau, on the plains of Pu'uepa in Kohala. It is said that the work took from sunset to sunrise and employed thousands of men who, in a human chain nine miles long, passed stones from nearby Niuli'i. Archaeologists believe that the heiau dates to the 1300s or 1400s. The massive Mo'okini was a vital center of political and religious power in the Kohala district; it was dedicated to the war god Kū. Alapa'inui is said to have overseen repairs to the heiau.

CAPTAIN JAMES COOK (1728–1779)

In the late 1700s, two to three thousand Hawaiians lived at Kealakekua—the Path of the God—around a lava-strewn shore, along a crescent-shaped bay north of Hōnaunau. The village of Ka'awaloa on the northern edge sheltered a residence for the high chief Kalani'ōpu'u. At the south side of Kealakekua, priests tended to the luakini heiau, Hikiau. Smaller shrines, freshwater ponds, springs, brackish pools, and well-maintained farm plots surrounded tranquil ocean waters.

On January 17, 1779, the annual Makahiki festival had just started and the war god Kū had relinquished his power to Lono, the god of farming, games, and peace. On this date, Captain James Cook sailed into Kealakekua Bay with the British exploration ships *Discovery* and *Resolution*. Hawaiian life would begin to change dramatically and irrevocably.

Cook, considered by many as the best navigator of his time, was making his third Pacific voyage. In January 1778, he had stopped at Kaua'i, where he named the islands the Sandwich Islands after his patron, the Fourth Earl of Sandwich, Britain's First Lord of the Admiralty. Over the summer he had explored Alaska, finding nothing but ice. He had now returned to the islands to escape the worst of winter before resuming his search for the Northwest Passage.

Hoping to provision his ships and make repairs, Cook had sent William Bligh (best known for his later role in the mutiny on the *Bounty*) ahead to see if the area would be suitable to fulfill the crew's needs. With his artist John Webber, his botanists, and his astronomers, he also wanted to secure permission to document the island.

Cook assumed that he could trade European objects with the Hawaiians, whom he had discovered to be especially fond of metal, which made wonderful weapons and tools. What he did not realize was that he had entered a culture built on the sharing of resources. When he accepted refreshments and lavish gifts, Hawaiians felt that he had accepted an obligation to be as forthcoming with his own supplies. The chiefs were happy with the gifts he did give, but puzzled by his refusal to share more freely. Some Hawaiians (low-ranking chiefs and commoners) took matters into their own hands and helped themselves to whatever they could quietly make off with.

"Leaving a village, the makahiki procession pauses on Hawai'i's rugged southeastern shore to gaze at Cook's Resolution, *also making a circuit of the island. At this time Cook's second ship,* Discovery, *was far behind and out of sight. The bearer in the foreground holds the akua loa, the standard of Lono. In the village the akua pa'ani, standard of the god of sports and games, has been set up, and festivities are about to begin."* Voyagers *[**Visitors from Another World**/Herb Kawainui Kāne]*

19

Captain Cook was honored for his accomplishments as a navigator and explorer. Strangely, for so famous a man, little is known of his personal life. His journals objectively comment on everything that he saw, yet provide little inkling of the deepest thoughts and character of the man himself. [Hawai'i State Archives]

The first days in Kealakekua proceeded well enough. The Hawaiians honored Cook as an important chief and a special guest from a foreign land. At Hikiau Heiau, the priests wrapped Cook in soft white kapa and adorned him with a red feather cloak. The islanders brought hogs, potatoes, taro, bananas, and coconut water. There was kava, a narcotic drink made from the 'awa root. When the high chief Kalani'ōpu'u, who had been absent on Maui, returned, further festivities were held at his residence.

The Hawaiians continued to swim under the ships to obtain metal, and Cook's sailors grew angry. They fired muskets at the Hawaiians. Some sailors went on shore and carried off some carved ki'i images from Hikiau Heiau, which they used for firewood. The Hawaiians were upset by the hostilities and dismayed by the Westerners' disrespect for sacred things.

Cook's crew of 180 men stayed for two long weeks, and Kalani'ōpu'u did his best to remain generous, as expected of a great chief. When the *Discovery* and *Resolution* sailed away on February 4, continual feasting and gift-giving, together with the necessity of feeding the retinue of Kalaniopu'u, had exhausted the local food supply.

Unfortunately for Cook, his ships were caught in a storm and the *Resolution's* foremast was dislodged. Knowing of no other safe place to anchor, Cook returned to Kealakekua Bay for repairs. This time, one week later, the welcome was cool.

When a Hawaiian took a pair of tongs and a chisel, the sailors opened fire and the man's canoe was seized. The ensuing fight was quickly subdued, but, after sunset, the *Discovery's* cutter disappeared. In the morning, the British blocked the bay to prevent anyone from escaping with the boat. When a Hawaiian tried to leave, one of the sailors shot him dead. Cook, meanwhile, had gone on shore with nine sailors and a loaded double-barreled musket. He took Kalani'ōpu'u hostage, hoping to get the cutter back, but succeeded only in alarming the chief's entourage. As Cook and his men retreated down the beach towards the water, someone thrust a dagger at Cook. In response, Cook fired in the air. A battle broke out, in which Cook was killed.

Cook died on February 14, 1779, along with four marines and more than twenty-five Hawaiians. Sporadic fighting continued for a week. Ka'awaloa village was completely destroyed. The British sailed off on February 22. A monument at Kealakekua Bay marks the events.

Thus ended the first major contact between the Hawaiians and Westerners, one that irrevocably change the Islands. Hawai'i was now on the map of the world, and contact with the "big world" brought foreign ships, new forms of warfare, trade, and religion, new status symbols, and terrible diseases.

◤◉◥◤◉◥◤◉◥◤◉◥◤◉◥

Left: The first documented contact between Europeans and Native Hawaiians took place between 1778 and 1779, during Captain James Cook's visits to the islands of Kaua'i and Hawai'i. The artist John Webber was aboard the ships of exploration, and his extensive drawings are an important illustrative source of ancient Hawaiian artifacts and lifestyles. In this dramatic scene, Webber depicts the formal arrival of the high chief Kalaniōpu'u to welcome Captain Cook on January 25, 1779, at Kealakekua Bay. Kalaniōpu'u leads two other large canoes filled with chiefs wearing rich feathered cloaks and helmets and armed with spears and daggers. In the second canoe the famed kahuna Kao'o carries sacred images, or ki'i, displayed on red cloth. "Kalaniopuu, King of Owyhee bringing Presents to Captain Cook, ca. 1781-83." Pen, ink wash, and watercolor. [Dixson Galleries, State Library of New South Wales, Sydney]

Below left: After coming ashore at Kealakekua, Captain Cook was taken in hand by kāhuna and escorted to Hikiau Heiau. An elaborate ceremony was performed, including the sacrifice of pigs and the offering of a feather cloak to Cook. At the time his officers believed their captain was being revered as the god Lono. Nineteenth-century American missionaries such as Reverend Hiram Bingham condemned Cook's apparent willingness to be so honored as a blasphemy that was punished by his later death. Some contemporary scholars and Native Hawaiians have challenged this view of Cook's "deification," arguing that this ceremony depicted by John Webber was to honor him as a great chief, not a god. [Hawai'i State Archives]

CAPTAIN COOK'S DEATH

On February 14, 1779, Captain James Cook was killed on the shores of Ka'awaloa at Kealakekua Bay on the island of Hawai'i. John Webber recorded this tragic scene, published in 1782 as an engraving, "The Death of Captain Cook." [Mitchell Library/State Library of New South Wales]

"Captain Cook was then the only one remaining on the rock. He was observed making for the pinnace, holding his left hand against the back of his head, to guard it from stones, and carrying his musket under the other arm. An Indian was seen following him, but with caution and timidity, for he stopped once or twice, as if undetermined to proceed. At last he advanced upon him unawares and with a large club, or common stake, gave him a blow on the back of the head, and then precipitately retreated.

"The stroke seemed to have stunned Captain Cook. He staggered a few paces, then fell on his hand and one knee, and dropped his musket. As he was rising, and before he could recover his feet, another Indian stabbed him in the back of the neck with an iron dagger. He then fell into a bight of water about knee-deep, where others crowded upon him, and endeavored to keep him under; but struggling very strongly with them, he got his head up, and casting his look toward the pinnace, seemed to solicit assistance. Though the boat was not above five or six yards distant from him, yet from the crowded and confused state of the crew it seems it was not in their power to save him.

"The Indians got him under again, but in deeper water. He was, however, able to get his head up once more and, being almost spent in the struggle, he naturally turned to the rock and was endeavoring to support himself by it when a savage gave him blow with a club, and he was seen alive no more."

— David Samwell, 1786, surgeon of the Discovery
A Narrative of the Death of Captain James Cook (London: 1786).

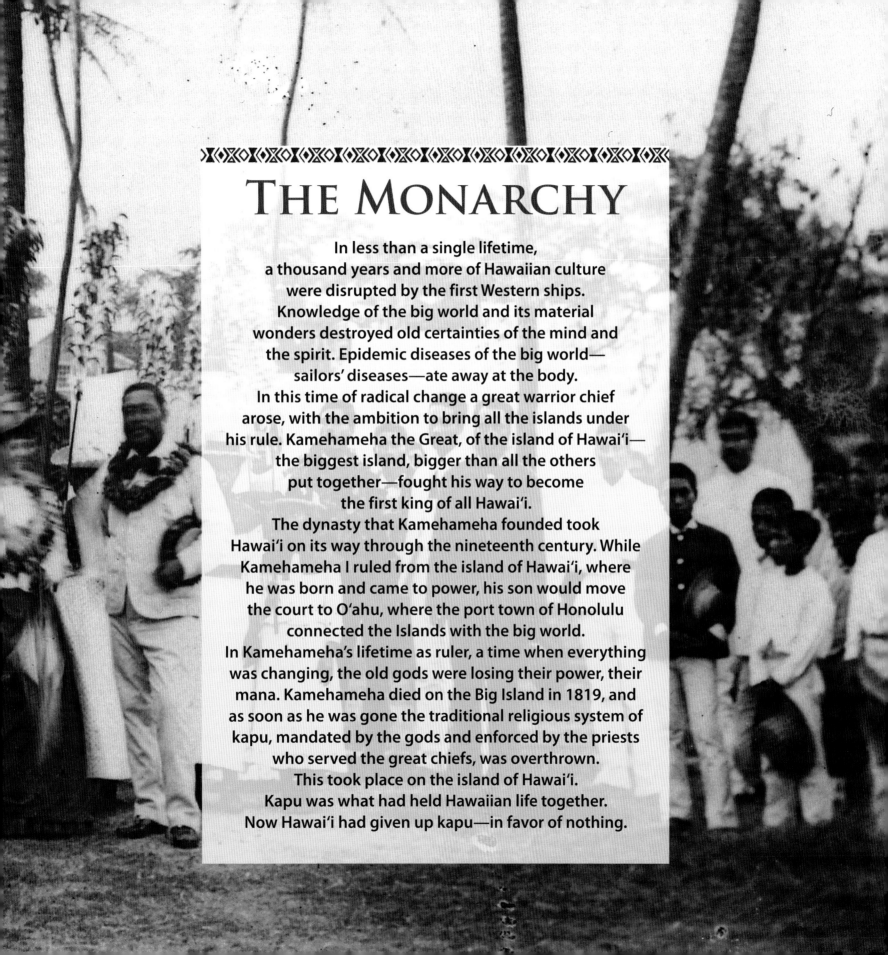

THE MONARCHY

In less than a single lifetime,
a thousand years and more of Hawaiian culture
were disrupted by the first Western ships.
Knowledge of the big world and its material
wonders destroyed old certainties of the mind and
the spirit. Epidemic diseases of the big world—
sailors' diseases—ate away at the body.
In this time of radical change a great warrior chief
arose, with the ambition to bring all the islands under
his rule. Kamehameha the Great, of the island of Hawai'i—
the biggest island, bigger than all the others
put together—fought his way to become
the first king of all Hawai'i.
The dynasty that Kamehameha founded took
Hawai'i on its way through the nineteenth century. While
Kamehameha I ruled from the island of Hawai'i, where
he was born and came to power, his son would move
the court to O'ahu, where the port town of Honolulu
connected the Islands with the big world.
In Kamehameha's lifetime as ruler, a time when everything
was changing, the old gods were losing their power, their
mana. Kamehameha died on the Big Island in 1819, and
as soon as he was gone the traditional religious system of
kapu, mandated by the gods and enforced by the priests
who served the great chiefs, was overthrown.
This took place on the island of Hawai'i.
Kapu was what had held Hawaiian life together.
Now Hawai'i had given up kapu—in favor of nothing.

KAMEHAMEHA I, THE ISLANDS' FIRST KING

⟩✕◉✕◉✕◉✕◉✕◉✕◉✕⟨

Previous pages: The monarchs often visited the other islands, on governmental business, to get away from Honolulu's political intrigue; to visit family, friends and well-wishers; or for governmental affairs. For King Kalākaua there were added factors—to lift the morale of his people suffering from population loss and the vanishing of the culture and encourage his subjects to "Hoʻoūlu Lāhui—To Increase the Race." Also, after riots followed his election to the throne, Kalākaua recognized the importance of inspiring his subjects in an effort to gain their support. His frequent tours to the Big Island were always received with a great outpouring of aloha and hoʻokupu, or gifts, in his honor. [Baker-Van Dyke Collection]

Opposite: An early nineteenth century portrait of Kamehameha I was probably a copy of one of the two portraits known to have been sketched from life by the artist Louis Choris, sailing with the explorer von Kotzebue. In this picture, Kamehameha is shown wearing Western clothing. In daily life, he preferred the comfort of the traditional malo, or loincloth, but formal portraits called for Western formal wear. [Bishop Museum]

Sometime between 1753 and 1758 a son was born to Keōuakalani, the grandson of the great chief Keawe, and Kekuʻiapoiwa Liliha, the daughter of a high-ranking Kohala family. The child was at first named Paiʻea, meaning hard-shelled crab. Later, he took the name Kamehameha, the lonely one.

He was a member of the Big Island aristocracy, 250 or so nobles who ruled over more than 100,000 people. Sometimes they served a great chief who ruled the whole island; sometimes they quarreled among themselves and split the island into warring districts. Local politics were complicated by intermarriages with the aristocracies of other islands, as well as by inter-island wars. More and more, chiefs were aspiring to rule more than just one island. Kamehameha was the first chief to rule all the islands.

When his parents died, he was fostered at the courts of his great-uncle Alapaʻinui and then of his uncle Kalaniʻōpuʻu, both of whom had managed to seize and retain control over all of the Big Island.

When Kalaniʻōpuʻu died in 1782, he bequeathed control of secular affairs to his son Kīwalaʻō, and the guardianship of the war god Kūkāʻilimoku to his nephew Kamehameha. Such divisions of political and religious powers had occurred in the past. Soon Kīwalaʻō and Kamehameha began to fight for the overlordship of the entire island. Kīwalaʻō was killed, but Kamehameha was unable to win over the chiefs who had supported his rival. A decade of battles followed, between Kamehameha, who ruled mostly over Kohala and Kona, and the chiefs who ruled Hāmākua-Hilo and Puna-Kaʻū.

In March 1790, Kamehameha took a cannon from the captured trading vessel *Fair American*, and seized two sailors familiar with cannons and Western-style warfare. Kamehameha adopted the irresistible new weapons and tactics. Soon, only the chief of Kaʻū, Kīwalaʻō's half-brother Keōua, stood against Kamehameha.

In 1791, Pele intervened: Kīlauea erupted, and a rain of ashes fell upon Kaʻū. Close to four hundred Hawaiians, Keōua's warriors and their families, choked or burned to death. Deeply shaken, Keōua ceased his offensive. Also in 1791, Kamehameha began to construct the enormous heiau of Puʻukoholā—the Hill of the Whale—on the site of an older, smaller heiau. He believed that the gods would favor him and grant him victory.

When the heiau was finished, Kamehameha invited Keōua to the dedication ceremony. Keōua arrived and was killed by Kamehameha's warriors before he had a chance to walk onto Kawaihae's shores. His body was then offered as a sacrifice on the altar of the new luakini heiau. The Big Island belonged to Kamehameha.

In 1795, Kamehameha seized Maui, Lānaʻi, and Molokaʻi, then sailed to Oʻahu. The battle for Oʻahu culminated on the pali, or cliff, of Nuʻuanu, where hundreds of Oʻahu warriors fell to their death, forced over the edge of the steep cliff by the onslaught of Kamehameha's armies. Only Kauaʻi was left to be conquered.

Kamehameha made several attempts to send a force to Kauaʻi. A planned attack in 1796 was foiled by a storm. Kamehameha renewed preparations, building canoes and gathering an armada. But an 1804 epidemic, one that killed thousands across the islands, also killed much of his invasion force.

Eventually, Kamehameha decided to compromise with the Kauaʻi chief, Kaumualiʻi. Kaumualiʻi would formally recognize Kamehameha as his sovereign; in return, he would be allowed to retain control of Kauaʻi. Finally, in the year 1810, Kamehameha had accomplished his task. The Islands had been unified.

Kamehameha returned to Kailua in 1812 to handle the ongoing task of keeping the Islands organized amid growing foreign pressures. He delegated the individual islands to governors, and relied on his trusted advisor, Kalanimoku, his prime minister, to manage the governors.

The king spent the last years of his life peacefully at his residence, Kamakahonu, near the sacred Ahuʻena Heiau in Kailua. He died May 8, 1819, after a long illness; he was probably about 61 years of age. In keeping with custom, his bones were bundled up and hidden by trusted retainers. His last words were "Endless is the good I have conquered for you to enjoy."

"The wars were over and the Kingdom of Hawai'i firmly established. At Kamakahonu, his estate at Kailua Village in Kona, Kamenameha devoted his last years to ruling his kingdom as a benevolent and just monarch, encouraging prosperity, conducting business with foreigners, and educating his son Liholiho as his successor. [Here he is] wearing [a] simple kapa garment [while] in conversation with his son Liholiho. Beside him stands his prime minister, Kalanimoku. The prince's attendant, wearing a short yellow cape, is John Papa I'i, who later became an important historian. The fish in the foreground represent the gifts brought daily to the court. Two ladies of the court are seated at the left. Kamehameha's residence was a complex of thatched structures around a tranquil cove at Kailua Bay. Across the cove stands 'Ahu'ena his private temple." Voyagers [**Kamehameha at Kanakahonu**/Herb Kawainui Kāne]

29

☗☗☗☗☗☗☗☗☗☗☗☗

Above left: "In the foreground Kamehameha's business agent John Young and a visiting foreign officer are in conversation with two guards beside one of the eighteen cannons that faced the bay. The thatched building in the distance at right is the king's retreat, the doorway concealed by a small guardhouse where Kamehameha could [secretly] keep watch over the traffic in the bay as well as view his upland plantations. The heiau, built on a platform of rockwork, was dedicated to patron spirits of learning, the arts, and healing.... The largest structure, the hale mana (house of power), required more than three hundred thousand ti leaves in the thatching. 'Ahu'ena heiau is now on the National Registry of Historic Places." Voyagers [**'Ahu'ena Heiau**/ *Herb Kawainui Kāne*]

En route to China in early 1790, the American trading ship *Eleanora,* owned by Captain Simon Metcalfe, anchored in Kealakekua Bay. Captain Metcalfe was there to meet the small two-master *Fair American,* commanded by his eighteen-year-old son. After several weeks of waiting, Metcalfe, impatient and short-tempered, sailed to Maui to obtain fresh water. There a Hawaiian chief took one of his cutters. In retaliation, Metcalfe killed hundreds of innocent villagers. Still seething, he returned to Kealakekua on March 16. When a Hawaiian chief from North Kona boarded the *Eleanora,* Metcalfe lashed out again. The chief swore to take revenge. The next American ship to pass by would be his.

Hours later, the *Fair American* sailed past North Kona's shores, and as it reached Ka'ūpūlehu, the chief attacked and killed six of the seven crewmen, including Metcalfe's son. Only the first mate, Isaac Davis, a sailor from Wales, survived, wounded and nearly blinded. Kamehameha took him under his protection, and claimed the ship, its cannon, and other armaments.

The following day, the boatswain of the *Eleanora,* John Young, an experienced sailor from Lancashire, England, obtained permission from Metcalfe to explore the lands around Kealakekua, oblivious to what had happened some seventeen miles north. Nor did he know that Kamehameha, afraid that Metcalfe would find out about the fate of the *Fair American,* had ordered that no canoes were to leave shore; Young could not return to his ship. After a

[Hawai'i State Archives]

couple of days, the *Eleanora* sailed off without him. Eventually, Young met Kamehameha and found Davis. Caught in an alien culture, the two Englishmen became close friends.

Aware of the unprecedented advantage in warfare and trading that the two Westerners could provide, Kamehameha made them his assistants. Young and Davis, armed with cannon and muskets, trained Kamehameha's warriors and led them in the fiercest battles. Confident that he could rely on them, Kamehameha attacked the Maui chief Kahekili that same year. His artillery, against which Maui's warriors had no defense,

wreaked havoc in a battle in the 'Īao Valley above Wailuku.

Other chiefs started to accumulate Western-style arsenals. In 1791, Kahekili thought he had acquired enough guns to challenge Kamehameha. In this he was aided by the chief of Kaua'i, who sailed to Waipi'o and desecrated a heiau said to have been built by Līloa. Kahekili sailed to Hālawa in Kohala, and plundered his way east.

But Kamehameha's generals, Young and Davis, had managed to buy many weapons from the trading vessels that stopped in Kealakekua Bay. Kamehameha was able to bring seven hundred

⟫⟨⟩⟨⟩⟨⟩⟨⟩⟨⟩⟨⟩⟨⟩⟨⟫

Left: Kamehameha led his war fleet to Maui with the intention of conquering the island. He stands aboard the Fair American, *a Western-style ship, with his trusted advisors and friends Isaac Davis and John Young. [**Kamehameha Aboard** Fair American/Herb Kawainui Kāne]*

Above: Queen Emma (1836-1885) was born and raised in Honolulu, but her roots lay in Kawaihae, in the Big Island, the home of her grandfather, John Young. During the Mahele, the land division of the 1840s, when lands were distributed to the king, chiefs, and commoners, Emma's uncle Keoni Ana, John Young's son, was given half of the Kawaihae ahupua'a; the other half was crown land. Emma later inherited Keoni Ana's Kawaihae landholdings, making her the largest landowner in the ahupua'a. [Joseph W. King/Bishop Museum]

canoes, heavy with firearms, and twenty thousand men to fight the Maui and Kaua'i chiefs. Young and Davis commanded the fight from aboard the *Fair American*. Hawai'i's first armed sea battle is remembered as the Battle of the Red-Mouthed Gun, due to the blood that was shed. For all the carnage, it was indecisive.

Although Young and Davis had tried to escape during their first year in the islands, they eventually resigned themselves to their fate. Kamehameha treated the two sailors as if they were high chiefs. He provided them with wives and granted them lands. Young, who built his homestead east and inland of Pu'ukoholā Heiau, was named 'Olohana, for his favorite command, "All hands." He was the king's most trusted advisor and served as Kamehameha's interpreter and liaison with Western visitors.

In 1802, Kamehameha named Young the Big Island's governor. Upon the king's return to the Big Island in 1812, the two men, both wiser and older, deepened the genuine friendship that had grown between them. When the king died in 1819, John Young sat at his side and was the last man to embrace him.

Young spent his last years with his daughter Grace and her husband, Dr. Thomas C.B. Rooke, in Honolulu. He died in 1835 at the age of 91. His eldest daughter, Fanny, became the mother of Emma Na'ea, who married Kamehameha IV in 1856. Emma gave birth to a royal heir, Prince Albert, in 1858, but the child died at age four. Today, there are no known descendants of Young.

Davis became governor of O'ahu. He died in 1810. It was rumored that he was poisoned, in revenge for his actions when he foiled a plot to kill the chief of Kaua'i. His three children were adopted by Young. In later years, Princess Ruth Ke'elikōlani took one of his grandsons as her husband.

THE MONARCHY AFTER 1819

Queen Kaʻahumanu (1768–1832) was born in Hana, Maui. Her father, Keʻeaumoku, was an aliʻi from the Big Island; her mother was a high-ranking Maui chiefess. Her father became one of Kamehameha I's strongest warriors and most trusted advisors. Her brothers were also prominent in Kamehameha's army. Kamehameha sealed his connection with this powerful clan by marrying Kaʻahumanu when she was only thirteen. Date unknown. [Hawaiʻi State Archives]

Among Kamehameha's five royal wives was the beautiful Kaʻahumanu, the daughter of the high-ranking Kona chief Keʻeaumoku. He had arranged their 1785 marriage when she was just thirteen, and within a few years, Kamehameha and Kaʻahumanu had become inseparable.

Kaʻahumanu was not only a large woman— six feet tall, with tattoos on her hands, legs, and tongue— she was also powerful and intelligent. Kamehameha respected her counsel and gave her the godlike power of puʻuhonua, so that her presence provided a sanctuary for those who had broken the kapu. He also learned to live with her frequent affairs, aware that their marriage, despite its stormy nature, was in his own interest.

Kaʻahumanu's strong will, free spirit, and determination would change the course of Hawaiian history. Through traders and sailing crews—John Young among them—news of another god had reached Hawaiʻi. Kaʻahumanu saw that the foreigners who did not heed the ancient kapu were not struck down by the Hawaiian gods. As her quest for power intensified, she realized that to advance herself, she must find a way to break the old kapu and gain privileges that, until then, only men enjoyed.

After Kamehameha's death in 1819, which was followed by a traditional period of sanctioned chaos, the time came for his eldest son, Liholiho, to ascend the throne and reinforce the kapu. Kaʻahumanu declared herself co-regent, and, with the support of the high priest, decided to challenge the Hawaiian gods once and for all.

Liholiho's mother was Keōpūolani, Kamehameha's highest-ranking wife. Her children by Kamehameha were of even higher personal rank than their father. But the king's heir, just twenty-two, lacked the courage and self-assurance of his parents. When Kaʻahumanu instructed Liholiho to eat with the chiefly women, he did not dare resist. On a November day in 1819, fortified with liquor, he staggered to the women's table, sat down, and partook of the women's food. Disaster did not follow. "'Ai noa," the guests shouted. "The kapu is broken." Across the island, upon Liholiho's orders, heiau and idols were torn down.

When the chief Kekuaokalani, who was in Kealakekua at the old luakini heiau of Hikiau, heard that Liholiho had broken the kapu, he marched north with his army to defend the old gods. Kekuaokalani fought the old-fashioned way, with spears and clubs; Liholiho brought artillery. In December 1819, at Keauhou Bay, the two forces met in what is now known as the Battle of Kuamoʻo. Kekuaokalani's army was massacred. Hundreds are said to be buried in the Lekeleke Burial Grounds of Keauhou, at the end of a desolate stretch of jagged lava fields.

The overthrow of the kapu, the value system that had given structure to daily life, left a spiritual void. . In 1820, four months after the kapu had been broken, Protestant Christian missionaries from Boston arrived. Keōpūolani became the first aliʻi to turn to the new religion. Liholiho, content with five wives and a life of luxury, gave the Christians permission to stay, but did not convert to their creed.

Kaʻahumanu kept her distance from the missionaries and their new religion until she fell seriously ill. She then learned to read and write, and was baptized in 1825. Two years later, she proclaimed new laws based on the Christian scriptures. She died on June 5, 1832, at her Mānoa Valley home in Honolulu, hours after the first edition of the missionaries' Hawaiian-language New Testament had come off the press. By then, secular and religious leadership had become deeply entwined, and Protestant Christianity had effectively become Hawaiʻi's state religion.

After the dramatic abolition of the kapu, Liholiho—Kamehameha II—shared rulership with Kaʻahumanu. Influenced by European and American traders, Hawaiʻi had changed substantially, and affairs of state required more guidance than the young king could provide. The kingdom was in turmoil. Diseases were beginning to claim commoners and chiefs alike. Foreigners were pressuring the new Hawaiian government. Liholiho's decisions would eventually hasten the end of the old Hawaiian ways.

In 1820, Liholiho moved the royal court to Honolulu to ensure control over merchant ships, which had

>X0I(>X0I(>X0I(>X0I(>X0I(>X

Far left: During the reign of Kamehameha II (Liholiho), the ancient kapu system was overthrown, the American missionaries arrived, and the sandalwood trade flourished. Liholiho also led a stormy voyage to Kaua'i to bring back as his vassal Kaumuali'i, the island's king. [Hawai'i State Archives]

Left: Kamehameha III, Keauikeaouli, and his wife, Kalama Hakaleleponi Kapakuhaili had two children, both of whom died as babies. The royal couple adopted three hānai children including his nephew, Alexander Liholiho, who eventually ascended the throne as Kamehameha IV; a girl named Kaimina'auao who died young; and Albert. During his long reign, the sandalwood trade declined, whaling practices rose and fell, the sugar industry grew, and the missionaries built churches and schools. [Hawai'i State Archives]

begun to favor the sheltered harbor at Honolulu over the Big Island's Kona coast. In November 1823, possibly seeking to escape from daunting responsibilities, he set out on a voyage to England with his favorite wife, his half-sister Kamāmalu. In July 1824, the royal couple died of measles in London.

Upon his brother's death, Kauikeaouli ascended the throne as Kamehameha III. He was only eleven years old. Born in a village on Keauhou Bay (the site is marked by a stone memorial)the young prince followed his older brother Liholiho to Honolulu when the royal court was moved. Though he visited the Big Island in 1820, he never lived there again.

Since his mother, Keōpūolani, had been an early convert to Christianity, Kauikeaouli had been taught by Protestant missionaries from the age of six. Although a nominal Christian, he was always torn between the old ways and the new. In order to ensure that his children would be of high rank, he cohabited with his half-sister Nāhi'ena'ena, a situation to which the missionaries strongly objected. He disobeyed

them in other ways as well, drinking and carousing with raffish friends, both Hawaiian and Caucasian. His legitimate children died and he left no direct descendants.

Kauikeaouli ruled longer than any other Hawaiian king: thirty eventful years, from 1824 to 1854. He signed Hawai'i's first written constitution. His sovereignty was threatened by foreign warships. In 1843, a British commander took control of the government at cannon point, though his government restored sovereignty after five months. The 1848 Mahele made private land ownership law, and the cash economy of Hawai'i began to depend on the outside world.

Many of Kauikeaouli's policies had a long-lasting effect on the Big Island. He parceled out land under the Mahele. To encourage the growing trade in beef and hides, he had Spanish-Mexican cowboys, vaqueros, brought in from California. Their influence is still felt in the paniolo (Hawaiian cowboy) culture—in its work habits, skills and crafts, and distinctive slack-key guitar music.

ROYAL VISITS

Right: Kalākaua's first coronation was a modest affair, thanks to the disputed election. Several years later, in 1883, he staged a coronation after his own heart: lavish, expensive, replete with European pomp and Hawaiian display. He scandalized missionaries by including hula performances in the ceremonies. He built 'Iolani Palace, then the last word in modernity and style, but also spent much time at his boathouse in Honolulu Harbor, where he drank, played cards, and relaxed with his friends. Date unknown. [Hawai'i State Archives]

Far right: Lili'uokalani was married to John Owen Dominis, the son of a sea captain who had settled in Honolulu. Much to her sorrow, they had no children of their own. She raised three hānai (adopted) children: Lydia Aholo, Kaiponohea 'Ae'a, and John Owen Dominis, Jr., her husband's son by another woman. 1881. [Baker-Van Dyke Collection]

David Kalākaua (1836–1891)

When Kamehameha V died without a declared successor in 1874, the Hawaiian Legislature was asked to elect a new king. After a passionately disputed election, they selected David Kalākaua, who came of a high-ranked lineage of Big Island chiefs. Under his reign, Hawai'i assumed a larger international role, economically and politically.

Kalākaua liked to travel to the Big Island for rest and relaxation. He remodeled Hulihe'e Palace in Kailua and staged frequent dances there. He often went up to Waimea, where his classmate and close friend, Samuel Parker, had inherited half of the island's largest cattle ranch. In Hilo, the kingdom's second-largest town, Kalākaua maintained a small royal residence, a cottage.

Kalākaua's reputation for Hawaiian joie de vivre earned him the nickname Merrie Monarch. This name was proudly adopted by the Hawai'i Island Chamber of Commerce when in 1963 they sponsored the Merrie Monarch Festival, now the world's premier hula competition.

Lili'uokalani (1839–1917)

Kalākaua's sister succeded him upon his death in 1891. She, too, often stayed at the royal summer house in Hilo, and came to care deeply for the town and its residents. Around 1911, she donated five acres of her personal lands to crate a garden there, it still exists today. A gifted musician and songwriter, she composed the most famous song of Hawai'i, "Aloha Oe." Her reign ended when in January, 1893, the Hawaiian kingdom was overthrown in a bloodless revolution at Honolulu, led by resident American businessmen backed by United States marines from a warship in the harbor.

PRINCESS RUTH "LUKA" KE'ELIKŌLANI

As the great-granddaughter of King Kamehameha I, Ruth Ke'elikōlani was devoted to her Hawaiian culture and heritage and wary of all things foreign, including the English language and Christian beliefs. She is still remembered for an 1881 visit to Hilo, then threatened by a flood of lava from Mauna Loa. She prayed and gave offerings to Pele, the volcano goddess; the lava stopped.

Her life was filled with personal tragedy. At age sixteen, Ruth married Leleiohoku, the son of Kamehameha I's prime advisor Kalanimoku. Ruth's second child died in infancy, her husband fell victim to a measles epidemic in 1848, and in 1859 her first-born was killed in an accident at age seventeen. Ruth remarried in 1856, but her second husband, a grandson of Isaac Davis, was abusive and they separated within a year.

[Hawai'i State Archives]

She had adopted the younger brother of David Kalākaua, whom she renamed Leleiohoku and whom she hoped would claim the throne, but he died in 1877 at age twenty-three.

From her first husband, Ruth had inherited vast estates, including the stone-and-mortar Hulihe'e Palace in Kailua. She herself became the Big Island's governor in 1855. Ruth, however, would not sleep inside Hulihe'e Palace, preferring a native grass house. She resided mostly in Hilo, and remained governor until 1869.

In the end, Ruth, said to have been "the largest and richest woman in the islands," had nothing but her wealth. When she fell ill, she left the enormous mansion that she had built in Honolulu and returned to Kailua and the Big Island. She died in her beloved grass house on May 24, 1883. Heir to her estates was her cousin Princess Bernice Pauahi Bishop, who, with Ruth's death, became the last remaining direct descendant of Kamehameha I. Thus almost all of Ruth's royal lands became part of the Bishop Estate.

Below: Hulihe'e Palace, a two-story stone mansion in the Western style, was built by Governor Kuakini in 1837–1838, on the seafront at Kailua-Kona. The building with a steeple is Makuaikua Church, also built in the 1830s by Kuakini. Hulihe'e Palace was the Kona residence of royal governors; it also housed the kings and queens of Hawai'i whenever they visited the Kona coast. Princess Ruth disliked the palace, and while governor of the Big Island, she lived either in her Hilo cottage or in a grass house on the Hulihe'e grounds. [Hawai'i State Archives]

Above: A visit to Captain James Cook's monument at Kealakekua Bay, 1886. King Kalākaua is in the white suit, to the right is Princess Lili'uokalani, and next to her is John A. Cummins. [Baker-Van Dyke Collection]

Right: King Kalākaua at the Amulus residence in Ho'okena, Kona (top of stairs), with Prince and Princess Henri de Bourbon on his left. They also visited Hulihe'e Palace. Circa 1886. [Hawai'i State Archives]

Left: Kalākaua (standing second from right) in Kailua, Kona, would visit friends, well-wishers, and his subjects, trying to win their loyalty and uplift their morale. Circa 1886. [Bishop Museum]

Below: Sam Parker's carriages pick up guests at Kawaihae Harbor for the trip to Parker Ranch. Prince Jonah Kūhiō Kalaniana'ole, Princess Ka'iulani, Princess Elizabeth Kahanu Kalaniana'ole. [Baker-Van Dyke Collection]

WESTERNIZATION

First had come the explorers. Then merchants and adventurers. Then, in 1820—the year after Kamehameha I died—came American missionaries, bringing word of a new god, the God of the big Western world.

The goal of the missionaries was to convert Hawaiians to Christianity. This meant dismantling and breaking up "pagan" Hawaiian culture.

The mission of the merchants was to use the Hawaiian islands to make money. First, a trade in aromatic sandalwood, for which there was a lucrative market across the Pacific in China. Then whaling, using the port of Honolulu for transshipment—a big business for decades.

The island of Hawai'i was the center of another Western business: cattle ranching. Parker Ranch in Kohala grew to be bigger than any other ranch of its time on the American mainland, and it was the birthplace of a distinctively Hawaiian cowboy culture: "paniolo" life.

Of all the impacts of the nineteenth-century "big world," the greatest and most devastating was disease. Epidemic diseases, one after another, came in at the port of Honolulu and spread through the islands.

By the latter part of the nineteenth century, the Hawaiian population was on its way to being devastated. On the island of Hawai'i, whole districts were emptying out. The old culture survived only partially, and only in scattered remote areas.

MERCHANTS, ADVENTURERS, AND TRADERS

◆〉X《◆〉X《◆〉X《◆〉X《◆〉X《◆

Previous pages: After the Kailua Church was destroyed in a terrible fire in December 1835, eager volunteers encouraged by Governor Kuakini built Mokuaikaua Church in its place. The cornerstone was laid January 1, 1836, and almost one year later the new church was completed, on January 31, 1837. It was built to last, constructed of lava rock walls and a koa roof supported by 'ōhi'a beams. Benches were introduced for the first time, replacing floor mats, but they restricted space for the more-than-4,000-person congregation so a lānai was constructed around the sides of the building to provide additional seating. [Tongg Publishing Co.]

Right: As the sandalwood trade waned, whaling became the economic mainstay of merchants in Hawai'i. Each season the crews of the American whaling fleets descended like locusts on the ports of Honolulu and Lahaina, seeking provisions and the sailors' traditional pleasures of the bottle and the flesh. [Hawai'i State Archives]

For centuries, isolated from the rest of the world, the Hawaiians had fished and farmed contentedly. They practiced their arts, lived in harmony with the land, and carefully managed their resources. Their barter economy was far removed from international, large-scale trade and cash-based industries. But during the course of the nineteenth century, in contact with Western technology and Western values, Hawaiian ways would undergo irrevocable and relentless change.

Word of the Sandwich Islands had spread quickly in Europe and America. In the 1800s, three groups—merchants, whalers, and missionaries—would seek out the islands in distinct, but not always compatible, ways. Overwhelmed, unable to resist, and struggling to understand, the Hawaiians adopted—for better or worse—the goods, skills, food, and teachings that the foreigners brought. Hawaiian men who decided to join the merchant and whaling crews came home with new ideas, which accelerated the changes.

The Hawaiians became caught between two worlds. Their traditions and customs started blending with those from the West—but not completely. Status symbols shifted. Money started to replace barter. One of the biggest shifts toward Western standards would come in the mid-1800s, with the privatization of land.

Hawaiians, used to feudal ways, did not understand the importance of keeping title to the land and readily sold it. More and more land was owned by foreign immigrants, who built new Western enterprises on Hawaiian soil.

The Sandalwood Trade

In the early 1800s, Western merchant ships frequently anchored off Kailua, Kawaihae, and Hilo. The island offered provisions, a respite from a rough life at sea, and the opportunity to make money—particularly by trading for 'iliahi, the fragrant sandalwood that the Hawaiians used to scent their kapa cloth. The merchants had discovered that Chinese merchants would pay high prices for sandalwood, which was used to make perfume, incense, and fans, among other things. The sandalwood tree grew abundantly on the Big Island, and the merchants convinced Kamehameha I to sell the sandalwood to them.

By 1809, 'iliahi was a regular trade commodity, for which the merchants paid with exotic merchandise that the chiefs could not resist. Silks, brocades, crystal vases, fancy clocks, gilded mirrors, European clothes, and furniture became far more valuable than taro lo'i, fish ponds, feathered capes, or even scented kapa cloth.

Kamehameha I initially kept the sandalwood trade as a royal monopoly for himself and his 'ohana. Ali'i were allowed to keep "four parts by weight for every ten collected." Prices rose. When his son Liholiho came to power as Kamehameha II in 1819, he was unable to keep the chiefs from carrying on the trade on their own behalf. Many Big Island chiefs forced commoners off their taro patches to work in the forests. Men and women carried heavy logs to the coast on their bare backs, often dying of dehydration and exhaustion. Fields were abandoned. By the late 1820s, the 'iliahi forests had disappeared. The chiefs, who had been buying on credit against future trees, could not pay back their debts.

There were attempts to replace the sandalwood trade with other resources. While sea salt gathered in lava pans along the Kīholo coastline hardly sufficed, tallow, hides, and salted dried beef from wild cattle proved valuable.

But none of these crops were sufficient to pay off the debts. Sandalwood forced the transition from barter to money—a wider-reaching currency—and created a desperate need for cash.

The Whalers

Sometime after 1810, the whalers came. They were rough, lonely men who were out at sea for three or four years at a time and found in the Islands a pleasant place to spend the winter before returning to icy hunting grounds. Although Maui's Lahaina would become the favorite whaling spot, thousands of whalers swarmed Hilo, Kawaihae, and Kailua, demanding liquor, supplies, and female company in exchange for cash. Brothels and bars came to line muddy tracks where Hawaiians had once bartered taro for fish. Many maka'āinana, commoner men and women, joined the whaling crews.

In the autumn of 1819, the *Balaena* anchored in Kealakekua Bay, harpooned one whale, and harvested 110 barrels of oil. Such a potential bonus added to the attraction of the Islands as a replenishing site.

The whalers, for whom it was said there was no god west of Cape Horn, were the curse of the missionaries, who began settling in 1820. Between 1852 and 1857, an annual average of sixty-five whaling ships moored in Hilo Bay. "Licentiousness and drunkenness are their besetting sins, and most of them are profane in the extreme," wrote missionary wife Sarah Lyman.

But the seamen brought in thousands of dollars, not just sins. A cash-based economy found its start. The sailors bought salt beef, tallow, and hides, spurring the island's young cattle industry. Small enterprises opened up that provided services in exchange for cash. Natives served as laundry men, barbers, blacksmiths, carpenters, ship builders, messengers, and guides. A few general stores opened up. Bustling villages grew up around Hawai'i's whaling ports. By 1850, money was the new standard.

Around 1876, oil had replaced whale products. The transition was accelerated by two disasters in the Arctic ice in which dozens of vessels and their crews were lost. The whalers stopped coming, but fortunately, Kamehameha III had earlier paid off the monarchy's accumulated trading debts.

THE MAHELE

In pre-contact times, the high chiefs held the ultimate title to land, which they handed out as estates to their retainers. The lesser chiefs then distributed land to the commoners who worked upon it. Every time a chiefdom was conquered, or a new chief came to power, land was redistributed. The foreigners who settled in the islands disliked this system as they wanted to own land in fee simple, not at the whim of a chief.

In 1848 Kamehameha III initiated the land reforms called the Great Mahele. Henceforth, land was to be held in fee simple. The reform took years to complete.

The king and the chiefs laid claim to vast tracts of land, though much of it was mountain, lava, forest, and dry uplands. Commoners claimed only slightly more than 2 percent of the total, but this land consisted of house lots and fertile valley parcels, the most valuable land at that time. Only in the late nineteenth century would the dry uplands become valuable, thanks to irrigation ditches and artesian wells.

The Hawaiians could not hold onto their land; they did not understand the new system. In the end, most of the kingdom's lands ended up in the hands of immigrant foreigners, Caucasian or Asian.

A Scotsman, James Wight, who was stranded in Kohala in the year 1850, started with 22.5 acres. Eventually his estate grew to 17,000 acres. One of the first foreigners to own land, John Palmer Parker, would expand his holdings to thousands of acres, forming the huge Parker Ranch.

HAWAIIAN WAYS: A THREATENED CULTURE

◆》X《◇》X《◇》X《◇》X《◇》X《◆

This photograph captures a moment in cultural time when ancient ways were first blending with the foreign influences that later inundated Hawai'i. A family dressed in Western clothing is shown in front of their hale pili, or grass house. Across the wooden bar connecting the two papaya trees in the foreground is a large throw net for fishing. [Bishop Museum]

The nineteenth century was tragic for the Hawaiian people. The big world ran roughshod over them and their small islands. Hawaiian culture and language were scorned; traditional values were trampled upon; the Hawaiian life of the land was uprooted.

By the end of the century, the very existence of the Hawaiians as a people was threatened—extinction was looming as a real possibility. The cause was simple and terrible: introduced diseases. Living in isolation for so long, Hawaiians had not been exposed to all the diseases of the "big world." Now those diseases came to the Islands by ship, carried by sailors, and they were fatal to Hawaiians. Epidemics, one after the other, devastated the population.

In 1778, the year of Captain Cook's first Hawaiian landfall, probably more than 100,000 people lived on the Big Island. By 1823, the visiting missionary William Ellis' estimate was 85,000. In the first missionary census in 1832, the figure was 45,600. In 1853, only 27,200 Hawaiians were left. In that year there were 2,726 deaths and just 586 births on the Big Island.

"It can scarcely be said," wrote George Kenway from Waimea in 1853, "that there is any Native population at all. The hill sides and the banks of watercourses show for miles the ruins of the 'olden time'—Stone

were also against traditional Hawaiian enjoyments. Under Calvinist influence, the government banned public performance of the hula. Sex outside Christian marriage could lead to jail time and work on road gangs. Surfing and other Hawaiian sports were denigrated. And the Hawaiian body, traditionally and healthfully exposed to the warm air of the Islands, was to be covered with hot, heavy clothing, in the interests of Christian decency.

To teach Christianity and to inculcate Christian civilization, the missionaries learned to speak and write Hawaiian. Hawaiians took to reading and writing in their own language with great appetite. But English was presented as the true language of civilization and Hawaiian was denigrated. And there were fewer and fewer Hawaiians to speak and write it. As the Hawaiian population dwindled and immigrants crowded into the Islands to work in the new base industry—plantation sugar—fluency in Hawaiian language faded; English and English-based pidgin became the lingua franca.

Young Hawaiians were leaving their rural homes for the excitement of town life. But out in the country, some small communities persevered in staying Hawaiian. People went to the missionary church on Sundays, but they also raised taro, pounded poi, and fished in the old ways. Deaths of close ones were mourned with the customary wailing. Keiki, or children, were joyfully adopted—gifts of their parents to the larger family, the community, the 'ohana.

Away from the watchful eyes of the missionaries, even going "underground," the old ways were practiced, taught, and preserved; tradition was kept alive.

◆》X《◆》X《◆》X《◆》X《◆》X《◆

A Hawaiian man holds a carrying pole and bundles; a calabash swings from one hand. His coat is made out of leaves. Date unknown. [Kona Historical Society]

walls half sunk in the ground, broken down and covered with grass.—large broken squares of trees and imperfect embankments.—remains of old taro patches and water runs now dried up and useless, and many other such tokens that like old coins old Castles and old books, impress one with a melancholy curiosity about a people that cannot now be found."

Among the things introduced by Westerners was alcohol, which had not been part of life in Hawai'i. By 1807, the Big Island was producing beer and distilled spirits, for a new kind of revelry—and a new way to drown sorrows.

The missionaries were against alcohol—and they

◆》Ⅹ《◆》Ⅹ《◆》Ⅹ《◆》Ⅹ《◆》Ⅹ《◆

Above and right: The Hawaiian concept of 'ohana, or family, encompassed kūpuna or elders down to keiki or children, living together under one roof, sharing experiences, wisdom, and life. An 'ohana extended beyond blood, to include neighbors and friends in a warm and secure embrace. It meant being constantly surrounded by people who truly cared, not out of a feeling of obligation, but from an inborn value that created an environment of genuine love. The 'ohana was largely responsible for keeping the Hawaiian culture alive during the dark days it faced. [Lyman House Memorial Museum]

Left: A Hawaiian family of Kapoho, Puna, photographed in 1894 with a visitor. The family is living in an old-style grass house, which would have been inexpensive but impermanent. The structure in the background may be an irrigation flume. The village of Kapoho was destroyed in 1960 by a volcanic eruption. [Baker-Van Dyke Collection]

THE HUKILAU

The shores along the Puna and Kohala coasts teemed with small fish as well as shrimp, crab, eel, and octopus. Hawaiians fished from canoes and boats, or waded out onto the reefs with spears, baskets, and small nets.

Sometimes communities held a hukilau, a group effort in which entire schools of fish were caught. The technique involved spreading a large net in a semicircle just off shore and then pulling the nets slowly towards shore, with the catch securely trapped inside. Dozens of people worked closely together and then shared the catch. To prolong the life of the nets, the fibers were soaked in a dye made from the pounded bark of the kukui nut tree. [Hawai'i State Archives]

MISSIONARIES

The Thurstons from Massachusetts arrived on the Big Island in 1820, with the First Company, but were soon moved to O'ahu. They did not return to the mission in Kailua until 1823. They were intensely dedicated and hardworking. They built churches and helped set up new missions along the Kona and Ka'ū coasts. Asa Thurston helped to translate the Bible into Hawaiian. He died in Honolulu, at age eighty, followed by Lucy eight years later. Over the course of half a century, she had kept a journal—a vivid, detailed account of early missionary days—which The Friend, a missionary publisher in Honolulu, published in 1934 as Life and Times of Mrs. Lucy G. Thurston. Of the Thurstons' five children, two died at a young age, and the others aided the mission. Their grandson, Lorrin Andrew Thurston (1858–1931), became Minister of the Interior, a leader in the overthrow of the monarchy in 1893, and, in 1900, publisher of the Honolulu Advertiser. The Thurston name remains prominent in the Islands today. [Hawaiian Mission Children's Society]

Sent from New England to establish Christian civilization, the men and women from the East coast of the United States brought a new religion to the Islands, and surrendered themselves body, heart, and soul to their task. The five months' voyage to Hawai'i was not a deterrent. The brig *Thaddeus* brought the First Company of New England Congregationalist missionaries, six couples, anchoring at Kawaihae on the first day of April, 1820. Over the next twenty-eight years, eleven more companies would follow, expanding the work of the ABCFM (American Board of Commissioners for Foreign Missions) over all of the Islands.

Mission work in all its aspects started immediately. The Big Island's first missionary wife, Lucy Thurston, was so shocked to see the Hawaiians' nakedness that she began to host a sewing circle for native women on April 3, 1820, before the missionaries had even gained permission to stay. As it turned out, the mission on the Big Island would be delayed.

After gaining Kamehameha II's support, Asa and Lucy Thurston, and the physician Thomas Holman and his wife, Lucia, stayed in Kailua, while the others sailed to Honolulu. The four foreigners spent their first night in Kailua in a flea-infested, dirt-floored native hut. They were unprepared for the scarcity of water, heat, and meals of dog meat. In July the Holmans fled. When Kamehameha moved his court to O'ahu, the mission feared for the Thurstons' safety and ordered them to O'ahu. They did not return to Kailua until September 1823.

The missionaries had been ordered by the mission board not to interfere with the kingdom or its government. However, caught in the struggle between the old ways and the new, sincerely anxious to protect their congregations from bullying foreign governments, avaricious traders, and rampaging sailors, they soon became political advisors and, before long, were deeply involved in matters of state. In some ways, their influence was beneficial—they were able to protect their charges from the worst of the Westerners. But they were rigorous in insisting on Protestant morality, forbidding anything they saw as "heathenish," thus contributing to the destruction of much of the old culture.

Several missionaries and their sons went into sugar planting. But others labored to help the Hawaiians keep their independence and their land. Most fought hard for schools, literacy, and Western medicine. By 1837, the northern district of the Big Island boasted 155 schools, over 5,010 students, and 10,000 textbooks.

Few missionaries abandoned their cause, even though the rugged, isolated vastness of the Big Island took its toll. Basic food supplies were always scarce, medical care was inadequate, and cultural differences made their life lonely and difficult.

In 1863, the American Board of Commissioners for Foreign Missions considered its work complete and transferred its responsibilities to the Hawai'i Evangelical Association. The ABCFM had supported missions all over the Big Island, even in such remote areas as the deep valleys of Kohala, the lava-strewn lands of Puna, and the desert of Ka'ū By 1882, only three of the original mission stations remained—in Kohala, Waimea, and Hilo.

The Journal of William Ellis (1794–1872)

The mission received unexpected help when William Ellis from the London Missionary Society arrived in 1822. Familiar with Tahitian—he had been stationed in the Society Islands—Ellis quickly mastered Hawaiian. On June 23, 1823, soon after the April 27 arrival of the Second Company, Ellis sailed to the Big Island to scout suitable station sites. Accompanied by three American colleagues—Asa Thurston, Joseph Goodrich, and Artemas Bishop—Ellis journeyed through all the districts, even into remote areas where no one had ever seen a white person before. His tour guide was Makoa, who for many years had been Kamehameha's personal messenger. Ellis became the first foreigner to climb Kīlauea volcano. The tour lasted two months, during which time Ellis recorded detailed impressions. His

Narrative of a Tour through Hawaii, or *The Journal of William Ellis,* is one of earliest and most reliable accounts of nineteenth-century Hawai'i. Ellis returned to England after eighteen months in the Islands.

Artemas Bishop (1795-1872)

Artemas Bishop from New York came with the Second Company and served on the Big Island from 1824 to 1836. Like most of his colleagues, he became fluent in Hawaiian and translated numerous books. Several times he repeated William Ellis' challenging tour, and trekked to rugged and isolated areas. Sereno Edwards Bishop, one of his sons, was the first missionary boy born in the Hawai'i to return to the islands after attending seminary in the northeastern United States.

The Hilo Mission: David and Sarah Lyman (1803–1884 and 1805–1885)

Arriving with the Fifth Company in 1832, David and Sarah Lyman were sent to Hilo. There they gave their steady, unwavering support to the Hawaiian community and their Hilo neighbors, as the town grew from a small fishing village into a bustling sugar port. The Hilo Boarding School for boys that David Lyman opened in 1836 was his principal passion, but he also supervised other schools and several churches. Daily farming was a critical part of the curriculum at the boarding school. About twelve boys enrolled in the first year. By 1841, sixty boys boarded full-time in

◆》✕《◆》✕《◆》✕《◆》✕《◆

Above: William Ellis did this drawing of a missionary preaching at Kailua-Kona. Circa 1827. [Bishop Museum]

Below: Ellis' sympathetic observations of native life, showing a people struggling to adjust to changing times, marked him as a man apart in the Hawai'i of his time, particularly among his missionary colleagues. [Hawai'i State Archives]

Hilo just to hear him preach. When on November 7, 1837, a tsunami struck during a service, killing thirteen people, Coan was quick to interpret the disaster as a warning from God. He used this to turn the mission around. Eight months later on July 7, 1838, Coan baptized 1,705 Hawaiians. History remembered these events as "the Great Revival." By 1840, Coan's congregation of seven thousand converts accounted for more than half of all church members in the Islands. In 1857, Coan found the support needed for the construction of Haili Church, which was dedicated on April 8, 1859, and is still in use today. He died December 1, 1882, soon after the publication of his autobiography, *Life in Hawaii.*

◆》✕《◆》✕《◆》✕《◆》✕《◆》✕《◆

Above: The Lyman family lived in a thatched-roof 'ōhi'a- and koa-wood house that David and Sarah had built in 1839 and expanded in 1855. This historic home is considered the oldest frame building on the Big Island and the second oldest in the islands. In 1931 it opened as a museum, still filled with period pieces and the original furniture. In this formal portrait sit David and Sarah Lyman and four of their children. Seven children survived them, staying in the Islands and joining the political and business elite. [Hawaiian Mission Children's Society]

Right: Titus Coan (1801–1881) with his first wife, Fidelia Church Coan (1810–1872). Titus remarried in 1873, to Lydia Bingham (1834–1915). Date unknown. [Hawaiian Mission Children's Society]

an enlarged schoolhouse. Sarah Lyman raised seven children (an eighth child died as a toddler), taught, and in later years educated Chinese immigrants.

Lyman's school led to similar manual-training boarding schools in the Islands and in America. The Hilo Boarding School closed in the 1920s. Sarah's personal journal and letters contribute to the most colorful descriptions of early nineteenth-century life in Hawai'i and give haunting descriptions of the loneliness of a missionary wife. After a four-month illness, David Lyman died on October 4, 1884, at age eighty-one. Sarah followed fourteen months later, on December 7, 1885, at age eighty.

Titus Coan (1801-1882)

Although the chiefess Kapi'olani had urged the Hawaiians of Hilo to convert to Christianity, and although the resident missionary, David Lyman, was an excellent preacher in Hawaiian, Hilo's natives remained reluctant to join the new church. In 1835, Titus Coan from the Seventh Company came to Hilo and spurred the religious awakening for which the Mission had been praying. Thousands flocked to

LORENZO LYONS

The Waimea missionary Lorenzo Lyons (1807–1886) wrote beautiful Hawaiian hymns that are still sung today. One of his most popular songs is "Hawai'i Aloha," which is sung even on secular occasions, such as the opening of the State Legislature. He lived in Waimea for fifty-four years and was known to his parishioners as Makua Laiana, Father Lyons.

He and his first wife, Betsey Curtis, arrived in Waimea in 1832. Lyons was often away, traveling. In those days, he was responsible for all of Kohala and Hāmākua. He was a small man, said to weigh only 110 pounds, but he covered his enormous district on foot with indefatigable zeal. He converted thousands of Hawaiians and built nineteen churches, some of which survive today.

His young wife gave birth to two children and did her best to make a home in what were to her the lonely, uncomfortable surroundings of Waimea. She died in 1837. Lyons married again, in 1838, to Lucia Garratt Smith, a young woman who had come to the islands as a missionary teacher. Lucia gave him two more children and survived her husband by several years, dying in 1892.

Lyons' home church, the stone church of 'Imiola in Waimea, survives today, though it was severely damaged by the 2006 earthquake. However, his most enduring monument may be one song, "Hawai'i Aloha."
[Hawai'i State Archives]

"Hawai'i Aloha"

E Hawai'i, e ku'u one hanau e,
Ku'u home kulaiwi nei,
'Oli no au i na pono lani ou,
E Hawai'i, aloha e.
Hui: E hau'oli na 'opio o Hawai'i nei.
'Oli e! 'Oli e!
Mai na aheahe makani e pa mai
nei mau ke aloha, no Hawai`i.

E ha'i mai kou mau kini lani e, Kou
mau kupa aloha, e Hawai'i,
Na mea 'olino kamaha'o no luna
mai , E Hawai'i, aloha e.
Na ke Akua e malama mai ia 'oe,
Kou mau kualono aloha nei,
Kou mau kahawai 'olinolino mau,
Kou mau mala pua nani e.

O Hawai'i, O sands of my birth,
my native home,
I rejoice in the blessings of heaven,
O Hawai'i, aloha.
Chorus: Be happy, youth of Hawai'i.
Rejoice! Rejoice!
Gentle breezes blow love always
for Hawai`i.

May your divine throngs speak,
your loving people, O Hawai'i,
the holy light from above,
O Hawai`i, aloha.
It is God who protects you,
your beloved ridges,
your ever-glistening streams,
your beautiful flower gardens.

HENRY OPUKAHA'IA (1792–1818)

In 1802, Kamehameha's armies killed the parents and baby brother of Opukaha'ia, a ten-year-old Hawaiian boy, in Ka'ū. From then on, fear and sadness haunted the child. It was, he said, "better for me to go." In 1808, after hearing about the Christian God, Opukaha'ia sailed off on an American trading ship. Acknowledged as the first Hawaiian Christian, he studied at Andover Theological Seminary, under a new name, Henry Obookiah. In 1816, the Congregational Church formed the American Board of Commissioners of Foreign Missions and opened a school in Connecticut, where boys like Henry could learn how to bring the Christian word back home. Opukaha'ia began translating the Bible into Hawaiian and prepared to return to the Islands. But on February 17, 1818, he died of typhus fever. He left behind a journal that lamented that his native land was still steeped in paganism and ignorance. Published as *Memoirs of Henry Obookiah and Supplement* that same year, it quickly sold over 50,000 copies and inspired the formation of First Company of missionaries for Hawai'i. These New England Congregationalists pledged themselves to fulfill the young Hawaiian's dream. [Hawaiian Mission Children's Society]

♦》✕《♦》✕《♦》✕《♦》✕《♦》✕《♦

Right: Elias Bond's Kohala Sugar Company opened in 1863. Many scoffed that the "missionary plantation" was bound to fail—and were proved wrong. In the end, the Kohala Sugar Company absorbed all its rivals. When it closed in 1971, it had operated for over one hundred years. [Hawaiian Mission Children's Society]

Below right: Missionary John C. Paris and his wife Mary arrived from New England in 1841 and were assigned to Waiʻōhinu, Kaʻū. Mary died in 1847 and Paris left the Islands for a long visit to the United States. He remarried and returned to Hawaiʻi in 1851. He was assigned to the Kona coast, where he built a new home on the hillside above Kealakekua Bay. Paris traveled up and down the Kona coast, preaching and building churches, until his death in 1892. One of his descendents still lives at the old Paris home, Mauna ʻAlani. Circa 1855. [Hawaiian Mission Children's Society]

Below far right: Kahikolu Congregationalist Church. This 1855 stone church, built next to Kealakekua Bay under the direction of missionary John Paris, replaced a dilapidated church built in 1840. It served Hawaiians living near Nāpoʻopoʻo Landing. In the late 1800s and early 1900s, the landing was a busy port and a community gathering place on steamer day. The church has recently been renovated and is listed in the National Register of Historic Places. [Baker-Van DykeCollection]

The Kohala Mission: Elias and Ellen Bond (1813–1896 and 1817–1881)

The peninsula of North Kohala, with its steep gulches, abundant rainfall, and rugged coastlines, did not receive a permanent mission until June 26, 1841, when Elias Bond and his pregnant wife Ellen arrived. Where those before them had abandoned the mission, the Bonds persevered. While Ellen raised nine children, Elias opened Hawaiʻi's first Normal School to train new teachers, a Boys' Boarding School, and a school for haole children. Kohala was struggling, however, as between 1832 and 1860 it lost 5,400 native residents to illness and migration, leaving less than 3,000 alive. In 1863, Bond started a sugar plantation in a desperate attempt to save his people by providing meaningful work. The plantation prospered.

Ellen's dream, a boarding school for native girls, became a reality in 1872. Parents sent their daughters from around the island for a Western education. Ellen died in 1881, at sixty-four. Her school ran until 1956, and has been restored as an educational center.

Elias Bond died at age eighty-two. Their son Benjamin served the district as a physician. The Bond Estate was designated a National Register Historic District in 1977 and is the only mission station in the Pacific that has remained almost intact.

GOVERNOR JOHN ADAMS KUAKINI (1791–1844)

◆》》◀《》》◀《》》◀《》》◀《》》◀《

Left above : A hula is performed for Kuakini, governor of Kailua. From an original drawing by William Ellis. 1827. [Hawaiian Mission Children's Society]

Left below: The inset sketch of Kuakini in Hawaiian costume appears to be a reworking of an engraving published in Ellis' A Journal of a Tour Around Hawaii. Kuakini is wearing an unconvincingly drawn Hawaiian feather cloak. [Bishop Museum]

After Kamehameha I's death, John Adams Kuakini, the brother of Ka'ahumanu and a chief of high rank, governed the Big Island from 1820 until his death in 1844. During this time he built the Western-style Hulihe'e Palace, which still stands today.

As a boy he had acquired the name John Adams, following the practice among Hawaiian chiefs to take a prominent English or American name. When the Congregationalist missionaries settled in Kailua, he welcomed and supported them. He was one of the first chiefs to read and write English and Hawaiian, and enthusiastically promoted the construc-

tion of schools and churches, for which he provided land.

Kuakini was not, however, a strict Congregationalist at heart. When Catholic missionaries arrived in 1840, he was generous with

them as well, giving them land and allowing them to preach—a generosity of which the fiercely anti-Catholic Congregationalists did not approve. As for his personal life, the Hawaiian historian Kamakau describes him as "a liquor-drinking, pleasure-loving chief, a hula dancer and a patron of thieves."

Kuakini was one of the first to grasp the implications of Hawai'i's burgeoning cash economy. He initiated a series of enterprises, including butter manufacturing, tobacco raising, sugar plantations, and cotton fields.

He died in 1844, at age fifty-three.

♦》X《♦》X《♦》X《♦》X《♦》X《♦

*A painting titled **Kapi'olani Defying Pele** by Herb Kawainui Kāne from his book* Voyagers. *[Herb Kāne]*

In 1824, the devoutly Christian chiefess Kapi'olani and fifty attendants journeyed from Kona to Hilo. On the way, they climbed Kīlauea to see the famous lake of lava. According to Hilo missionary Joseph Goodrich, who later met Kapi'olani at the crater rim, some local Hawaiians "tried to dissuade Kapi'olani from going up to the volcano. They told her that Pele would kill her and eat her up if she went there. She replied that she would go, and if Pele killed and ate her up, they might continue to worship Pele, but if not, i.e. if she returned unhurt, then they must turn to the worship of the true God." Kapi'olani, undaunted, climbed to the edge of the crater. She led the party in a hymn. The party then descended and proceeded to Hilo.

Goodrich's first-hand account is matter-of-fact. Other missionaries embroidered the story, and later storytellers dramatized it even further, adding new characters and incidents. Still, even in its earliest and simplest form, the story is compelling. Kapi'olani was threatened with Pele's wrath and ignored the threats, confident that her new god was stronger than Pele.

52

CATHOLICS

When, in 1827, French Catholic Sacred Hearts priests arrived at Honolulu, they were met with fierce resistance. Relations with France grew tense, and even after a tentative agreement was reached in 1839, the rivalry for the souls of the Hawaiians continued with near-violent vehemence. To Kailua in 1840 came Father Robert A. Walsh and Father Louis E. Heurtel. Close to Protestant Moku'aikaua Church, they held the island's first Catholic mass. Less than a year later, Governor Kuakini gave them land for the island's first Catholic church, St. Michael's, a simple grass house. Although the two priests managed to convert 650 Hawaiians and expand their message across the island, the mission continued to be thwarted by Protestant decrees. Only in remote places, such as Ka'ū, did they achieve success. By 1846, two-thirds of the Hawaiians in Ka'ū were Catholic.

The ritual, the images, and the icons of the Catholic Church resonated with the Hawaiian spirit. Less rigid than the Protestants, the priests admitted those whom the Congregationalists rejected. In Hilo, in 1846, Father Charles Pouzot happily took in the smoking, drinking sinners whom Titus Coan refused. Pouzot dedicated Hilo's first chapel in 1848. The larger Saint Joseph's Church was completed in July 1862. Slowly more Catholic churches appeared.

Father Damien

Father Damien is remembered for his selfless devotion to the sufferers of ma'i pākē, or Hansen's disease, at Kalaupapa on Moloka'i. Born in Belgium in 1840 as Joseph De Veuster, Father Damien came as a missionary to the Big Island's Puna district in 1864. There he learned to speak fluent Hawaiian and immersed himself in Hawaiian culture. On March 19, 1865, Damien was transferred to Kohala, where he labored for eight years.

In January 1866, the kingdom authorized a quarantine settlement for victims of the disease. Hundreds ended up on the isolated Kalaupapa peninsula on the island of Moloka'i, left alone to die without medical care, spiritual support, or adequate shelter. On May 10, 1873, Father Damien left Kohala for Moloka'i, pledging himself to tend to the sufferers. He persevered despite enormous obstacles. He eventually contracted Hansen's disease himself and died of the disease on April 15, 1889, in the Kalaupapa settlement where he had done so much good. In 2009 he was canonized—made a saint.

Father Damien. [Hawaii State Archives]

◆》X《◆》X《◆》X《◆》X《◆》X《◆

Above: In August of 1819, Captain Louis de Freycinet of the French warship L'Uranie sailed into the waters of Kawaihae, on the island of Hawai'i. There, he learned from John Young that Hawai'i's ancient religious system had just been overthrown. Young warned the captain that the political situation for the new King Kamehameha II was very tenuous, as defenders of the old religion were mounting armed resistance. At Young's urging, a Catholic baptism was held for Chief Kalanimoku onboard the ship. Its chaplain officiated with the "utmost simplicity." In attendance were Ka'ahumanu, the queen regent; Boki, governor of O'ahu; and the interpreter Monsieur Jean Rives. Yet, even as the participants in this ceremony, as depicted by Jacques Arago, were being introduced to Catholicism, a brig filled with Protestant missionaries readied to set sail on an historic mission from Boston to the Hawaiian Islands. [Bishop Museum]

RANCHING AND PANIOLO

In 1793, Britain's naval captain George Vancouver gave a fateful gift to the aliʻi nui Kamehameha on the Big Island—five cows and a bull, sick and weak after the long voyage from California. Kamehameha turned the animals loose and placed them under a ten-year kapu; no one was to hurt or kill them. They were to be allowed to breed freely. Feasting on native shrubs and trees, plowing through taro and sweet potato fields, the cattle fattened and multiplied. The kapu was lifted, but the cattle still thrived. By the early 1820s, herds of wild bullocks trampled, plundered, and destroyed forests and farm lands. Gardens and homes were no longer safe, despite hastily effected lava-rock walls.

The aliʻi found a new trading commodity in the form of dried salted beef, sold to American whaling ships wintering off the Big Island. Ranching began with the herding of wild beasts into improvised corrals. Vaqueros came from Spanish California to teach Hawaiians to rope and ride. Other ranch hands were a mixed bunch—sailors who had jumped ship, and later, sugar plantation workers looking to escape the cane fields, and Portuguese immigrants from the Azores with a background in cattle handling.

By 1851, an estimated eight thousand domesticated and twelve thousand wild cattle roamed the uplands. Hawaiians carried barrels of beef on bare shoulders down to the shore, for sale to ship captains. The market for tallow and hides grew. In 1859, the Big Island exported 222,171 pounds of hide. Dairy products became important as well, especially butter. Cattle and sugar met on steamer days at the ports, when passengers could find themselves waiting for hours amid bags of sugar and piles of cabbages, or herds of cattle and mules.

The Big Island ranching community developed a distinctive culture. At its center were the Hawaiian cowboys, paniolo. And at the center of paniolo culture was music. The Spanish vaqueros of the

Below: Ioane Haʻa, a paniolo from Puʻuoʻo Ranch of Mauna Kea. Hawaiians took to cattle ranching with great enthusiasm. [Hawaiʻi State Archives]

CAPTAIN GEORGE VANCOUVER

One of the most important early Westerners to come to the Big Island was the British naval commander George Vancouver. He had sailed with Cook, and was at Kealakekua when Cook was killed. He had met Kamehameha briefly then, and when he came back in the winters of 1793 and 1794, the two became friendly. Vancouver built Kamehameha a European-style ship, the *Brittania*, and as part of his mission to establish trade, he brought cattle and sheep. [Hawaiʻi State Archives]

1830s had brought the guitar. The Hawaiians took to it and re-tuned it, and that was the beginning of slack key guitar, which became an instantly identifiable sound in Hawaiian music–still played, more popular now than it has ever been, the material of Grammy CDs.

As for the roping and riding Hawaiian cowboy, he made his permanent mark on the Big Island–and beyond. At the 1908 steer roping world championship in Cheyenne, Wyoming, the winner was a Big Island paniolo, Ikua Purdy. A song was written about him in Hawaiian; and a statue of him in action, bigger than life, stands at Parker Ranch in the Waimea district, the heart of ranching territory.

By the middle of the twentieth century, demand for Hawaiian beef has fallen, as tastes changed to fat-marbled corn-fed beef from the feedlot. The cost of shipping cattle feed became prohibitive, making it cheaper to import Mainland beef. Some ranchers sought to diversify with agricultural crops, while others created a niche for specialty beef and meats.

Today, following a fortunate trend, Big Island ranchers promote locally raised, grass-fed beef once more, their revenues further supported by leisure ranch activities for tourists.

◆》✕《◇》✕《◇》✕《◇》✕《◇》✕《◆

Left: In the early 1800s, Kamehameha invited skilled Spanish-Mexican vaqueros to help with the capture and slaughter of cattle. Expert horseback riders, they also tamed the wild horses introduced to the Islands in 1803. Known for their strength, endurance, and agility in the saddle, they taught the Hawaiians the use of bridle and lariat. With skills passed on to the next generations, a new breed of Hawaiian cowboys evolved, the paniolo (the Hawaiian way of saying "español"). The sound of the guitar and the 'ukulele would soon accompany evening meals of salt beef and kalo root. In 1908, paniolo Ikua Purdy placed the Hawaiian cowboy on the world map by winning the world steer-roping championship at the Cheyenne Frontier Days celebration. He won by roping, busting, and hog-tying an animal in 56 seconds. His larger-than-life bronze statue at the Parker Ranch Center in Waimea commemorates Hawai'i's paniolo heritage. [Baker-Van Dyke Collection]

Below left: Hawaiian cowboys, or paniolo, branding cattle in old Waimea. [Baker-Van Dyke Collection]

◆》X《◆》X《◆》X《◆》X《◆》X《

Above: Loading cattle at Kailua-Kona near the American Factors warehouse. Date unknown. [Hawai'i State Archives]

Right: Cattle shipping, Kailua Bay, Kaiakeakua Beach. Circa 1935. [Bishop Museum]

Left: From ranch to ship—the cattle swim. Since the main market for beef was in Honolulu, live cattle had to be herded to one of the two dozen boat landings where inter-island steamers anchored safely away from the reefs. To get from shore to ship, strong paniolo and intrepid sailors worked with well-trained horses and sheer force to drag each animal into the water. They swam the cattle to a small skiff where they were lashed on by the horns—four animals to a side. Half swimming, half drowning, the cattle struggled along as the skiff pulled out, and were then hoisted onboard the steamer with slings. The cattle ships transported passengers as well—an eighteen-hour, noisy, smelly voyage. By the 1930s, piers and chutes replaced the cattle swim, one of the most colorful features of Hawai'i's old ranching days. Eventually tugs and barges took the place of cattle boats. [Baker-Van Dyke Collection]

Below far left: At Kawaihae, cattle were tied to the sides of whale boats by paniolo for the passage to the small steamship offshore, which transported the beef to markets in Honolulu. (Hawai'i State Archives)

Below left: Hoisting cattle aboard ship. (Bishop Museum)

PARKER RANCH

Right: Colonel Sam Parker, famed host and part-owner of Parker Ranch. He was the grandson of the founder of Parker Ranch, and shared ownership of the ranch with his uncle, John Palmer Parker II. The ranch would eventually pass to Sam's granddaughter Thelma and then to his great-grandson, Richard Smart. 1891. [Baker-Van Dyke Collection]

Opposite: Inside the house built for Mary Parker at the time of her marriage to Charlie Maguire. On the easel is a portrait of Sam Parker. [Baker-Van Dyke Collection]

In 1809, John Palmer Parker, a nineteen-year-old sailor from Newton, Massachusetts, deserted a sandalwood ship on the west coast of the Big Island, became friends with Kamehameha I and stayed to tend the king's fishponds in Hōnaunau. Restless, he left after two years. In 1814, after two years in China, he returned to the Big Island with a new musket, and became the first to gain royal permission to shoot cattle. He started trading beef.

From Kamehameha, Parker received land in Wai'āpuka, Kohala. In 1818, he married Kamehameha's granddaughter Rachel Keli'i Kipikāne Kaolohaka, and acquired two acres in Mānā, at the foot of Mauna Kea in Waimea, plus another 640 acres, as a royal wedding gift. Parker lacked the capital to start his own ranch and so, in 1835, he joined forces with William French, a successful entrepre-

neur who traded with whalers at the port of Kawaihae. Parker prepared hides, tallow, and beef for French and took cattle as his pay, thus paving the way for a future as an independent rancher. He diversified his first cattle operations with peach orchards and a dairy that produced butter and cheese. By 1847 he had accumulated enough assets to buy land and set up his own ranch. Over the years, he and his heirs bought more land, until Parker Ranch became bigger than any ranch under single ownership on the American mainland.

At the time of Parker's death in 1868, Parker Ranch had grown to over two hundred thousand acres. His son, John Palmer Parker II, and young grandson—handsome and charming Samuel—were equal heirs. The ranch suffered under Samuel's management. He was a bon vivant, much preferring social life to ranching. He and his wife Panana spent most of their time in

Honolulu, in the circle of Sam's friend, King Kalākaua. In 1899, a prominent Oʻahu lawyer, Alfred Wellington Carter, came to manage Parker II's half of the estate. Ranch affairs turned around, but Carter's efforts initially cost a great deal of money, which enraged Samuel and led to years of tedious legal battles. John Parker II had legally adopted Sam's son John Parker Palmer III. When John Parker II died, ownership of his half of the ranch passed to the adopted son—who died young, leaving a baby daughter, Thelma. Sam Parker, always short of money, sold his share in the ranch to his granddaughter for $600,000. The ranch prospered and, at one point, spanned 327,000 acres.

Carter died in 1949 and was succeeded by his son Hartwell Carter. In the 1960s, Richard Palmer Smart, Parker Ranch's sole heir, returned to Hawaiʻi after a career on Broadway, and in the early 1990s he replaced the ranch's single ownership with a foundation trust. Today, the ranch—about half its peak size—operates on a much smaller scale, and is open to visitors.

◆》✕《◆》✕《◆》✕《◆》✕《◆》✕《◆

Below: Mānā Hale was the original Parker Ranch homestead. John Palmer Parker and his Hawaiian wife lived in a Hawaiian hale pili, grass house, until 1847, when Parker built a New England-style cottage for his family. This sturdily-built, slate-roofed, koa-wood cottage was known as Mānā Hale, the House of the Spirit. Later, new wings and outbuildings were added. John Palmer Parker's heirs, John Palmer Parker II, and his grandson Samuel Parker, did not get along. Samuel Parker lived in Honolulu for much of the year, but periodically descended upon the ranch with his socialite friends, disrupting ranch business and irritating John Parker II, who actually managed the ranch. John Parker bought a new house, twelve miles away, called Puʻuʻōpelu. This had been built in 1862 by a Englishman called Notley, on a grand scale, like an English country house. The center of ranch activities moved to Puʻuʻōpelu and Mānā Hale was left to slow decay. The last of the Parkers, Richard Smart, moved back to the ranch in 1959 and later decided to move the original Mānā Hale to Puʻuʻōpelu. The building was disassembled and moved, plank by plank, to the new location. Most of the outer siding had to be replaced. Hence the Mānā Hale that is shown to visitors at the Parker Ranch Center is part-original, part-replica. Richard Smart also extensively renovated Puʻuʻōpelu. [Baker-Van Dyke Collection]

Right: Waimea was a thriving settlement before Westerners arrived. Hawaiians captured the streams flowing from nearby Kohala Mountain (one of the rainiest places in the islands) for irrigation, and raised large crops of dry-land taro and sweet potatoes. The pre-contact population, at its height, may have been seven to ten thousand. In this 1886 photo of the town, Imiöla church is to the right, and to the left, amid the vegetation, is the residence of Lorenzo Lyons. [Baker-Van Dyke Collection]

Below right: In 1894, Robert Hind, Jr., and Eben Low signed a lease on forty thousand acres of the Pu'uwa'awa'a ahupua'a, upland of Kïholo on the Kona coast. They planned to run cattle on the dry stony land. Here Eben (right) and James Hind (left), Robert Hind's son, relax with an unidentified friend (center) after a wild turkey hunt. The turkeys hang from the posts of the lānai. Eben Low, incidentally, had lost his left hand in a roping accident, but he was still known for his skill with a rope, horse, and steer. [Baker-Van Dyke Collection]

Above: Prince Kūhiō on horseback at Parker Ranch. Date unknown. [Baker-Van Dyke Collection]

KAHUĀ RANCH

In 1928, two young men from Oʻahu, Atherton Richards and Ronald von Holt, purchased a fifty-acre homestead on the misty slopes of windward Kohala, as well as leases for the surrounding cattle lands. About fifty cowboy families joined the twelve thousand-acre ranch at Kahuā. A school and a store opened. In the late 1950s, when it became increasingly difficult to make a profit at beef, and other ranches merged or sold, Atherton's nephew, Montague "Monty" Richards, became manager. He eventually opted to diversify with pioneering steps that enabled the ranch to survive. Windmills provided electricity. Sheep joined cattle. Tourists were invited. In 1989, Kahuā Ranch divided its lands to create Ponoholo Ranch, run independently by Pono von Holt, Ronald's son. Kahuā—now with about a dozen houses—is one of the last remaining ranch villages of old Hawaiʻi.

◆》》《《◆》》《《◆》》《《◆》》《《◆》》《《◆

The Parker family patriarchs and matriarchs pose for their portrait on the lānai of their homestead. Elizabeth Dowsett Parker's (far right) grandson, Richard Smart, was the last heir to Parker Ranch. His home, Puʻuʻōpelu, was expanded and modernized and became known for housing one of the finest private art collections in Hawaiʻi. He died in 1992. He left the home and an estimated $400 million estate in a trust to benefit the Waimea community. Date unknown. [Baker-Van Dyke Collection]

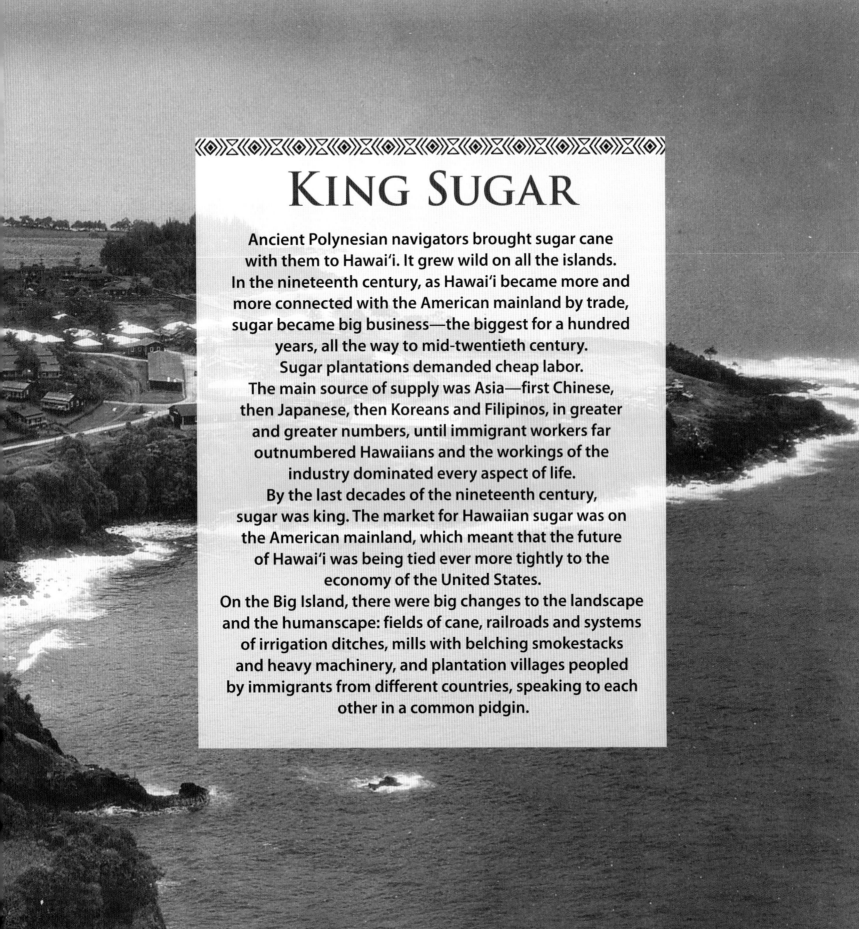

KING SUGAR

Ancient Polynesian navigators brought sugar cane
with them to Hawai'i. It grew wild on all the islands.
In the nineteenth century, as Hawai'i became more and
more connected with the American mainland by trade,
sugar became big business—the biggest for a hundred
years, all the way to mid-twentieth century.
Sugar plantations demanded cheap labor.
The main source of supply was Asia—first Chinese,
then Japanese, then Koreans and Filipinos, in greater
and greater numbers, until immigrant workers far
outnumbered Hawaiians and the workings of the
industry dominated every aspect of life.
By the last decades of the nineteenth century,
sugar was king. The market for Hawaiian sugar was on
the American mainland, which meant that the future
of Hawai'i was being tied ever more tightly to the
economy of the United States.
On the Big Island, there were big changes to the landscape
and the humanscape: fields of cane, railroads and systems
of irrigation ditches, mills with belching smokestacks
and heavy machinery, and plantation villages peopled
by immigrants from different countries, speaking to each
other in a common pidgin.

SWEET SUCCESS

Previous pages: In 1933 Pepe'ekeo Sugar Mill and its surrounding cultivated acres were one of the many sugar plantations that had transformed the Hāmākua coast from a sparsely populated series of Hawaiian villages to a thriving coast of plantation labor camps and incessant agricultural activity. The growth of the sugar industry gave Hawai'i its many ethnic groups while establishing and perpetuating an oligarchy of white racial, social and political dominance. [Baker-Van Dyke Collection]

When Westerners arrived, they found sugar cane growing wild on the wet windward side of the Big Island, in Hilo, Hāmākua, and Kohala. Sugar cane was one of the crops that the early Polynesians had brought with them, and it had made itself at home in the new land.

In 1804, a Russian explorer who had dropped anchor off Kealakekua noted that sugar cane might give the Hawaiians great wealth. Two years earlier, a Chinese man—one of several who jumped ship in the Islands—had milled the Islands' first sugar crop, on Lāna'i. Missionary Joseph Goodrich in Hilo was the first to build a mill on the Big Island. By 1829, he was grinding sugar.

Sugar did not become a real industry until the mid-1830s. In 1837, Big Island governor Kuakini employed a Chinese sugar master to run mills in Hilo and North Kohala. Almost all of these early startups were defeated by fluctuating markets and inadequate tools. Sixteen operations with primitive mills came and went before 1876—the year that Hawai'i signed a reciprocity treaty with the United States. The treaty allowed tariff-free export to America and became the foundation for a sugar-based economy.

The 1870s saw an explosion of new plantations and mills financed by foreign investors. The sons of missionaries became entrepreneurs, expanding their acreages by acquiring land from Hawaiians, building economies of scale.

Sugar became the new king, altering the Big Island in more dramatic ways than had sandalwood, whaling, or cattle. It changed demographics, politics, socioeconomics, the landscape, the language, and even the cuisine.

The rugged Big Island, with its steep terrain and diverse climate, forced planters to employ a variety of methods to grow cane. Planters performed amazing technological feats, building railways over precipitous coasts and digging irrigation ditches through lava. By 1884, the Big Island had more than thirty plantations, most in the Hilo and Hāmākua areas. Acre by acre, sometimes by less than savory methods, plantation owners (most of them Caucasians) bought land from the Native Hawaiians, expanding their acreages in search of economies of scale. Finding enough labor-

ers to hoe, plant, weed, cut, carry, and cultivate cane cheaply was an ongoing challenge. From 1852 onward, immigrants, mostly from Asia, came by the thousands to fulfill three- or five-year labor contracts.

Plantation owners saw themselves as good, caring employers; they developed a paternalistic system in which the sugar companies provided housing, medical care, and company stores. At the same time, they used ethnic difference among their labor force to "divide and rule," so that their workers would not be able to unionize; and the police clamped down harshly on "disorder."

In the early 1900s, mechanization and improved transportation—gone were the bullock wagons to transport cane—caused plantations to consolidate. Plantation funding mostly came from large Honolulu-based investment companies (called factors) who recouped debts in stock and gradually came to dominate the mills. From these factors came "The Big Five" companies that controlled the Islands' economy: C. Brewer & Company, Theo H. Davies & Co., H. Hackfeld & Co., Castle & Cooke, and Alexander & Baldwin. Centralizing their smaller assets into giant units, they eventually owned not just plantations but mills, railroads, and shipping companies. The island's economy thrived thanks to these mergers, and by 1936, sixteen consolidated mills produced close to thirty-four percent of the Territory's sugar.

Ongoing Big Five consolidations in North Hilo led to the 1973 formation of C. Brewer's Hilo Coast Processing Company. Hamakua Sugar Company came to manage all of Hāmākua, plus a few lands in North Hilo, Kohala Sugar Company absorbed all of Kohala's mills, Puna Sugar Co. formed in the Puna district, and Ka'u Agribusiness Company farmed Ka'ū.

The sugar industry also made itself responsible for many public improvements still in use today. Com-

Above: Built right at the water's edge, the Hakalau Sugar Mill shows the collection point at the end of the flume below the railroad track, circa 1920s. [Richard Otaki Collection]

Left: Sugar cane leaves are sharp! Cane workers protected themselves from the leaves, as well as from the sun, with boots, overalls, long sleeves, gloves, scarves, and big hats. [Hawai'i State Archives]

>X(®)X(®)X(®)X(®)X(®)X(

Right: The "picture bride" system was
initiated to locate suitable mates for
thousands of single Asian immigrant
men. These women traveled to Hawai'i
to begin a marriage with a man they
had, in most cases, never seen except in
a photograph. After a quick ceremony,
they were expected to perform the
domestic duties of a wife, and also
work on the plantation. [Hawai'i State
Archives]

Below: Workers planting sugar cane
pose for the camera. Date unknown.
[Kona Historical Society]

panies donated lands to the then Territory of Hawai'i
and to Hawai'i County for public parks and community projects. The companies often constructed roads,
bridges, harbors, schools, parks, and churches.

Mechanization caused a dramatic decrease in the
demand for labor. Between 1932 and 1942, production of sugar jumped from 19.9 tons to 33.0 tons per
employee, while the number of employees per plantation fell to almost half. Workers left for Honolulu.

In 1853, the Big Island's 24,450 residents accounted
for 33.4 percent of all Hawai'i residents. By 1970, the
Big Island's 63,468 residents formed only 8.2 percent of
the state's population. Changing economics—Hawai'i
could no longer compete with other sugar-producing
countries where labor was cheaper—led to the end of
sugar on the Big Island in the mid 1990s. In 1996 Ka'ū
became the last district to cease sugar farming.

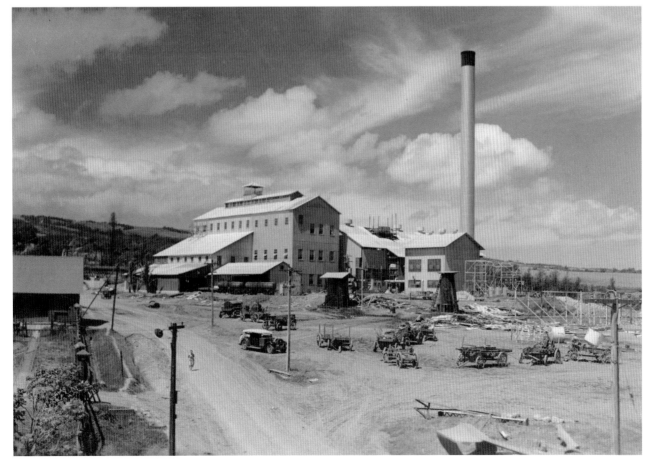

>X<(>)X<(>)X<(>)X<(>)X<

Above left: Charles F. Hart, the proprietor of Niuli'i Plantation, at first owned only sixty acres of land, on which he built the Niuli'i Mill. He depended on the Hawaiian landowners of Niuli'i for a steady supply of sugar cane; he was often disappointed. He attempted to buy out the independent growers and largely succeeded. They did not understand the complexities of Western business, took on mortgages, and were eventually forced to sell. Hart sold his share of the plantation in 1899. The plantation later merged with the Union Mill and then with the Kohala Sugar Company. Circa 1890. [Bishop Museum]

Below left: The Kohala Sugar Company operated from 1863 to 1973. Kohala Sugar Mill was built on the North Kohala coast near Hala'ula village. The closest towns, Kapa'au and Hāwī, were located further up the mountainside. Today, the mill ruins can be seen near the Kauhola Point Lighthouse. Only foundations are left. Smokestacks like the one pictured were common. One of the last ones remaining on the Big Island collapsed in the 2006 earthquake. 1938. [Bishop Museum]

><(<)><(<)><(<)><(<)><(<)><

Right: Beginning in 1913, Pa'auilo's mill and transportation center was the northernmost terminus of the Hawaiian Consolidated Railway Limited. Hamakua Mill Company's product was shipped to Hilo via this railroad until it shut down in 1946 after a tsunami destroyed much of the tracks and several trestles. [Baker Van-Dyke Collection]

Below: Honomu Sugar Company was established on two thousand four hundred acres by M. Kirchoff & Company in 1880. By 1890, the plantation was producing 2,000 tons of sugar yearly. For more than twenty years to 1923, this efficient small plantation never missed paying a dividend. Maximum production of 10,218 tons was reached in 1942, during World War II. From 1929 to 1936, Honomu Plantation Company was managed by Andrew T. Spalding. He was one of several Spaldings prominent in the sugar industry. During World War I, he served as an army officer. He organized the first National Guard company on the Big Island. Later, he organized and commanded the 299th Regiment. During World War II, Spalding commanded the First Regiment Hawaiian Rifles and was one of several Spaldings prominent in the history of the sugar industry. In 1946 C. Brewer & Company closed down the Honomū mill, and merged operations into the neighboring Pepe'ekeo Sugar Company. [Richard Otaki Collection]

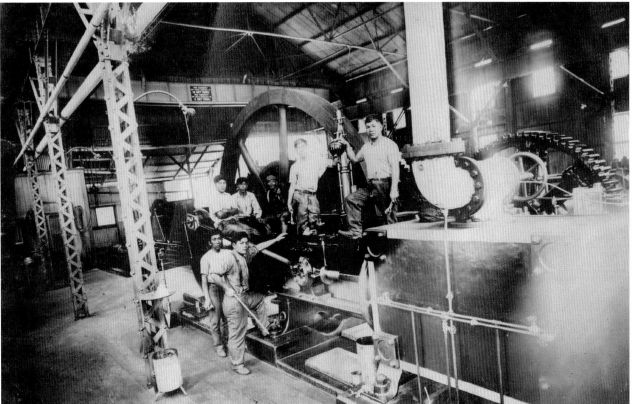

Above: In 1933, when "King Sugar" ruled the Hāmākua Coast, mills like this one at Papaaloa were Hawai'i's most powerful and important economic engines. Note the arrow and mileage to Hilo painted on the roof of the mill for the purpose of guiding airplanes flying by night. [Baker-Van Dyke Collection]

Left: It was often so hot inside Honomu Mill that one worker—who shoveled bagasse (dried, crushed cane stalks) into the sugar boilers—usually worked naked. His co-workers would call out for him to dress whenever visitors arrived. The mill was closed in 1948 and later dismantled. Circa 1920. [Ishii Family Collection]

SUGAR TOWNS

Until the late 1800s, the plantations kept their workers on site, around the mill, where a camp store provided merchandise; purchases were deducted from monthly wages. Immigrants who had finished their contracts would move from camp to camp by horse or foot, to peddle fish, produce, hogs, milk, poi, and other goods. In the early 1900s, transportation became easier. The first cars came—clumsy, large Model-Ts for the plantation managers, little trucks for the peddlers. The peddlers opened stores—centrally located, sometimes exactly between two or three mills—where they catered to the managerial elite, while continuing to make deliveries to camps. Eventually, bustling sugar towns developed, with soda fountains, theaters, and shops that sold sake, pork, pastries, coffins, rice, kerosene, corned beef, clothes, nails, brooms, and fabric by the bolt. There were tailors, chop suey eateries, bakeries, coffee shops, bars, garages, and billiard rooms. Small hotels served salesmen and business travelers. Occasionally there was a hospital. Horses would be tethered to hitching posts, next to carriages or gleaming autos, as residents visited the post office to check for mail on steamer days (usually once or twice a week). Island-wide, camp life was shifting, from inward-looking ethnic settlements towards ethnically mixed communities, communities rapidly developing their own local food, pidgin, and culture.

The sugar towns thrived throughout the heyday of the early 1900s, but in the aftermath of the centralizing mergers and the decline of sugar in the 1970s, towns on the periphery emptied out. Today, they are not much more than memories, with perhaps a couple of surviving dry goods stores. A handful of towns—Honoka'a, Honomū, Pāhoa, Nā'ālehu, Holualoa, Hāwī, and Kapa'au included—survived the hard times. Here, Japanese merchants still run small mom-and-pop stores and Portuguese malasadas are still made according to old recipes. Some old storefronts that once sat abandoned have been spruced up by newcomers in recent years; galleries, art centers, and modern coffee shops fill the dusty spaces of old.

A man and children beneath a sign advertising a chop suey restaurant on Main street, Pa'auilo, on the Hāmākua coast. Electricity has already come to this rural community. Downtown Pa'auilo also boasted a bar and a movie theater with wooden seats. A few of these buildings still stand today, though many of them are vacant. Circa 1929. [Nakahara Family Collection]

Above: The Ah Foo Restaurant building still stands today on Mamane Street, Honoka'a. The elevated sidewalks with their two-step curbs were convenient for passengers in horse-drawn wagons. Circa 1920. [Hal Yamato Collection]

Right: The Akita Store was a Honomū landmark in the early 1940s. It was a combination grocery store, bar, and gas station, as well as a soda fountain where a banana split cost about 30 cents. The store was a popular stop both for local people and for the U.S. Army soldiers stationed nearby during World War II. There were many such combination gas stations and stores along the old Māmalahoa Highway. [Yugawa Family Collection]

Above left: The S. Miura Store provides a backdrop to this view of 1930s Pāhoa town. [Richard Otaki Collection]

Below: L. Ahuna, proprietor of the Kim Choy Kee Store, sits with his family on the store's lānai. Date unknown. [Kona Historical Society]

SUGAR TRAINS

During sugar's first decades, the Big Island's plantations struggled to transport cane from the mills to Honolulu-bound steamers. Bullock wagons had to traverse steep gulches to reach small, dangerous landings, where little skiffs or cable-and-pulley systems were invariably challenged by choppy waters and shallow reefs. Sugar transport was inefficient and expensive.

In 1878, Samuel G. Wilder, Minister of the Interior, initiated new transportation laws and charters. Soon after, he resigned from the Cabinet to go into building railroads. Conveniently, Wilder already owned an inter-island steamer company.

The Big Island eventually had four railroads that brought cut cane from the fields to the mills: the Hawaiian Railroad Company operating in Kohala, the Hilo Railroad Company, the West Hawaii Railway (which ran from 1906 to 1926 but could not rescue the Kona Sugar Company), and a small line in Ka'ū.

Kohala's Railroad (1878-1941)

With Samuel Wilder as principal shareholder the Hawaiian Railroad Company in Kohala, the Big Island's first railroad, serviced five mills and delivered all of Kohala's sugar to Māhukona harbor in the leeward west. Work on the thirty-six-inch narrow gauge line started in April 1881, at Māhukona. For twenty-one months, one hundred Chinese graded, dug, blasted, built, and laid track, slowly progressing from hot, dusty, boulder-strewn land to the greener shoreline of Kohala's most eastern plantation in Niuli'i, a distance of nearly twenty miles. At its completion on January 13, 1883, the railroad crossed seventeen gulches—one of them eighty-four feet deep—and wound around twenty-five sharp curves. Plantations paid $2.50 per two thousand pounds of sugar transported regardless of distance, a strategy that so outraged John Hind of Hawi Mill that he chose not to participate. Even so, Kohala's revenues soared. Screeching, grinding wagons also transported passengers; Wilder envisioned Māhukona as a commercial hub with stores and restaurants.

Wilder died in 1888. He had managed to acquire the whole company, which now belonged to his family. It soon became clear that his railroad records, including notes about shares, were either incomplete or

absent. Over the next few years, alleged co-owners of Kohala's sugar mills, struggled with the betrayal. Lacking support and good management, the railroad's income dwindled.

In 1912, Kohala Sugar Company's powerful factor, Castle & Cooke, took over the railroad and offered John Hind of Hawi Mill 45-percent ownership and the presidency. Under new management, the railroad climbed out of debt within three years.

Its newly gained stability allowed it to weather the consolidation of Kohala's five sugar mills, and enabled the building of spur lines that ran closer to the cane fields. The reprieve was temporary. Sugar companies were switching to trucks. By 1940, trucks were hauling 50 percent of the cane. The railroad was unable to compete. It shut down in December 1941, the day after the Japanese attack on Pearl Harbor that started World War II in the Pacific.

High trestle bridges, such as this one near Hakalau sugar plantation, were great feats of engineering. Thanks to the bridges and the railway, the Hāmākua coast could be traversed in hours rather than days. Before the railway, travelers had to take narrow switchback roads down to the bottom of the deep ravines that dissected the coast, cross the streams, then go up more switchback roads to reach the level uplands again. The railroad was largely destroyed by the 1946 tsunami, but several old railroad bridges, widened and remodeled, are used by today's Belt Highway. [Baker-Van Dyke Collection]

Hilo's Railroad

The Big Island's second common carrier railroad proved to be the most ambitious in the Islands. In 1899, the crews of Honolulu entrepreneur Benjamin F. Dillingham started laying standard gauge track for the first phase of the Hilo Railroad Company. The track ran to 'Ōla'a, eight miles south of Hilo. By 1902, Dillingham had bought two new sugar mills, built a bridge over Wailoa River to reach Hilo's bayfront end at Wailuku, extended the railroad from Waiakea to Kapoho, and laid track uphill to the town of Glenwood to capture the tourist market drawn to Kīlauea. This was more than thirty-seven miles of railroad. It seemed that nothing could stop Dillingham.

Poor sugar crops forced Dillingham to explore new ventures, including the building of a large break-water that would, he hoped, transform Hilo into a principal shipping port. Congress granted permission on condition that the railroad be extended along the steep-gulched Hāmākua coast, another fifty miles. Work began in 1908. Challenges and costs exceeded all estimates. The railroad reached Pa'auilo in 1913. At that time, it included thirteen steel bridges, 3,100 feet of tunnels, and sharply curved trestles that negotiated daunting cliffs. It also cost a record $60,361 per mile, leaving the venture bankrupt. In 1916, the company was sold and reincorporated as the Hawaii Consolidated Railway. The new owners targeted tourism, creating the Hamakua Scenic Express, complete with a carpeted dining wagon that served pot roast on china plates. But the passenger line lost its customers to the automobile and enjoyed a brief turnaround only during World War II, when soldiers needed transportation between Hilo and Waimea.

On April 1, 1946, a tsunami washed away all shoreline construction and led to the railway's sudden and permanent end. To commemorate it, a small museum in Laupāhoehoe opened in 1998.

Above: Onlookers admire a steaming, shiny Hilo Railroad 4-6-0 Ten-Wheeler No. 192; this oil burner was delivered by Baldwin in 1912. [Richard Otaki Collection]

Right: The Hilo Railroad train pulls out of a station along the Hāmākua coast. Although hauntingly beautiful, not even the coastline could turn the railroad's luck around. The railroad's finances improved in the 1920s, but the automobile won. [Baker Van-Dyke Collection]

A kindergarten class with teachers and perhaps parents poses around the Hilo Railroad train at what is believed to be Glenwood Station. In 1902, Benjamin F. Dillingham opened a railroad extension from Hilo for tourists wishing to visit Kīlauea Volcano and the famed Volcano House. The line ended at Glenwood, where passengers had to disembark and continue nine more miles by wagon or horse to reach their destination. Circa 1920s. [Baker-Van Dyke Collection]

SUGAR WATER

Sufficient water supplies were key to the success of the Big Island's sugar plantations, as cane cultivation demanded hundreds of thousands of gallons per day per acre. The Kohala Mountain watershed, around which the Kohala and Hāmākua plantations were clustered, is drained by numerous surface streams. Plantation engineers built tunnels and ditches to divert the stream flow, away from the ocean and onto the thirsty cane lands.

The early 1900s saw the construction of four irrigation aqueducts. Hundreds of Japanese laborers recruited from the plantations hand-drilled and dynamited through solid lava rock, persevering despite extreme heat and harsh rains, dangerous rock-slide-

✕⟨◇⟩✕⟨◇⟩✕⟨◇⟩✕⟨◇⟩✕⟨◇⟩✕

Below: Cane was harvested by hand, cut into short lengths, and dumped into the flume that carried it downhill to a collection point. [David Weiss/Final Harvest]

prone terrain, and treacherous river crossings. They suffered from hypothermia and "powder consumption," a muscular rheumatism caused by nitroglycerin fumes. They earned about $1 a day.

Although only two ditches proved successful, sugar revenues soared. The ditches did not just bring irrigation, they also improved the transportation of sugar cane. Through V-shaped gutter-like slides known as flumes, the diverted stream water pushed freshly-cut mauka (inland) cane downhill, directly from field to mill, reducing expenses for cumbersome wagons and labor. The ditches also brought drinking water and sewer systems, and fueled hydroelectric plants.

The Kohala Ditch Company

As early as 1889, engineers had proposed to gather the waters of the Kohala streams to provide for all of Kohala's plantation needs. They admitted that it would be expensive to blast through the mountain's high, perpendicular cliffs. Only John Hind, owner of Hawi Mill, pursued the idea; he incorporated the Kohala Ditch Company in 1904, with Michael M. O'Shaughnessy as chief engineer. O'Shaughnessy, incidentally, is the same man later responsible for the Hetch-Hetchy project in California's Bay Area.

Construction started in January 1905. For eighteen months, six hundred Japanese laborers burrowed deeper and deeper into the mountains, along trails carved on the edge of thousand-foot-high cliffs. Fourteen men died; the names of only a few are known. Upon completion, the ditch ran for twenty-two and a half miles, with fifty-seven tunnels spanning sixteen miles, six miles of open ditch, and twenty-nine flumes. More than thirty miles of trails, contributory tunnels and bridges, telephone lines, and fourteen isolated maintenance cabins supported the system. Its maximum delivery capacity was seventy million gallons per day.

Cane yields nearly doubled after the Kohala Ditch opened. But ditch water was flowing at a loss. Plantations had subscribed for more gallons of water than the ditch could deliver, at prices that were too low. Three more laborers died during improvements at the ditch. Hind had to rely on his own investments and started to sell electricity from a hydroelectric plant. In 1921, he placed the ditch under the umbrella of the Big Island's Public Utilities Commission.

In the mid-1950s, Hilo Electric Light took over electricity sales, and the ditch merged with Castle & Cooke's Kohala Sugar Company. After the closure of the Kohala plantation in 1975, Castle & Cooke kept Kohala Ditch going, then sold it with its other assets to a new landowner, Chalon International, now known as Surety Kohala Corporation. Ranchers and farmers drew water from the ditch and kayakers floated down it, until, on October 15, 2006, a 6.7-magnitude earthquake destroyed the system. The ditch was restored in late 2008.

The Hamakua Ditch System

In 1904, the Hamakua Ditch Company was founded to serve the numerous plantations around Honoka'a and Pa'auilo. Investors hastily built what became known as the Upper Hamakua Ditch. But the fifteen-plus miles of unlined ditches and galvanized flumes, completed in 1907, deteriorated rapidly. Maintenance expenses were prohibitive. Reconstruction

Above: A few of the Japanese ditch laborers with Jorgen Jorgensen (front) and his righthand man Mizuno-san (to his right). [Bishop Museum]

appeared useless. Eventually, the Territory of Hawai'i took over the water licenses, and in late 1908 spent several million dollars on repairs to serve Waimea farm lots.

The Lower Hāmākua Ditch incorporated the lessons learned, with the investors working under a new name, the Hawaiian Irrigation Company. Using twelve hundred workers and fourteen thousand barrels of cement, it was completed in 1910, after fourteen months of construction and the digging of forty-five tunnels. At least three men died—among them the ditch's engineer. Difficulties arose after completion, when Hāmākua's numerous companies fought over just allocations and costs. Controversy was stanched only by a series of mergers. Contention over the 25-mile-long Lower Hāmākua Ditch rose again after the collapse of sugar in Hāmākua in the mid-1990s. The poorly maintained ditch had been repaired to tap directly into Waipi'o streams, leaving independent taro farmers dry. The ditch had to be restructured. It now supports diversified agriculture and ranching in Hāmākua's former cane fields. New Waipi'o stream management seeks to restore parts of the original watershed.

Kehena Water Company, Ltd.

Co-investors for the Kohala Ditch opted for a second aqueduct in the upper Kohala mountains to bring water to ranches on the western side of Kohala. By 1914, after two years of construction, Kehena Water Company Ltd.'s fourteen-mile ditch meandered through rugged pasture land down to Puakea Ranch. However, its reservoirs leaked, the boggy ground absorbed the run-off water, and the rain was too seasonal. It was abandoned in the late 1960s.

NEWCOMERS

The increased productivity of sugar plantations soon led to a labor shortage. To fill this need, thousands of Chinese immigrants were signed to three- or five-year contracts. After completing their contracts, many moved to urban centers or took up independent rice and coffee farming. By the 1890s, Chinese were no longer considered "reliable" plantation laborers, and the government passed "An Act Restricting Chinese Immigration," limiting numbers to five thousand a year for agricultural labor only. In this photo, Chinese men arrive in Hawai'i in 1901 on the S.S. America Maru. [Hawai'i Sate Archives]

As early as the late 1820s, two Chinese sugar masters had planted sugar in Waimea and erected a mill. Governor Kuakini—always in search of new economic opportunity—employed a Chinese sugar master to run several mills in the Hilo and Kohala districts by 1837. Once it appeared that sugar was a viable crop, Chinese men were recruited to serve five-year contracts out in the fields. Pay was less than ten dollars a month for twenty-six ten-hour days of work. In 1852, about three hundred Chinese arrived in the Islands. Thousands followed, especially after 1876.

Working and living conditions were often harsh. Sickness, tardiness, or even pausing to talk or stretch one's back while on the job warranted verbal and physical abuse or fines. The Kohala missionary Elias Bond, who founded and co-owned Kohala Sugar Company, tried to protect the laborers. In an 1866 letter to his co-owners, he wrote: "Above all, flogging is to be abandoned. We must train men, and not brutes. A man flogged for stealing and rendered sulky by such treatment, undoubtedly set fire to the carpenter shop recently. This style of management must be abandoned." But Bond failed to change any minds. "[T]he business of the Plantation must go on, morals or no morals," Castle & Cooke wrote back.

The Chinese

The earliest Chinese lived close to the mill, in barracks without running water, kitchens, or sewage systems. They were lonely in a foreign land, and to alleviate their misery they often gambled and turned

≫⟨◈⟩≪≫⟨◈⟩≪≫⟨◈⟩≪

Left: A Chinese family in front of their plantation house. The Chinese were among the early foreign settlers to make Hawai'i their home. As early as 1787, Chinese were coming to Hawai'i on foreign ships, sometimes as cooks or seamen. Some Chinese merchants established small businesses in Island ports, while others developed rice or coffee farms in Waipi'o Valley or Kona. They also freely intermarried with Hawaiian women, thus establishing many Chinese-Hawaiian dynasties that have survived until today. Date unknown. [Lyman House Memorial Museum]

Below: A Chinese man with a carrying pole in Kohala. Circa 1915. [Bishop Museum]

possible, pooled finances to help families back home. The first true tong temple on the Big Island, Tong Wo Society, was founded in 1886 in Hālawa, North Kohala, and has been recently restored. The Ling Hing Society in Hilo, organized in 1899, was destroyed by a tsunami in 1960. Tongs existed in Hāmākua and Kailua, and as far south as in Nā'ālehu in Ka'ū.

Some of the Chinese married Hawaiian women. A few sent word home for picture brides. Most stayed in the Islands. In the early 1880s, Hawai'i's government decided that the Chinese had become too numerous—25 percent of the total population. This led to immigration restrictions in 1883 and, in 1900, complete prohibition. By then, more than 25,000 Chinese lived in the Islands, close to 17 percent of a total population of 154,000. 30 percent of the Chinese resided on the Big Island.

to opium. Tongs, or club-houses and fraternal Chinese societies, cropped up, retreats where the men smoked, kept memories alive, secured political ties, arranged funerals, and, if

A Japanese woman and her child sit outside their grass-thatched home on a sugar plantation. Tens of thousands of young contract laborers from Japan immigrated to Hawai'i beginning in 1868, eventually becoming the largest ethnic group in the Islands. They transplanted a rich tradition of values, foods, language, architecture, clothing, customs, and beliefs. [Hawai'i State Archives]

The Japanese

As early as 1868, a handful of Japanese laborers came as part of a first group of 153 immigrants from Japan. However, word of plantation conditions reached the Japanese government, which prohibited further emigration until, in 1885, a new agreement was reached. The second group, the *kanyaku imin,* or government-contract Japanese, were lauded by the planters as "the principal check upon the Chinese, in keeping down the price of labor." Between 1885 and 1894, over twenty-nine thousand Japanese arrived on the Big Island.

The Japanese sent home for their wives and children. Thousands of picture brides also came. When contracts were finished, many found that they did not have the resources to leave. Staying, they soon outnumbered the Chinese. By 1896, they formed the Islands' dominant race. A third group of Japanese immigrants, the culturally distinct Okinawans from the Ryukyu islands, also immigrated in great numbers. In 1920, of the Big Island's 65,000 residents 33,000 were Japanese.

Many Island residents resented the Japanese influx and would have preferred to stop the immigration, but cheap workers were hard to find. The plantations tried to keep the Japanese under control. The sugar industry developed a new identification system, bango numbers—metal tags with embossed numbers that laborers had to carry around their necks. The men were addressed by number, not by name.

Around the island, Hongwanji temples and Jodo Missions opened up. In 1893, a Christian minister in Kohala opened the Islands' first Japanese-language school for American-Japanese *nisei,* offspring of the first generation or *issei.* By 1910, 140 schools throughout the islands kept Japanese children connected to their roots.

When their contracts were up, many Big Island Japanese moved to Kona to grow coffee. Others opened little mom-and-pop stores, grew crops on ranch lands around Waimea, or became tenant cane growers in Hāmākua and Kohala.

In 1924, the United States government prohibited further Japanese immigration. An estimated two hundred thousand Japanese had come to the Islands by then. In World War II, the *nisei* 442nd Regimental Combat Team played a a heroic role in the European theater. Japanese traditions such as New Year's mochi pounding, celebration of Boy's Day, bon dancing, and other cultural practices characterize Big Island town life to this day.

Left: The Wainaku homes of Japanese plantation workers were built of local materials but resembled Japanese farmhouses rather than Hawaiian hale. The banners at the center of the photograph may have marked a community bath. A wooden flume and pipes brought water from the hill. Circa 1890. [Bishop Museum]

Below far left: Young Japanese women, cane workers, with their cane knives. As thousands of "picture brides" immigrated to Hawai'i from Japan and Okinawa between 1900 and 1924, the number of women employed on the plantation steadily grew. By 1915, women were 38 percent of the total Japanese sugar plantation workforce. The women also made extra money doing laundry for single men. [Lyman House Memorial Museum]

Above: Hard-working plantation women are washing clothes in a small stream. The nattily-dressed gentleman with a dog has stopped to observe. Perhaps he is a friend of the photographer who captured this rural scene. [Hawai'i State Archives]

83

The Portuguese

In 1877, the sugar plantations turned to Portugal's Madeira and Azores Islands for laborers. The planters reasoned that the Portuguese were already skilled cane hands and would offset the overwhelming numbers of Chinese.

The Portuguese came with their families and traditions, determined to stay. Most arrived between 1878 and 1886, bound to the same ten dollar-a-day, twenty-six-day work contact offered to the Chinese. However, the Portuguese soon became luna, or foremen, and would form a new class, intermediate between Asian laborers and predominantly American managers and owners. The plantation hierarchy grew more complex.

By 1888, some North Hilo Portuguese owned their own mill and operated it as the Hilo Portuguese Sugar Company. By 1920, 7,046 Portuguese lived on the Big Island, representing more than 26 percent of the Territory's total Portuguese population. Independent, they were drawn to the coffee farms in the Kona district and to the ranches around Waimea, Pa'auilo, and Honoka'a. In Honoka'a, Portuguese language was still spoken in the 1960s. Today, over 18 percent of its residents are of Portuguese ancestry.

Right: Manual Pico, a rancher and a business associate of the Greenwell family from Kona, with his family. Date unknown. [Kona Historical Society]

Below left: A mother carries a basketful of sweetbread that has been baked in an outdoor brick oven. By sharing an oven, families could economize on fuel and labor. Ovens were fired once a week; each housewife would bake enough bread in a single day to supply her family for a week. [Bishop Museum]

Below right: The Portuguese in the islands clung to many of their national customs here in the Islands. These Portuguese women are baking pao doçe or sweetbread in a backyard oven, 1908. [Hawai'i State Archives]

Left: A Portuguese family gathering circa 1890. The young ladies, dressed in immaculate white Sunday-best dresses, are posed on the lānai steps with their instruments: zither, accordion, and guitar. [Hawai'i State Archives]

Below: Portuguese women workers from the Atlantic islands of Madeira and the Azores wearing the picturesque hats of their distant homeland. Many Portuguese customs survived, particularly food. [Bishop Museum]

The Filipinos

After 1898, young and impoverished men from the Philippines' agricultural provinces became a new resource for Hawai'i's plantations, which were still looking for a cheap, steady, and racially diverse labor supply. The first group of just fifteen men arrived in December 1906, to work at 'Ōla'a Plantation near Hilo.

During the next fifteen years, *sakadas*—Filipino sugar plantation workers—arrived by the thousands. They were paid eighteen dollars a month—equal to a year's pay back home—and guaranteed three years of work. But they also found themselves at the bottom of the plantation hierarchy, living in the harshest housing conditions. Disillusioned, many Filipinos chose to leave Hawai'i. The Filipino population jumped from twenty-five thousand in 1910 to sixty-three thousand in 1930—17 percent of the total Territory's population.

Six thousand Filipinos lived on the Big Island.

The majority of these workers were single men, without wives or families. A new service industry grew up around the Filipino camps. Japanese women, wives of plantation workers, took in laundry and made lunches. Bathhouses opened—25 cents for a month of baths. There were even dance halls where, for a dime a dance, men could enjoy female company for the length of a song.

The Filipino men became known for their roosters and cockfights. They celebrated Rizal Day in honor of their revolutionary hero who was slain by the Spanish. They also met and mingled with other ethnic groups, discussing sports and movies, sharing food and music.

By the late 1930s, Filipinos formed 70 percent of the Big Island's plantation work force.

Below: Filipino fishermen display a string of goby, caught near a stream near the Hāmākua coast town of Pepe'ekeo. The fish is called bonog *in Ilocano. Hawaiians called the fish 'o'opu. Circa 1950s. [Cabatu Family Collection]*

Below right: A Kona coast Filipino family, dressed in their best for a formal portrait. Date unknown. [Kona Historical Society]

The Koreans

Plantation owners turned to Korea to help neutralize the overwhelming presence of Japanese. The first 102 Koreans arrived in the islands on January 17, 1903. Not bound by contracts, they chose to settle in distinct Korean communities. There were Korean settlements in Hilo, in Hōnaunau in South Kona, and in Kehena between Waimea and Hāwī. They kept to themselves; their attention was often focused on the tense political situation back home in Korea. In 1905, when just seven thousand eight hundred Koreans had settled in the Territory, Korea prohibited further emigration.

The Koreans followed the Methodist Christian faith, and by 1904, had established the Korean Methodist Episcopal Church. Fifteen years later, the Hilo Korean Church opened. Across the island, the Korean flag waved at clubhouses where folk songs and theater plays kept the culture alive. Language schools ensured that new generations knew Korean politics and history.

For every ten Korean men, there was only one Korean woman. Between 1910 and 1924, during a second wave of immigration, close to one thousand Korean picture brides immigrated to Hawai'i.

Others

The plantations turned to other places for labor. In the 1870s, they recruited more than two thousand South and Central Pacific Islanders. Homesick, these men did not see the point of slaving for the planters and left after about six years.

In the early 1880s, the plantations tried their luck with Europeans, hoping that they would reinforce the Caucasian minority. Along the Hāmākua coast, the Scots settled in as managers. Kohala became known as "Little Britain." The Scandinavian people stopped coming after just two ships' worth, six hundred men, women, and children in all. Most of the Germans started out in Kaua'i. The Europeans augmented the Caucasian presence but did not become laborers.

In 1898, Puerto Rico became a territory of the United States, and, in December of 1900, the first fifty-six Puerto Ricans arrived, destined for O'ahu and Maui. In early January 1901, a second group of 387 laborers landed in Kohala; most of them were assigned to the Hāmākua and 'O'ōkala plantations. They earned about sixteen dollars a month. Eleven ships came that year, carrying five thousand immigrants. By 1920, the Big Island was home to twenty-one hundred Puerto Ricans. They were already a racially-diverse group, in which Indian, Caucasian, Spanish, and African blood mingled. They brought their own music, dance, and food, including pasteles, a type of ground-meat tamale.

In 1901, John Hind of Hawi Mill in Kohala urged plantations to bring in Blacks from the mainland. About two hundred arrived that year from Tennessee, but, unhappy among so many foreigners, they left quickly.

Finally, after 1907, a few hundred Spanish immigrants, mostly from Malaga and Granada, came to the Big Island where they took skilled positions and blended with the Puerto Rican and Filipino cultures.

Left: Three years after Japan annexed Korea in 1910, Dr. Syngman Rhee came to Hawai'i to serve as an educational minister. Instrumental in the Don Ji Hoi, a nationalist political organization for the Korean Independence Movement, Rhee lived on the Big Island where he initiated a charcoal enterprise in Mountain View to help finance Korea's cause. By 1919 about three thousand Koreans had raised $34,000, and Rhee left Hawai'i the following year. He eventually became the Republic of Korea's first president. [Hawai'i State Archives]

Below: In December 1900, the first group of Puerto Rican laborers arrived in Hawai'i. By 1905, they numbered fifty-two thousand men, women and children who sought better opportunities in the Islands following devastating hurricanes in their homeland. [Hawai'i State Archives]

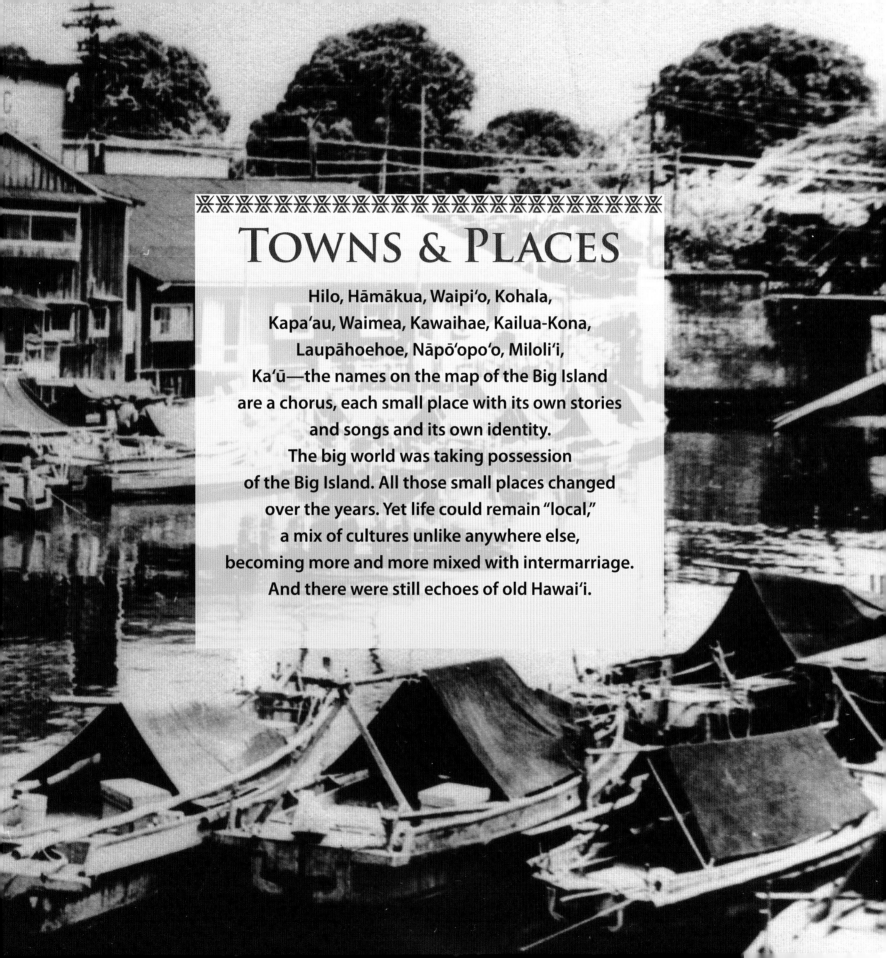

TOWNS & PLACES

Hilo, Hāmākua, Waipi'o, Kohala,
Kapa'au, Waimea, Kawaihae, Kailua-Kona,
Laupāhoehoe, Nāpō'opo'o, Miloli'i,
Ka'ū—the names on the map of the Big Island
are a chorus, each small place with its own stories
and songs and its own identity.
The big world was taking possession
of the Big Island. All those small places changed
over the years. Yet life could remain "local,"
a mix of cultures unlike anywhere else,
becoming more and more mixed with intermarriage.
And there were still echoes of old Hawai'i.

HILO

※※※※※※※※※※※

Previous pages: Hilo Harbor. Hilo's growth exploded in the early 1900s. In 1908, construction of a massive breakwater got underway, combined with dredging of a landing built on the Wailoa River in the 1840s. Hilo emerged as a leading commercial port, though its crescent bay lost its traditional value as a diving and surfing spot. [Richard Otaki Collection]

Below: The village of Hilo, as depicted in this 1854 engraving in Edward T. Perkins' **Na Motu** *or* **Reef-Roving in the South Seas**, *was nestled at the base of Mauna Loa along the peaceful Waiākea River. Although today a modern town, Hilo has been able to retain its unique Pacific flavor. [Baker-Van Dyke Collection]*

The village of Hilo—for that is all it was—gained its name in legendary times, "hilo" being the word for the first night of the new moon. The crescent bay, of course, resembles the crescent moon. In olden times, the bay was fringed with green taro lo'i, fishponds, and tidy thatched houses.

Hilo had long been home to powerful chiefs. From its mauka forests came the koa wood for Kamehameha I's final conquest fleet of eight hundred canoes. Its nearby black sand beach drew hundreds seeking paddling, surfing, and horseback-riding opportunities. Princess Ruth officially moved her court to Hilo in 1855, around the same time that commerce began to flourish and dozens of ships anchored offshore. For affluent travelers en route to the volcano, Hilo provided a natural place to rest. The town eventually became the Kingdom's second city.

Life continued unhurriedly into the early 1900s. The railroad that had opened in 1899 boosted sugar profits and drew new residents to the town. Improvements to Hilo's harbor transformed the town's appearance, as did the opening of new ethnic stores and shops. A "downtown" developed, complete with automobiles. Service industries—such as the Japanese fishermen who took their sampans to Waiākea Pond at the mouth of Wailoa river and provided Hilo with fish—catered to the surrounding plantations. Cheap and reliable sampan buses—modified Model-T cars —provided transport along the Hāmākua coast.

But in 1946 and 1960, two tsunamis erased the sampans, the train, and the bayfront stores and homes. A greenbelt buffer zone, with a recreation center around Wailoa River, took their places. The ending of sugar was to bring new economic hardships.

Tourists would continue to come to Kīlauea—airport development started in 1937—but after the war, rainy Hilo would compete for visitors with Kailua-Kona, which was sunny and dry and eventually became the Big Island's prime hotel destination.

Education and research created a new industry when, in the 1960s, astronomers turned their attention to Mauna Kea. In 1970, the University of Hilo—a vocational school since 1945—opened to accommodate scientists and students. The university has since expanded year after year. "Downtown" was revitalized around 2000 with spruced-up buildings, educational centers, and new galleries and shops. Hilo remains the seat of the Big Island's county government, and its forty-four thousand residents comprise 30 percent of the island's total population.

❊❊❊❊❊❊❊❊❊❊❊

Above: In 1875 Hilo town extended right to the edge of the bay. On the left is the American Consulate. After three devastating tsunami in the twentieth century, the commercial district was moved back from the imperiled coastline. [Baker-Van Dyke Collection]

Left : A very rare image of the ship loading dock that extended from Waiänuenue Avenue into what was formerly known as Byron's Bay. Circa 1900. [Richard Otaki Collection]

✳✳✳✳✳✳✳✳✳✳

Above: A Hilo waterfront panorama taken in the 1880s. [Baker-Van Dyke Collection]

Right : Another rare image of a hukilau at Hilo Bay. On the left are the twin towers of the old St. Joseph's Catholic Church built in 1862 facing Bridge Street (now Keawe Street) in downtown Hilo near Waiānuenue Avenue. The church was relocated (rebuilt) at Kapi'olani and Haili Streets in the late 1890s. Circa 1890s. [Richard Otaki Collection]

Above left: The famed "Kona nightingale," or donkey, was the essential mode of transportation of the coffee industry. Here one of them resists human persuasion on a Hilo Street. [Lyman House Memorial Musuem]

Above right: Mule-drawn carts were used to haul or dump anything and everything as in this rural Manono Street scene. Circa 1900. [Richard Otaki Collection]

Left : Kamehameha Avenue looking like the wild, wild west. Circa 1900. [Richard Otaki Collection]

✕✕✕✕✕✕✕✕✕✕✕

*Waiākea River was known for its fish-
ponds, referred to as the Royal Ponds.
These spring-fed inland ponds included
Hoʻakimau pond (Piʻopiʻo), Mohouli,
Kalepolepo, and Waihole ponds as
well as the largest pond, Waiākea. The
ponds were stocked mainly with fry
of mullet and milkfish caught along
the sandy shores at the mouths of
the streams of Hilo Bay. The mullet in
these latter four ponds were reserved
for the king's use, and remained so for
Kamehameha's sons and grandsons; the
mullet of Hoʻakimau pond belonged to
Kaʻahumanu and to her heirs. [Hawaiʻi
State Archives]*

*Right : Hilo town from Wailuku river,
1880. [Baker-Van Dyke Collection]*

❊❊❊❊❊❊❊❊❊❊

Above Left : Swimming off Wailoa Bridge at the mouth of the river was a favorite pastime. Visible at right are sampans docked at Suisan. Date unknown. [Richard Otaki Collection]

Below left: Construction of the Wailuku River railroad bridge, looking north towards the Hāmākua coast. Date unknown. [Richard Otaki Collection]

※※※※※※※※※※※※

Fishing was one of the important industries developed by Japanese immigrants. Utilizing skills developed in their homeland, sampan fishermen began providing the commercial needs of major population centers such as Honolulu and Hilo. The small, highly maneuverable boat was ideal for navigating island currents and could be handled by fewer men than most other watercraft. Until the tidal waves of 1946 and 1960 reshaped the Hilo waterfront, the sampan fleet would be crowded into Wailoa River and Hilo Bay. Although throwing a fishing net has been seen as a Hawaiian skill, the smaller throw net was also the contribution of Japanese immigrants. Like the sampan, the throw net fishing technique was quickly adapted by other ethnic groups to become one of the many multicultural aspects of Island life. This 1908 photograph shows the sampan fishing fleet at the Hilo Fishmarket on the Wailoa river. [Bishop Museum]

Left: The fertile sugar fields of the districts of Hāmākua and ʻŌlaʻa were rapidly expanded as capital, labor, and technology poured into the windward coast of the island of Hawaiʻi. The commercial center of this plantation growth was Hilo town, which felt the impact of rapid urbanization as small ethnic businesses, automobiles, construction, and congestion transformed the main thoroughfare, Kamehameha Avenue, pictured here in 1926. [Baker-Van Dyke Collection]

Below: 1930's Kamehameha Avenue looking south as it bends around Hilo Bay. [Richard Otaki Collection]

Kaʻū

✖✖✖✖✖✖✖✖✖✖✖

Right: Honuʻapu landing in the Kaʻū district, 1908. [Baker-Van Dyke Collection]

Below left and right: Lee Chong's general store in Pāhala, Kaʻū. Pāhala was a sugar plantation town until 1996. The store was operating as early as 1903 and seems to have prospered, as Chong opened up several branch stores and operated a hotel, a gas station, and a restaurant. He died in 1950. Date unknown. [Baker-Van Dyke Collection]

SOUTH KONA

✳✳✳✳✳✳✳✳✳✳

Left: **Village de Kearakekoua,**
lithograph by Langlume after L'Auvergne, 1836. A view of the Hawaiian fishing village of Ka'awaloa, built on low ground in Kealakekua Bay. The village is now gone, and the promontory holds only the Cook Monument, marking the spot where Captain Cook was killed. [Bishop Museum]

Below: When this photograph was taken in 1888, the village of Ho'okena was second in size only to Kailua Village on Hawai'i's west side. A popular landing for passengers and goods from inter-island steamships, Ho'okena included a school, two churches, two stores, a wharf, a courthouse, and many fine homes. In 1890, a tourist guide called it "the last specimen on the islands of a purely Hawaiian community," which might have attracted Robert Louis Stevenson to visit for a week in 1889. [Bishop Museum]

This photo near Hoʻokena shows the contrasts between the old and the new. Note the grass house frame under construction. This is steamer day, and the town has turned out. People gather with their trunks and other luggage, waiting their turn to be rowed out to the vessel in the harbor. [Baker-Van Dyke Collection]

※※※※※※※※※※※

Right: At this funeral, mourners gather in front of the Hawaii Coffee Mill Company. Later the building housed the Post Office. Date unknown. [Kona Historical Society]

Below: The Manago Hotel in Captain Cook was founded in 1917 by Kinzo and Osame Manago. It is still in operation, run by a third generation of Managos. Date unknown. [Kona Historical Society]

Kealakekua Bay with Nāpō'opo'o in the foreground and the Captain Cook Monument across the bay at Ka'awaloa. 1933. [Baker-Van Dyke Collection]

KAILUA-KONA

Boat Day at Kamakahonu Beach at Kailua Village was a popular biweekly event for this busy West Hawai'i shipping center. A colorful and noisy jumble of coffee bags, goat and cow hides, wool bales, orange crates, and live cattle joined passengers draped in colorful flower lei, waiting to be rowed out to an inter-island steamer in the bay. In the background, historic Moku'aikaua Church (right of center with steeple), constructed in 1837, rises over the village. Along the shoreline, the two-storied Hulihe'e Palace on the left, built in 1838, awaits its royal guests, including King Kalākaua, who hosted many lively parties on its grounds later in the century. [Hawai'i State Archives]

Sheltered by the slopes of the 8,271-foot volcano Hualālai and lacking permanent streams but with plenty of sun, Kailua relied on dryland terrace farms to provided sustenance to its large Hawaiian population.

With its little beaches and calm waters, ideal for swimming and surfing, the village of "two seas" became a favorite residence for chiefs around 1600, making it one of the island's most significant political, social and cultural areas.

Less than a mile inland, a five-mile lava wall stretching from Kailua village to Keauhou in the south protected agricultural crops from pigs and dogs. Later it was enlarged, becoming known as Kuakini's Wall, barring cattle, sheep, and goats.

Kailua, with its calm waters and little beaches is great for swimming and surfing. The village of "two seas" became a favorite residence for chiefs around 1600, making it one of the island's most significant political, social, and cultural areas.

After Kamehameha I unified the Islands and returned to the Big Island in 1812, he chose Kamakahonu at the north side of Kailua Bay as his court. There he rebuilt its sacred 'Ahu'ena Heiau and dedicated it to Lono, the god of agriculture and peace. Here he lived and ruled until his death in 1819. Six months later, his son and two of his wives would break the kapu. This was also the location of the first missionaries' arrival. As were Hawaiians throughout the Islands, the Hawaiians of Kailua were ravaged by introduced diseases. In 1823, Asa Thurston estimated Kona district's total population to be about 20,000. By 1835, a missionary

census counted just 11,000, and in 1853, 7,223.

Around Kahalu'u, just south of Kailua, a fishing community thrived, and its chiefs made offerings at Ku'emanu Heiau to ensure good surfing waves. According to legend, the menehune, mythical beings living deep in the mountains, built a massive breakwater here. In the late 1800s, King Kalākaua built a summer cottage in Kahalu'u.

The old royal quarters crumbled in the late 1850s. Hulihe'e, a new stone-and-mortar palace nearby, served as a far more comfortable retreat. However, it was not to the taste of Princess Ruth Ke'elikōlani, appointed island governor in 1855, who preferred to live in a grass house nearby, or in Hilo.

Kailua Bay became one of the island's most important ports. From here, upland produce was shipped to Honolulu. Ranchers shipped cattle for slaughter on O'ahu. Twice a week, when inter-island steamers anchored off shore, the beach was packed with passengers and produce such as oranges, coffee, goat and cow hides, wool, and butter. Noisy cattle-loading operations added further color to the scene. In the village itself, merchant stores, boarding houses, and bars opened up. In the bustle, sacred or traditional Hawaiian sites were erased. A large concrete pier was built.

In 1957, to differentiate Kailua from a town on O'ahu that was also named Kailua, the U.S. Postal Service gave the town a new name: Kailua-Kona. In 1960, a high-rise hotel was built over the ruins of Kamakahonu, the old royal complex. Little merchant stores gave way to tourist shops, and busy Ali'i Drive was built alongside the historic seawall. Only a replica of 'Ahu'ena Heiau remains.

※※※※※※※※※※※

Right: Kailua-Kona at dawn of the twentieth century. In the middle of a quiet, dusty street, two men on donkeys. Many years later, the Kona Inn was built on this spot. 1908. [Baker-Van Dyke Collection]

Below: The old Kailua-Kona courthouse, known as Hale Halawai. This beautiful, late-Victorian wooden building, probably built in the 1880s, was torn down in 1960 when Hale Halawai Park was created. Date unknown. [Baker-Van Dyke Collection]

X166-KAILUA LANDING-J.A.GONSALVES-PHOT.

※※※※※※※※※※※※

Above, below, and above on following page: Once a small port village, by the 1920s Kailua-Kona was emerging as a commercial center for its surrounding districts. As well, its sunny, dry weather and beautiful oceanfront were beginning to attract tourists, particularly after the Kona Inn was built. Its historical past could be felt everywhere. It was here that the kapu was overthrown, where Christianity was introduced to the Hawaiian people by the Thurstons a few months later and where Hulihe'e Palace was located. Donkeys and carriages once dominated tree-lined dusty lanes. Yet the town was not much different from when the British traveler Isabella Bird described the place in 1873 as "a land where all things always seem the same...a region of endless afternoons...people speak in hushed thin voices and move as in a lethargy, dreaming, too!" [Hawai'i State Archives]

107

✳✳✳✳✳✳✳✳✳✳✳

Right: Kailua village, as seen from the second story of the old Hackfield building near the wharf. A temporary cattle pen sits next to Kaiakeakua Beach. Sometimes sumo matches were held in the pen, as entertainment on boat days. Date unknown. [Kona Historical Society]

※※※※※※※※※※

Left: An early aerial view of Kailua-Kona. The resort hotel behind the wharf, towards the top of the picture, was later demolished. In the foreground is Moku'aikaua Church. Date unknown. [Kona Historical Society]

Below: Kailua-Kona was a sleepy country town when this 1933 photo was taken. In later years, missionary descendant and newspaper magnate Lorrin P. Thurston built a magnificent home on the point of land in the center of the photo. [Baker-Van Dyke Collection]

NORTH KONA

※※※※※※※※※※※

Right: A Japanese family, possibly the proprietor's, in front of Hanato Store, Hanalo. Date unknown. [Kona Historical Society]

Below: Heiji Yamagata, the issei proprietor of Kona's Yamagata Store, with his produce and "Kona nightingale." Circa 1930. [Bishop Museum]

✕✕✕✕✕✕✕✕✕✕✕

Above: A Fourth of July parade in Kainaliu. 1924. [Kona Historical Society]

Left: Hōlualoa's Japanese community gathers for a ceremony. The building on left was originally the Tanimoto Store (circa 1900-1925), then became the S. Morikami Store (1928-1964). Date unknown. [Kona Historical Society]

111

✳✳✳✳✳✳✳✳✳✳✳✳

Above: The shoreline stretching from Kīholo to Honokōhau Beach had many settlements, some dating as far back as the twelfth century. Their inhabitants relied on fishponds like those at Kaloko and 'Aimakapā. [Kona Historical Society]

Right: The Kaloko fishpond lies next to the remains of a Hawaiian fishing village, believed to have been settled in the 1200s. Fishponds belonged to chiefs, and fed the chiefs and their numerous dependents. The ponds were managed by skilled konohiki who maintained water quality, protected the fish, and harvested them when needed. Among the many fish species protected there were 'anae, or mullet, and awa, or milk-fish. This pond was in use until 1961. It is now part of a national historical park. [Kona Historical Society]

MĀHUKONA

500 MAHUKONA - HAWAII.

Māhukona was once a thriving harbor. It was the terminus of Kohala's Māhukona to Niuli'i railroad, built in 1880–1882. Sugar from North Kohala plantations was shipped to the port, where it was loaded onto inter-island steamers for transshipment to Honolulu. In 1941, the port was closed by the U.S. military authorities, who feared a Japanese invasion. Nothing is left of the port except wharf remnants, some structures, a sugar warehouse, and a railroad office. [Hawai'i State Archives]

Kawaihae

※※※※※※※※※※※

Above: Kawaihae is one of the driest spot in the Hawaiian islands, with an annual rainfall of less than 20 inches. Thanks to good fishing offshore, a small Hawaiian community once eked out a living there. In the late eighteenth century, Kawaihae became one of Kamehameha I's residences and the location of his great heiau, Pu'ukoholā. Kawaihae was a busy port all through the nineteenth and early twentieth century. In the 1950s, the old village and shoreline were destroyed when a new, larger harbor was dredged and expanded port facilities were built. Kawaihae is now the second-busiest port on the Big Island. [Bishop Musem]

Right: A Kawaihae Hawaiian family in front of their neat, whitewashed waterfront house. A boat lies nearby, perhaps the family fishing boat. [Hawai'i State Archives]

※※※※※※※※※※※

Left: Bringing supplies ashore at Kawaihae. The Puʻukoholā Heiau is in the background, at right. [Baker-Van Dyke Collection]

Below: Landing goods at Kawaiahae Harbor, in front of a building originally built by French and Company. 1870. [Bishop Musem]

WAIPI'O VALLEY

※※※※※※※※※※※※

Right: Remote Waipi'o Valley was one place where the traditional way of life was able to sustain itself in the nineteenth century. This etching is from a drawing by Reverend William Ellis, who in 1823 was the first foreigner to visit the royal village of Waipi'o. It illustrates a land still rich in cultivation, though depopulated since the arrival of foreigners in the islands. [Bishop Museum]

Below: A pandanus tree is reflected in the still waters of Waipi'o Valley. The stone oven next to the tree was built by Chinese rice growers for smoking whole pigs. [Hawai'i State Archives]

Waipi'o Valley, the Land of Curving Water, is a large and stunning ahupua'a several miles long on the northern tip of the Big Island between Hāmākua and Kohala. A population of thousands was once sheltered there, nurtured by abundant water and food.

Celebrated in legend, myth and song, Waipi'o was home to high-ranking kings and the traditional deities believed to live there. Some of the most sacred heiau on Hawai'i Island were in Waipi'o, including Paka'alana, which was a temple of state, the most significant heiau and also a pu'uhonua After the kapu was abolished in 1819, sacred sites of Waipi'o continued to be centers of Hawaiian worship.

There were an estimated 4,000 residents in Waipi'o at the time of European discovery, when Captain Cook's ships passed offshore in 1779. In 1823, missionary William Ellis wrote of 1,325 residents in the valley. Thirty-five years later, the population had fallen to 640, according to Elias Bond, another missionary.

Above: Heavily populated by ka poʻe kahiko, or the ancient people, Waipiʻo Valley was terraced with lush taro fields fed by the cool waters from the ever-replenished streams. Accessible only by canoe or down the steep ascent of the valley walls, the floor of Waipiʻo was described by the Reverend William Ellis in 1823 as "one continued garden, cultivated with taro, bananas, sugar cane, and other productions of the islands, all growing luxuriantly." By 1901, when this photograph was taken, the population of the valley had greatly diminished. Waipiʻo became an enclave of a Hawaiʻi from another, quietly fading era.
[Hawaiʻi State Archives]

Left: Sand hills and bluffs. Circa 1880.
[Hawaiʻi State Archives]

117

A home with the twin falls of Hiʻilawe and Hakalaoa in the background. Hiʻilawe, with a vertical drop of more than one thousand feet, is the tallest waterfall in Hawaiʻi. [Hawaiʻi State Archives]

※※※※※※※※※※※※

This dramatic aerial illustrates why Waipiʻo is referred to as a V-shaped or amphitheater valley. Muliwai Pond is on the right and Lālākea Pond is on the left. Lālākea was used in the 1970s for growing lotus root. It is now overgrown with weeds and cattails. [Baker-Van Dyke Collection]

Right: Waipi'o Valley is still home to several taro farms. Some farmers live down on the valley floor; others live up on the ridge above. They use 4WD vehicles to descend and ascend the steep, zig-zag road to the valley floor. Waipi'o taro is still a Big Island favorite, prized for poi and laulau. [Bishop Museum]

Below: A mule train packed with goods slowly makes its way up the steep trail out of Waipi'o. 1936. [Baker-Van Dyke Collection]

CHINESE RICE FARMERS

Left and below: Rice planting was backbreaking labor. The fields had to be flooded to just the right depth, then the young rice seedlings set out in neat rows. [Hawai'i State Archives]

When their plantation labor contracts were up, the Chinese often started businesses. Some ran their own small sugar operations and hired their own gangs. Others became itinerant food-peddlers or storekeepers, or left for Honolulu. They also started growing rice in the wet Kohala valleys of Waipi'o, Waimanu, and Pololū. At the height of production in 1890, rice farming employed five thousand Chinese workers. Rice production ended in the 1920s, due to competition from California-grown rice.

Hin Chun, known to the Hawaiians as Ahina, first came to Waipi'o in the 1890s. He leased rice land from the Bishop Estate and, aided by his hardworking wife, Kwok Shee, and his five sons, eked out a living raising and milling rice for the Island market. It was a precarious living. Island rice faced increasing competition from California rice farmers. Storms occasionally flooded the valley, destroying crops. Hin Chun lost his entire crop in 1914. He planted one more crop, then died in 1915—after having advised his sons to go to school rather than plant rice for a living.

No rice grows in Waipi'o Valley today.

LAUPĀHOEHOE

Right: Laupāhoehoe is a small, flat, lava-rock peninsula that juts out into the ocean from the Hāmākua coast. It was formed by a lava flow from the now-dormant volcano, Mauna Kea, that looms over the coast. Its name means "leaf of lava," fitting since it is a leaf of lava reaching into the ocean. It is reached by a steep, switchback road leading down from the uplands. It has been inhabited since pre-contact times. During the late 1800s and early 1900s, it was part of the Hāmākua coast's robust sugar economy. The low-lying peninsula was devastated by the same 1946 tsunami that destroyed much of downtown Hilo. An elementary school had been built close to the waterfront; when the tsunami hit, it destroyed four teachers' cottages and swept across the school playing fields. Four teachers and twenty students were killed. This photo shows Laupāhoehoe in 1880. It was a thriving village, with thousands of residents and a hotel, a restaurant, and a post office. [Baker-Van Dyke Collection]

Below right: A slightly later photo of Laupāhoehoe. 1890. [Bishop Museum]

ONOMEA

Just a few miles north of Hilo lies scenic Onomea settlement fronting Onomea Bay. Onomea Plantation, once one of the more profitable sugar plantations on the Hāmākua coast, is long gone, but the shallow bay that served as the plantation's port is still called Onomea Bay. The old Hawaiian fishing village and port town, Kahaliʻi, that stood on the edge of the bay is also gone, a victim of the 1946 tsunami. It had ceased being a port long before, when the railroad was built. Circa 1900s. [Richard Otaki Collection]

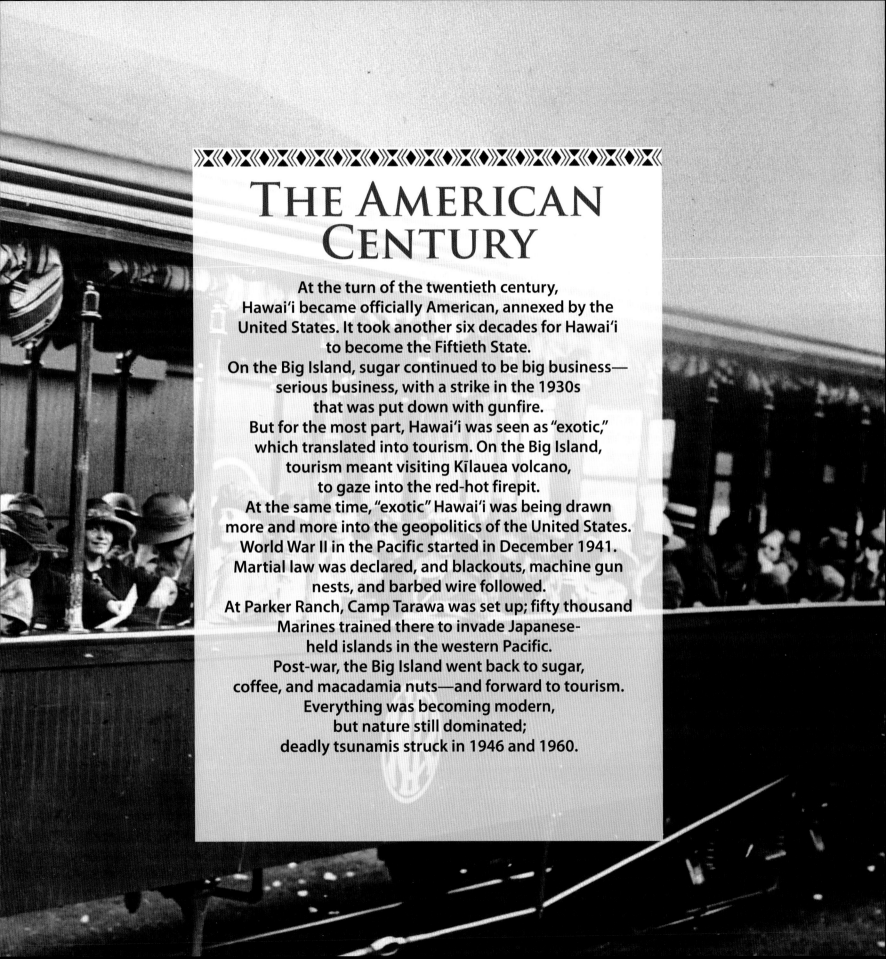

THE AMERICAN CENTURY

At the turn of the twentieth century,
Hawai'i became officially American, annexed by the
United States. It took another six decades for Hawai'i
to become the Fiftieth State.
On the Big Island, sugar continued to be big business—
serious business, with a strike in the 1930s
that was put down with gunfire.
But for the most part, Hawai'i was seen as "exotic,"
which translated into tourism. On the Big Island,
tourism meant visiting Kīlauea volcano,
to gaze into the red-hot firepit.
At the same time, "exotic" Hawai'i was being drawn
more and more into the geopolitics of the United States.
World War II in the Pacific started in December 1941.
Martial law was declared, and blackouts, machine gun
nests, and barbed wire followed.
At Parker Ranch, Camp Tarawa was set up; fifty thousand
Marines trained there to invade Japanese-
held islands in the western Pacific.
Post-war, the Big Island went back to sugar,
coffee, and macadamia nuts—and forward to tourism.
Everything was becoming modern,
but nature still dominated;
deadly tsunamis struck in 1946 and 1960.

HAWAIIAN WAYS: CULTURAL TRADITIONS

Previous pages: Tourists during the first three decades of the twentieth century were mostly Americans with enough leisure time and resources to afford an extended vacation in the Pacific. Travel to and from the Islands in cruise liners from ports on the West Coast took about ten days. Once tourists arrived, they occasionally toured beyond Waikīkī and Oʻahu, exploring the island of Hawaiʻi with its active volcano region, and the lush gardens and rainforests of Hilo. 1926. [Baker-Van Dyke Collection]

Right: Taro was the ancient basis of life—legends describe kalo as being the brother of the first human beings, buried and transformed into the nutritious plant. Whether planting, weeding, harvesting, or cooking taro, it was the work of families. Several generations within an ʻohana, as shown in this photograph in Hilo, gathered to clean, cook, and pound the kalo into a thick substance called poi. 1890. [Baker-Van Dyke Collection]

At the start of the twentieth century, Hawaiians were a minority on their own land—a few tens of thousands of people in a population of hundreds of thousands, all living under the American flag.

For Westerners on the Big Island, times were good; sugar equaled prosperity. For the families of Asian immigrant sugar workers born in the Islands, Hawaiʻi became their true home. For Hawaiians, as the century went on, there was more and more displacement. Asphalt roads were built over trails. Surfing and fishing spots became commercial harbors or hotel sites. Tourism co-opted parts of Hawaiian culture and commercialized it for entertainment.

Yet, it was still possible for some Hawaiians to make some kind of peace with the world around them and to find contentment with the life they were given to live. In small villages or enclaves nestled in the mountains or at the foot of a steep amphitheater valley, one could find modest wooden houses, shelters for the horses and other livestock, and the white spire of a small New England-style church, where the Sunday hymns were sung in Hawaiian. There existed a peaceful aura amid rich vegetation, the days hot and languid, the star-filled evenings warm with the pungent aroma of flowering plants.

The sounds of the village were a mixture of ease, excitement, joy, prayer, and the laughter of children. The men, or kāne, were active with shouts of direction to those working in the loʻi, the irrigated terraces for taro, or mounting their horses for ranch work in the hills. The women, or wāhine, took care of the infants, joined in the village work, and exchanged stories. When the village family, the ʻohana, gathered for feasts, music, dance, or prayer, their voices would be raised in rollicking laughter, melodious song, "talk story," or solemn concern. Away from the confusion, competition, and drive of the outside worlds, the fabric of life in those small Hawaiian villages was woven through shared values, shared work, celebrations, and mournings.

The Hawaiʻi of those Big Island villages hardly exists anymore. Only in a few remote places, shielded from progress, or in the vivid memories of the elders, can the sounds, smells, tastes, and feelings of the past be recalled. Photographs—moments captured over decades—give us a precious glimpse.

The faces of Hawaiian elders or kūpuna reflected the wisdom gained through life. During their lifetime, Hawai'i had undergone vast changes. They or their parents personally experienced what Westernization meant. Elders in these photos (above and left below) were the bearers of love and knowledge needed more than ever as cultural shock faced their people in the nineteenth century and knowledge of the old ways was being lost or forgotten.

Left: Three generations of the Hawai'i Kupuka'a Family. 1920-1921. [Bishop Museum]

Below left: A Hawaiian couple at Pāhō'iki, Puna, Hawai'i. Date unknown. [Baker-Van Dyke Collection]

Below right: In rural or outlying areas, families might still be large. A Kona mother sits with her five children. 1934. [Baker-Van Dyke Collection]

XXXXXXXXXXXXXXXX

Above: Twentieth-century Hawaiians in Western clothes pay their respects to tradition at Kilauea volcano. Circa 1930. [Baker-Van Dyke Collection]

Right: Hawaiian women mastered the craft of ulana, the traditional plaiting or weaving of lauhala, the durable and pliable leaves of the pandanus tree. Leaves were gathered, stripped of veins and thorns, softened, rolled, and later cut into strips for weaving. Lauhala was used for mats, baskets, sails, bed coverings, and other useful articles. A Puna family rolls and strips lauhala for weaving. 1932. [Baker-Van Dyke Collection]

Far right: A woman shows a child how to prepare lauhala leaves for weaving. Note the rolls of finished leaves on the lānai. [Baker-Van Dyke Collection]

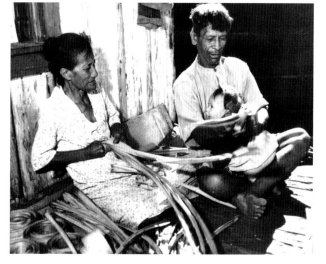

XOXOXOXOXOXOXOXOXOX

Throughout Polynesia, the earth oven, or imu in Hawaiian, is the way to cook large quantities of food. In the old days, it would have been prepared daily; now, it's a special occasion, reserved for festive lūʻau. [Baker-Van Dyke Collection]

Left: The imu starts with a deep pit filled with smooth river rocks. A fire is built on top of the stones, heating them red hot. The hot stones are covered with a layer of banana stumps and leaves, then leaf-wrapped food is put on top. Typical foods would be whole pigs, fish, taro root, breadfruit, and sweet potatoes, or tasty combinations of foods in leaf-wrapped laulau. The food is then covered with more leaves, and earth is piled on top. Heated from below, insulated on top, the food both roasts and steams. When the oven is uncovered and the food taken out, it has an inimitable smoky, moist, kālua taste. 1928. [Baker-Van Dyke Collection]

Far left: "Ua ola no o kai ia kai—Shore-dwellers find sustenance in the sea" was still a strong tradition in the first decade of the century as fishermen prepared their nets and canoes for a day of harvesting. Date unknown. [Hawaiian Historical Society]

Left: As the sugar planting became dominant, the land and water devoted to taro cultivation was drastically reduced. Scenes such as this Hawaiian woman in the taro field with her children became increasingly rare, as even the production of poi turned into a business, often owned by independent Chinese farmers. Circa 1900. [Hawaiʻi State Archives]

129

Above left: Two men paddle a Hawaiian outrigger canoe. This canoe is an old-fashioned dugout canoe, carved from one tree trunk (probably koa). The gunnels, booms, and outrigger are lashed to the canoe body. Traditional lashings were ingeniously designed to give just the right mix of strength and flexibility. [Bishop Museum]

Above right: A man poses with his paddle and Hawaiian canoe. He is sitting on the kaupo'i, a removable cover for the bow that helped keep heavy seas from filling the canoe. [Hawaiian Historical Society]

Right: Two men at the Makaokūikalani Stone. Hawaiian watermen were noted for their strength and skill. [Bishop Museum]

Far right: Members of the Hōnaunau Canoe Club. 1936. [Kona Historical Society]

Top: A crowd follows as the first King Kamehameha Day Parade makes its way to Hulihe'e Palace. 1914. [Kona Historical Society]

Above: Outrigger canoes approach the Kailua-Kona shore as part of the festivities of the first Kamehameha Day. 1914. [Kona Historical Society]

Left: Hōnaunau Canoe Club. Date unknown. [Kona Historical Society]

EARLY TOURISM

Below: Matson Navigation Co. advertised it's "Direct Line" between San Fransisco and Hilo. Date unknown. [Richard Otaki Collection]

Below right: Inter-Island Airways served Kohala's elite, offering flights to Hilo and Honolulu on a pair of eight-passenger Sikorsky amphibian planes, the Hawaii and the Maui. In 1930, a one-way passenger fare to Honolulu would have been $25—more than two weeks' wages for a plantation worker. [Richard Otaki Collection]

In the mid-1800s, a handful of explorers noted their discoveries about the Big Island's two active volcanoes in journals that circulated around the world. The volcanoes became a tourist draw for a growing stream of visitors.

In 1825, the British ship commander Lord George Anson Byron from England (a cousin of the poet George Gordon Byron) anchored in Hilo Bay and embarked on a scientific volcano study. In the winter of 1840, Charles Wilkes, in charge of an American expedition, brought along the famous artist Titian Ramsay Peale to create some of the earliest illustrations of the crater. These early travels were dangerous and required elaborate support—hundreds of Hawaiians to carry tents and gear. When Wilkes found Kīlauea without fire and continued to Mokuʻāweoweo, he lost two men to Mauna Loa's Arctic summit conditions.

Samuel Langhorne Clemens, aka Mark Twain, toured the island in 1866 and wrote lively travel pices. His entertaining prose was followed by the impressionistic and poetic 1873 accounts of Isabella L. Bird and Charles Nordhoff. Around the same time, the first tourist guidebooks to the Islands started to appear.

In 1915, the Big Island began to promote tourism. Advertisements did not mention rugged, unpaved roads. As roads improved, automobiles became common. Tourist numbers jumped when in 1929 Inter-Island Airways (now Hawaiian Airlines) introduced the first inter-island commercial airplanes–two Sikorsky amphibians. Automobiles became common as roads improved. Five years later, Pan American Airways shortened travel time from the mainland USA to Honolulu with the first commercial transpacific flights. (A direct connection from the Mainland to the Big Island would have to wait for another thirty-seven years.)

The Big Island's first lodgings were located around Hilo and the volcano. The district's rainy climate and lack of white beaches were not tourist-friendly. In balmy Kailua on the Kona coast, the Kona Inn opened in the late 1920s with barely any surrounding infrastructure support. Not until the 1950s did developers turn to Kona in earnest. The old seashore road to the harbor was transformed into Aliʻi Drive. A decade later, resorts and golf courses along the sunny Kohala coast followed. Today eighty percent of the Big Island's tourists stay in west Hawaiʻi and visit the volcano for a day or two. In 2005, almost 1.5 million visitors visited only the Big Island.

Kailua-Kona

The east side of the Big Island had the volcano. On the west side, Kailua-Kona had sunshine and beaches, but no good roads and a shortage of drinking water.

Kona coast tourism made a modest debut in 1928, when the Inter-Island Steamship Navigation Company opened the luxurious Kona Inn. Designed by the Territory's famous architect Charles Dickey, and drawing water from Kona's former sugar mill, which had closed in 1904, its saltwater swimming pool and tennis courts drew an upscale crowd. It closed in 1976 to make room for a shopping mall.

Despite the Inn's success, Kona remained poor; one inn could not compensate for limited agriculture and bad roads. Infrastructure to boost tourism became a priority. In 1948, construction began on a commercial airport strip. Hotels followed, as well as a county water system. Kailua soon hosted thousands of visitors a year. In 1960, the King Kamehameha Hotel opened with 105 rooms. After Hawaiʻi became a state in 1959, efforts to turn Kailua into a tourist attraction intensified Little seaport bars and tackle shops along the old seawall road were replaced with tourist shops. A new airport at Keāhole, a large harbor at Honokōhau, and several more hotels opened within the next twelve years.

By 1966, one hundred thirty-seven thousand tourists came to Kona, bringing new prosperity. In 1983, United Airlines started direct flights from the west coast to Keahole Airport. Today, more than a million tourists arrive at Keāhole, and more than one hundred seventy thousand come from cruise ships. By 2000, most of Kona's thirty-seven thousand residents worked in tourism-related jobs. About 40 percent of the Big Islands' accommodation units are in the Kailua-Kona area.

Left: When tourists boarded the Hilo Consolidated Railway in 1926, they were serenaded on their ride along the picturesque Hāmākua coast by the Hawai'i Orchestra from the S.S. Haleakala. [Tai Sing Loo/Baker-Van Dyke Collection]

Below: The commercial center of the growing sugar industry was Hilo town, which urbanized as new small ethnic businesses, automobiles, construction, and congestion transformed the main thoroughfare, Kamehameha Avenue. On boat days or to pick up passengers from the trains going to the volcano area, cars and their drivers would park awaiting their fares. 1926. [Hawai'i State Archives]

Right and below: Transportation for the carriage trade between Honolulu and Kona and Hilo was essential to develop tourism on the Big Island. An Inter-Island Airways plane arrives in Kailua-Kona. Boat Day in Hilo at the Inter-Island Steamship docks. 1934. [Baker-Van Dyke Collection]

Left: An early Hawaiian Airlines flight to the Big Island. Date unknown. [Kona Historical Society]

Below: Waimea in 1938 had a modest hotel for business travelers and the few tourists to the district. [Baker-Van Dyke Collection]

KONA INN

Right: The Kona Inn, designed by famous Island architect Charles Dickey, opened in 1928. It solved the water shortage that had throttled Kona tourism by diverting water from an abandoned sugar mill. The Inn's luxurious facilities made tourism comfortable and convenient for a country-club crowd. Here, guests spend their afternoon relaxing on the main lānai. The Inn closed in 1976 and was replaced by a shopping complex. [Baker-Van Dyke Collection]

Below left: A fisherman shows a string of colorful reef fish to two young guests. [Baker-Van Dyke Collection]

Below right: The sitting room was decorated with lauhala mats, wicker furniture, and colorful chintzes and cretonnes, combining Island comfort with contemporary notions of casual elegance. [Baker-Van Dyke Collection]

Left: Entertainers, including children, perform at nighttime for a large audience on the Kona Inn grass lawn stage, located on the ocean side of the hotel. [Baker-Van Dyke Collection]

Below: A Hawaiian-style grass house serves as backdrop. Date unknown. [Kona Historical Society]

CAPTAIN COOK SESQUICENTENNIAL

Captain James Cook first landed on Kaua'i on January 20, 1778. In 1928, Hawai'i's Territorial Government celebrated the 150th anniversary of the occasion with some pomp. A Captain Cook Sesquicentennial Commission organized local celebrations throughout the Islands, as well as arranging for the issue of a memorial U.S. half dollar (now rare and valuable) and a commemorative stamp. Scholarly essays in honor of Cook were solicited and printed in an album subsidized by the Commission and the Archives of Hawai'i.

In 1928, it had been thirty-five years since the overthrow of the Hawaiian monarchy. Hawai'i had been annexed by the United States and was now a U.S. territory, but not yet a state. Political power rested firmly in the hands of the predominantly Caucasian political and business elite. From their Western point of view, Cook had "discovered" Hawai'i—early Polynesian voyagers notwithstanding—and his arrival marked the true beginning of history in the Islands, a history which by 1928 had culminated in complete Western political and cultural dominance.

The 1928 celebrations on the Big Island, actually held six months later than Cook's visit to the Big Island, focused on the site most closely associated with Cook: Kealakekua Bay, where his ships had anchored and where he had died. An outrigger canoe regatta paddled into the bay, headed by a local Native Hawaiian in chiefly costume. Big Island dignitaries assembled next to the Cook Monument and celebrated with oratory. It is highly unlikely such a commemoration or celebration would be held today or would receive the participation of Hawaiians.

Right: The obelisk monument to Captain Cook at Kealakekua Bay dates from 1874. It is said to be on the spot where he was killed. [Baker-Van Dyke Collection]

Below: The scene of Cook's death has attracted visitors since the early nineteenth century. It was the site of a sesquicentennial observance in 1928. [Baker-Van Dyke Collection]

IN MEMORY OF THE GREAT CIRCUMNAVIGATOR, CAPTAIN JAMES COOK, R N., WHO DISCOVERED THESE ISLANDS ON THE 18TH OF JANUARY, A.D. 1778 AND FELL NEAR THIS SPOT ON THE 14TH OF FEBRUARY, A.D. 1779. THIS MONUMENT WAS ERECTED IN NOVEMBER A.D. 1874 BY SOME OF HIS FELLOW COUNTRYMEN.

Top left: During the 1928 event, Hawaiians reenacted the first contact with Captain Cook at Kealakekua Bay. [Baker-Van Dyke Collection]

Top right: Outrigger canoes idle in the bay. A British cruiser and a U.S. Navy battleship decked with festive flags can be seen in the background. [Baker-Van Dyke Collection]

Left: Automobiles are lined up near Nāpōʻopoʻo Landing to drive visiting dignitaries to Kīlauea. [Baker-Van Dyke Collection]

Above: Dignitaries arrive by boat at a temporary dock next to the Cook Monument. [Baker-Van Dyke Collection]

VOLCANO LANDS

*Above: An early visit by foreigners to Kīlauea. This engraving—***Na Motu** *or* **Reef-Roving in the South Seas***—was published in 1854 by Edward T. Perkins'. [Baker-Van Dyke Collection]*

Powers with far more impact than traders, missionaries, or sugar interests work side by side on the Big Island and, when least expected, make their presence known. These are earthquakes and tsunamis.

The Big Island's earthquakes are usually caused by the local volcanoes. Three of the island's five volcanoes—Kīlauea, Mauna Loa, and Hualālai—are active. Mauna Kea, which last erupted four thousand to six thousand years ago, lies dormant. Kohala has not erupted in the last one hundred twenty thousand years. The inactive or dormant volcanoes are eroding away, but the active volcanoes are still adding acreage to the island, as their lava pours into the ocean. Magma-induced tremors and earthquakes often precede volcanic eruptions. In a detailed logbook, missionary Sarah Lyman in Hilo reported about four to five earthquakes a year between 1833 and 1861, some mere shocks that "sloshed milk out of half-full pans." Since a record fatal earthquake in 1868, nine earthquakes of magnitude 6 or higher have struck the Big Island. An earthquake of magnitude 7.2 struck Puna in 1975, and a 6.7 earthquake 39 km below sea level and off Kīlolo Bay struck in 2006.

Large earthquakes sometimes displace huge masses of ocean water, resulting in a tsunami—liter-ally meaning a "great harbor wave." The Big Island is subject to tsunamis caused both by local earthquakes and faraway quakes. According to reports dating back to the early 1810s, more than eighty-five tsunamis have hit the Islands. At least fifteen were deadly; since record keeping began, 291 lives have been lost. Hilo Bay is particularly vulnerable to the giant waves, and Hilo's downtown has been destroyed twice.

Kīlauea

Kīlauea—the name can be translated as "spewing"—is arguably the most active volcano on earth. It first erupted three hundred to six hundred thousand years ago. In historical reckoning, it has erupted sixty-one times, from two rift zones and the summit. In the Puna district, its lava flows have erased the sites of heiau, petroglyphs and villages, as well as modern subdivisions and a popular black sand beach. On the other hand, lava pouring into the ocean has created more than 550 acres of new land.

Magmatic action at the summit crater, Halema'uma'u—sometimes a liquid glow in the dark, sometimes a boiling lava lake—drew intrepid explorers to the island in the 1800s and did not abate until 1924. Kīlauea's eruptions were usually more gentle, claiming lives only indirectly through heat, fumes,

and crumbly lava shelves. But in 1790, a sudden rain of ashes surprised and killed up to four hundred warriors and their families.

The winter of 1959 saw an unexpected outburst at Kīlauea, preceded by a series of earthquakes. On November 14, the summit vents at Kīlauea Iki came ablaze with cascading fires, lava, and lava fountains that eventually shot upward more than eleven hundred feet. A lava lake arose, at times climbing more than sixty feet a day. Activity abruptly stopped on December 20. The following year, another eruption took the village of Kapoho in Puna.

In more recent years, volcanic summit pressure at Halemaʻumaʻu has found relief through Kīlauea's east rift, at the Puʻu Oʻo vent. Active since January 3, 1983, Puʻu Oʻo has been pushing forth molten lava at an average of fifty-five thousand to one hundred ten thousand gallons a minute.

Mauna Loa

Measuring fifty-six thousand feet from the ocean floor, Mauna Loa—the "Long Mountain"—covers half of the Big Island. Despite its seemingly gentle dome, sometimes covered in mantles of snow, Mauna Loa is one of the most active volcanoes on earth. Since 1843 it has erupted thirty-three times, mostly from its summit crater Mokuʻāweoweo.

In 1859, lava cascaded down the Kona coast, reaching the ocean in eight days, and filled the large Kīholo fish pond, building a new point of land, Laehou. In the spring of 1881, a slow lava flow came within seven miles of Hilo town, hit the area's rivers, and accelerated amid hissing, dangerous steam and rock explosions. It was traveling as fast as five hundred feet a day, straight toward Waiākea Sugar Mill. Missionary Titus Coan and his congregation prayed, but prayers did nothing to stanch the flow. Hawaiians asked Princess Ruth for help. The formidable princess, who was residing in Honolulu at the time, took a steamer to Kona, traveled by horse wagon to Hilo, then went up to the flow with offerings to Pele. Prisoners had to help pull her carriage uphill. The flow stopped a mile and a half away from Hilo Bay.

In 1950, Mauna Loa erased a small fishing village in South Kona and, as recently as 1984, threatened Hilo again, halting just four miles from the city. During this most recent eruption, which lasted just twenty-one days, from March 24 until April 15, an intensely red glow could be seen in many parts of the island and curtains of lava fountains reached 160 feet high along the mountain's main rifts. Mauna Loa is currently inflating.

>≫◇≪◇≫◇≪◇≫◇≪◇≫◇≪◇≫

Above left and right: The series of eruptions of Kīlauea Volcano in the first half of the century drew visitors from around the world. One of the most frightening series began in 1924, when the Kīlauea caldera cracked, making the "lake of fire" visible for many years in Pele's legendary home of Halemaʻumaʻu Crater. As the lava subsided, it came into contact with underwater streams, which caused a tremendous explosion. Within moments the crater doubled its size, as volcanic bombs were hurled into the air so fast that the friction caused lightning to appear in the skies above the crater. As a gigantic cloud of steam billowed out of the earth, Volcano House shook so violently that many believed it would fall into the crater. The Hawaiʻi Volcanoes National Park was evacuated for several weeks before visitors were allowed back in May 1924 to gape at the devastation and to be photographed in front of the incredible cauliflower cloud. [Baker-Van Dyke Collection]

VOLCANO HOUSE

Right: The first Volcano House at Kīlauea Crater opened in 1861 as a grass-thatched building made from 'ōhi'a wood. It hosted among its most famed guests the author Samuel Langhorne Clemens—"Mark Twain." In 1877, a more sturdy wooden hotel was constructed, which many years later would be used as the Volcano Arts Center. In 1883, the Wilder Steamship Company purchased the unique hostelry, which at that time offered beds and bedding, a well-selected library and a "superior melodeon" to as many as thirty-five guests. [Lyman House Memorial Museum]

For one dollar a night, visitors to Kīlauea Volcano in the mid-1800s could find shelter in a grass hut erected by a savvy American entrepreneur, Benjamin Pitman, Sr. He gave it the name Volcano House. In 1866, three partners invested in a two-bedroom structure of 'ōhi'a, with a parlor, a fireplace and comfortable chairs. Mark Twain wrote in his 1866 *Letters from Hawaii*, "The surprise of finding a good hotel in such an outlandish spot startled me considerably more than the volcano did."

The Halema'uma'u Crater lake continued to brim with lava. In 1877, a new Volcano House with six rooms and a spacious verandah replaced the small inn; it was renovated around 1885 by Samuel G. Wilder, owner of the inter-island Wilder Steamship Company.

In 1921, after a new macadamized road and a new railroad increased access to the volcano, new owners moved the original 1877 structure and added a new two-story wing. It was lost to fire in 1940, and only the 1877 wing was spared. It has since been preserved as an arts center. The current Volcano House opened in 1914. Tradition has it that a hearth fire started in the 1877 fireplace is still going today, its embers burning through the decades.

Above (both) and left: A new, larger, and more luxurious hotel, photographed in 1903, was constructed. It stood until it was destroyed by fire in 1940. On its grounds at the edge of Kīlauea Crater, visitors could enjoy the panoramic view of the world's arguably most active volcanic crater with the magnificent vista of the world's largest mountain, Mauna Loa, in the background. Inside Volcano House, visitors could relax in the parlor or enjoy musical entertainment as this Congressional party is doing. [Above left: Baker-Van Dyke Collection; Above right: Hawaii State Archives; left: National Archives]

Right: In this undated photo, a group of women in Hawaiian-style mu'umu'u and lei stroll along the edge of Halema'uma'u Crater. Circa 1920s [Baker-Van Dyke Collection]

Below: An old-style musical interlude at Volcano House. Seated at right, with 'ukulele, is the famed composer of Hawaiian songs, Helen Desha Beamer. Circa 1926. [Baker-Van Dyke Collection]

"UNCLE" GEORGE LYCURGUS (1859-1960)

When a restored Volcano House opened for business in 1941, eighty-two-year-old George Lycurgus tried to harness the steam power of Kīlauea to heat his new hotel. Such practicality, however, did not mean that he did not believe in Pele. He insisted that he had actually seen the goddess, in 1908. Since George and Pele were both fond of gin, Uncle George would toss a bottle of gin into the great caldera at each eruption. He also made offerings of Pele's favorite food, 'ōhelo berries, in a traditional Hawaiian gesture of respect. On his one-hundredth birthday, Pele honored her old friend by causing fountains of fiery lava to burst from the earth. Uncle George was assisted to the crater's edge, where he offered his tribute of gin and 'ōhelo berries. It was the last exchange between the goddess and the Greek. [Baker-Van Dyke Collection]

In 1893, George Lycurgus, a Greek immigrant who had been living in California, settled on O'ahu. He had been invited there by his old friend, sugar transportation baron John Spreckels. He arrived only two weeks after Queen Lili'uokalani had been deposed.

He changed Hawai'i's hotel industry. He first became a hotelier in Waikīkī, where he opened the popular Sans Souci beachhouse. He later moved his operations to the Big Island. In 1901, Lycurgus bought property in Hilo and opened the Demosthenes Hotel (demolished in 1924). In 1904, he bought stock in Volcano House, where he thrived as a convivial host and manager-owner for 56 years, until his death on August 6, 1960, at the age of 101. He was known as "Uncle George," and his charisma alone attracted hundreds, including presidents, princes, and celebrities.

Lycurgus joined Lorrin Thurston, publisher of the *Honolulu Advertiser,* and scientist Dr. Thomas A. Jaggar in lobbying for establishment of a national park to protect the volcano summits. He entertained fifty congressmen and their wives with a Hawaiian lū'au, cooked over volcanic steam vents. In 1916, Congress created Hawai'i National Park, the U.S.'s thirteenth national park.

In 1921, Lycurgus sold Volcano House to the Inter-Island Steamship Company, which immediately poured $150,000 worth of renovations into the old hotel. When Lycurgus returned to Kīlauea in 1932, Kīlauea had ceased erupting and tourists had stopped coming. Lycurgus bought back his new old home for $300 at a sheriff's sale where he was the only bidder.

Two years later, with Pele still not making her presence felt, Lycurgus wandered to the rim of Halema'uma'u with offerings for the goddess. To the traditional 'ōhelo berries he added a bottle of gin. Kīlauea erupted the following day.

Lycurgus rode his horse daily for four miles until the age of ninety-three. In his late nineties, old and frail, he would still sit at the hotel's fireplace to greet his guests. On his one-hundredth birthday, he traveled to the crater one last time with his 'ōhelo berries and gin.

KONA COFFEE

Around 1813, the Spaniard Don Francisco de Paula Marin, an avid gardener, introduced coffee plants to the island of O'ahu. Twelve years later, an English agriculturist, John Wilkinson, planted coffee beans from Brazil on the estate of Chief Boki in Mānoa Valley, inland of the town of Honolulu. Cuttings from these saplings came to the Kona District in 1828 by way of missionary Samuel Ruggles, who was in search of ornamentals for his gardens south of Kailua.

Coffee thrived on Kona's volcanic slopes, where the climate allowed for cloud-covered afternoons and dry, cool summers. By the 1830s, the crop was commercially planted for brew. Hāmākua, on the other side of the island, also started to explore coffee as a commodity.

Early successes, however, turned out to be beginner's luck. Investors soon found out that Hawaiian coffee was subject to wild fluctuations in prices, and labor was always short. By the late 1840s and 1850s, the mostly Western investors left. Coffee was soon growing wild; Hawaiians continued to harvest the crops.

In 1892, Typica, a new type of coffee bean from Guatemala, was introduced. It grew well, sold well, and enticed new entrepreneurs. Two mills came to dominate the market: Captain Cook Coffee Company and H. Hackfeld and Company (later American Factors). Many Japanese sugar plantation families interested in independent farming joined Portuguese and Chinese immigrants in leasing three- to five-acre lots.

Kona coffee was never as lucrative as sugar. In 1899, when the world coffee market crashed and sugar prices happened to soar, many of the coffee fields around Hōlualoa were replaced with cane. The enterprise was doomed from the start, given the district's arid conditions, and in 1926, sugar ended. Attempts to grow cotton, sisal, tobacco, oranges, and pineapple also failed.

Meanwhile, early Japanese coffee farmers had little choice but to hang on since they did not have the funds to return to Japan. By 1909, Kona was home to 273 Japanese coffee growers. Five years later, coffee orchards covered thirty-eight hundred Kona acres, 80 percent of them tended by Japanese farmers. Kona became a prosperous district, despite the failures of other agricultural crops. But when coffee prices rose significantly in the 1920s, the Japanese farmers did not benefit. The two big mills that had survived the

decades controlled the lands, financial institutions, and even daily groceries. Lease agreements tied up dozens of farmers, regardless of coffee prices. Small Japanese-operated general stores worked under contracts to extend customers credit against coffee beans.

At the start of the 1930s, when Kona counted thirteen hundred growers, coffee prices tumbled. Entire families had to work the fields, and schools shifted vacations to coincide with the harvesting season. Even so, the small Japanese farmers ran into debt and their number decreased by 50 percent between 1929 and 1938. Persuaded by growers lobbying on the Big Island, American Factors canceled all but 2 percent of the farmers' debts. Coffee prices recovered in the late 1930s, and during World War II the Army proved an excellent buyer. Still, to thrive, the farmers needed independence from Kona's two dominant mills. In the 1950s, the first cooperatives were formed. In 1968, in an effort to ensure steady sales and prices, independent millers contracted with a Mainland firm to supply Kona coffee for inexpensive blends to be sold under the name Kona Coffee. Even these efforts were not enough to save coffee, which was once Hawai'i's third-leading crop behind sugar and pineapple. By 1975, coffee in Kona was all but gone.

Fortunately, a new taste for specialty coffees emerged. Idealistic newcomers from the Mainland and young third-generation farmers moved back to Kona to revive neglected coffee lots. They promoted a pure Kona coffee product, distinctly different from the ubiquitous blends. Today, about 650 farmers and thirty-six hundred coffee acres make Kona coffee viable once more. Cooperatives continue to buy the bulk of the beans, while about one hundred farmers create estate-grown coffee. Hāmākua coffee has also been revitalized.

This coffee label, possibly from the 1900s, was most likely designed by someone from the Mainland, as the picture on the label features Honolulu's Diamond Head rather than any recognizable Kona landmark. [Hawai'i State Archives]

LAUHALA WEAVING

During World War II, many Big Island Japanese men were in the armed services; some were interned, suspected of disloyalty. Many *issei* and *nisei* women were alone on their coffee farms in Kona. To supplement their income, they turned to lauhala weaving. Troops training on the island loved loved the baskets, hats, and mats. By the end of the war, over 60 percent of all lauhala goods manufactured in Hawai'i originated in Japanese households in Kona.

〉〉〈◆〉〈◆〉〈◆〉〈◆〉〈◆〉〈◆〉〈◆〉〈◆〉〈◆〉〈

Above left: Coffee shacks and mills dotted the uplands above Kealakekua and Hōnaunau. Carried on by Japanese and Chinese independent farmers, the coffee industry became an important economic resource for the Big Island. Date unknown. [Hawai'i State Archives]

Above right: Japanese immigrants took over the Hawaiian coffee industry in Hāmākua and Kona on the island of Hawai'i. First planted by missionary Samuel Ruggles in Kona, coffee was the one crop in the district that survived as an important industry, beating out sugar, cotton, pineapple, tobacco, oranges, and sisal. Nearly thirty-eight hundred acres of Kona and Hāmākua lands were in coffee cultivation by 1914, with 80 percent of the crop being produced by Japanese farmers. Date unknown. [Bishop Museum]

Left: Picking coffee beans. Date unknown. [Hawai'i State Archives]

Above left: Matsuko Kubota in her coffee-picking outfit at Captain Cook, Kona. December 1936. [Bishop Museum]

Above right: A Kona nightingale with young riders pauses near a "modern" car on a Big Island road. Date unknown. [Baker-Van Dyke Collection]

Right: Donkeys became the means of transportation for Kona's early independent coffee farmers. Called Kona nightingales—possibly because of their voices—they hauled coffee from the fields to the roadside, where the millers would pick it up. They delivered coffee to the stores, where farmers used coffee to buy their groceries instead of cash. The little town of Kainaliu formed the commercial center of the coffee belt; donkeys became integral to its economy. Numerous establishments provided donkey hitching posts to facilitate daily business. After World War II, however, jeeps replaced the sturdy animals. Today, a few wild descendants of the original animals roam in a reserve on Kona's lava-strewn shores. [Bishop Museum]

Left: Japanese coffee farmers created self-sustaining homesteads on leased lands that averaged three to five acres. The coffee-processing area often included a pulping facility, the kuriba, and a drying platform, the hoshi-dana. Under the auspices of the Kona Historical Society, a farm built around 1900 has been preserved. It features restored buildings from the 1920s and is open to visitors. Known as the Kona Coffee Living History Farm, it is the first permanent exhibit funded with support from the National Endowment for the Humanities. Date unknown. [Hawai'i State Archives]

Below left: Coffee beans were laid out to dry and had to be periodically raked and stirred so that they would dry evenly. The local coffee industry provided much-needed full- and part-time jobs for young people. Sometimes schools were closed during harvest season. Circa 1935. [Bishop Museum]

MACADAMIA NUTS

The crunchy, creamy macadamia nut, which has become one of Hawai'i's largest agricultural and international industries, traces its origins on the Big Island to the year 1879, when William H. Purvis came to Honoka'a from Australia, bringing with him a few kernels of macadamia, also known as the Queensland nut. The tree flourished in Australia, where it was popular as an ornamental. Planted as ornamentals at Purvis' newly established Pacific Sugar Mill plantation in Kapulena, close to Waipi'o Valley, the trees thrived on Hawai'i's volcanic soils. The nuts grew larger and sweeter than in their native land.

In 1912, the Hawaiian Agricultural Experimental Station gave macadamia nut seedlings to Kona farmers. At Honokaa Sugar Company, the first macadamia nut harvest took place fourteen years later. By 1948, Honoka'a was producing crops for resale, making the Big Island the site of the world's first commercial macadamia nut plantation.

Consumers loved the new product, which was 80 percent oil and 4 percent sugar. The number of macadamia nut orchards steadily rose, especially in Hāmākua, Mauna Loa, South Kona, and Ka'ū. Today, the Big Island has about seventeen thousand acres in macadamia nuts, the equivalent of 1.2 million macadamia nut trees. It contributes approximately 95 percent of the state's total annual production, and harvests average over 45 million pounds per year. A search for additional uses for the macadamia nut has led a Big Island technology startup to open a manufacturing plant that turns macadamia nut shells into premium-grade granular activated carbon.

Right: A bin of macadamia nuts for sale at a local store. Date unknown. [Kona Historical Society]

Below left: Factory workers packing macadamia nuts in glass jars, Honokaa Sugar Co., Hawai'i. 1953. [Bishop Museum]

Below right: This variety measures just over ten feet tall. 1949. [Hawai'i State Archives]

TOBACCO

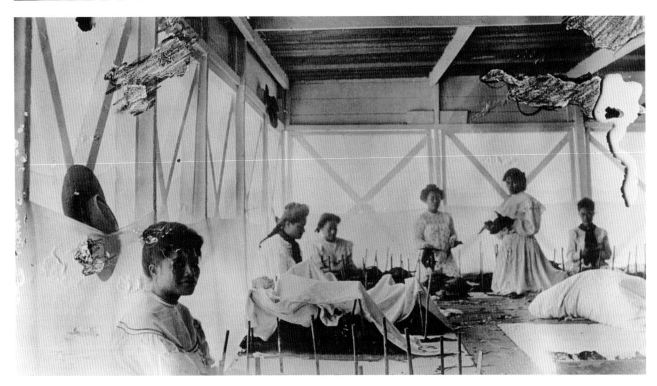

New York-born Jared G. Smith came to Hawai'i in 1901 as a U.S. Government botanist. In 1908, he quit his job to start the Kona Tobacco Company. He hired workers, built facilities, and planted a variety of Cuban tobacco called Vuelta. The company went bankrupt in 1912, after its storage shed burned to the ground, together with two years' worth of stored tobacco leaves. It was re-organized as the South Kona Tobacco Company in 1917, but that company also went out of business, leaving behind only the name of a road, Old Tobacco Road, in Hōnaunau.

Left: Hawaiian tobacco workers process leaves. Circa 1908-1912. [Kona Historical Society] Below: The Kona Tobacco Company's storage shed. Circa 1908-1912. [Kona Historical Society]

HAWAI'I'S MELTING POT

The Kohala Female Seminary, later called the Kohala Girls' School, was established in 1874 by Kohala missionary Elias Bond and deeded to the Hawaiian Evangelical Association in 1887. It was a boarding school for Hawaiian girls aged six through eighteen. Enrollment was normally sixty to eighty girls. Graduates were expected to marry, enter domestic service, or attend a teachers college to be trained as public school teachers. The school survived until 1955. The old wooden buildings that housed the school were then left vacant and deteriorating. They have recently been purchased and renovated by the New Moon Foundation. Circa 1912. [Baker-Van Dyke Collection]

Few regions could match Hawai'i's record as a melting pot, in which ethnicities from all over the world have settled and mingled. Thousands of Chinese, Japanese, Portuguese, Puerto Ricans, Koreans, Filipinos, and Caucasians brought their different religions, languages, traditions, festivals, values, and beliefs to the Islands, and learned to live together, in plantation communities or polyglot cities like Hilo and Honolulu. As each new ethnic group arrived, it added a new layer to daily life. Children in public schools soon started to mix their cultures in games, stories, and foods to create the basis for a unique "local" culture.

Initially, language was an obstacle to communication, as plantation workers spoke a dozen languages and dialects. But they quickly developed a plantation pidgin based loosely on Hawaiian, English, Japanese, Chinese, Filipino, and Portuguese words. Beginning in the second generation, pidgin evolved into a distinct language, Hawai'i Creole English. It is still widely spoken, and is still called pidgin.

Daily food connected each ethnic group simultaneously to its own culture. At schools and in the fields, during the short half-hour break for lunch, recycled Crisco cans and aluminum pails filled with ethnic specialties were passed around. Gradually, ingredients from different cultures mingled—flavors, spices, methods of cooking. White rice with umeboshi, pickled kimchee, poke, salted duck eggs, fried noodles, kalbi, teriyaki, tofu, plum sauce, Portuguese bread, sushi, smoked pork, manapua, musubi, and saimin—all were to become part of a "local" cuisine.

As cultural differences melted, a new identity emerged: "local." "Local" was anyone with plantation-worker roots, regardless of race. "Local" became a way of life, reflected as much in the ethnic make-up of the government as in choices in merchandise, arts, infrastructure, architecture, and fashion. Rows of different churches peacefully lined up together along "Church Rows." Buddhist temples welcomed everyone for annual Bon dances. County fairs featured music that blended Asian or Puerto Rican or Filipino elements with slack key guitar and Hawaiian song, as well as American music. Slowly and steadily, old cultures merged and a new one took shape.

≫≪◇≫≪◇≫≪◇≫≪◇≪

Above: In this photo of Waimea School students, one can see the multi-ethnic society that was emerging on the Big Island as well as over all the Islands. The children reflect several racial and ethnic groups; some are the offspring of mixed marriages. Circa 1920–1921. [Bishop Museum]

Left: Filipino plantation workers staged illegal cockfights at arenas like this one in Pāpaʻikou. Every other Sunday, this was the big draw at the camp park for all workers regardless of ethnicity. The promoter, or houseman, presided over the betting, then took a percentage of the winnings. Circa 1930s. [Hawaiʻi State Archives]

Right: Congregation members stand on the porch of Kohala Church. Part of the Americanization of immigrants and their children was to adopt the Christian religion, although some still held to the religious beliefs of their homeland. Circa 1899. [Bishop Museum]

Below left: In Honomū, a kimono-clad woman poses in front of a car. In her time, no driver's license was necessary. A car buyer would simply go to a Hilo dealership, and drive off in a new Packard or Model T. The winding drive from Hilo to Honomū took a little less than two hours. Circa 1920s. [Yugawa Family Collection]

Below right: Three Japanese girls dressed in kimono. Hilo, 1903. [Baker-Van Dyke Collection]

INTERMARRIAGE

"Local" also meant interracial marriage, officially sanctioned in 1840. At the time of the first immigrant arrivals, the Hawaiian population was still dwindling, due to epidemics. On the Big Island, the population plummeted from 24,450 in 1853 to 16,001 in 1872. While many Chinese and Caucasian men married Hawaiian women, the Japanese and Koreans preferred their picture brides. The Portuguese and Puerto Ricans brought their families with them. The Filipinos, the last large group of laborers to arrive, would eventually marry either women of Hawaiian or Filipino descent, and, in later generations, incoming Filipinos married women with mixed Hawaiian-Filipino blood.

Ethnic boundaries became increasingly diffused, as the children of intermarried couples intermarried again. By 1920, of the Big Island's population of sixty-five thousand, 66.8 percent were of Asian descent. Caucasians made up 17.9 percent, and just 15.1 percent had Hawaiian or part-Hawaiian blood. Ten years later, 25 percent of reported births on the Big Island were of mixed ancestry. In 1950, just 14 percent of the population was pure Caucasian. After 1955, more than one third of all marriages were interracial.

Today, at least half of all marriages are of mixed ethnicity. In 2000, almost 48 percent of the Big Island's 149,000 residents described themselves as being partly Asian, 52 percent considered themselves partly white, and 31 percent reported that they were of Pacific Islander descent—including Hawaiian blood. Chances are strong that any baby born in Hawai'i today traces its roots back to numerous ethnicities.

⫸⬦⫸⬦⫷⬦⫸⬦⫸⬦⫷

Above left: Japanese school students dressed for a festival. Circa 1916. [Bishop Museum]

Above right: Japanese sumo wrestling was popular in Hāmākua coast planta-tion communities. In this 1920 photo, Honomū sumo wrestlers stand inside a sumo ring probably erected on the grounds of the Honomū Hongwanji. The wrestlers may not all have been Japanese. One Hawaiian wrestled under the name of Dairiki. 1920. [Ishii Family Collection]

Left: The congregation of the Honomū Japanese Christian Church gathers for a formal photograph. In 1993, the old church was demolished and replaced by a modern building. Circa 1930. [Ishii Family Collection]

Right: A Filipino community gathers to celebrate Filipino Independence Day. 1966. [Kona Historical Society.]

Below left: Lunchtime for Kohala's sugar workers. The sampling of each ethnic group's food led to a distinct local cuisine, and the bonding brought about by the sharing of food helped pave the way for a multicultural society. Circa 1900. [Bishop Museum]

Below right: A Filipino man holds his fighting cock. Date unknown. [Kona Historical Society.]

Above: Multi-ethnic Big Island school-children at recess. Date unknown. [Lyman House Memorial Museum]

Below: Mochi pounding at the Hakalau Jodo Mission, probably just before World War II. Some families still keep up the tradition, pounding cooked sweet rice into tasty mochi paste for Japanese New Year celebrations. Circa 1940. [Sugino Family Collection]

LABOR UNREST

>X«»X«»X«»X«»X«»X«
Striking laborers who have lost their jobs march. 1947. [Hawai'i State Archives]

Dissatisfied with the early harsh labor conditions, immigrant workers from the start had demanded justice and better working conditions. Unacknowledged, they rebelled with cane fires, work slowdowns, fights, and gang strikes. Many ran away. Plantation owners responded by flogging, docking pay, making promises, and, above all, setting workers against each other.

Indentured servitude was abolished in 1900. As laborers rallied for fair treatment, worried managers offered incentives and bonus pay. It was not enough. After the first Japanese strike on O'ahu in 1909, young Japanese laborers from five Hāmākua plantations established Hawai'i's first organized labor association in 1919, asking for higher wages and shorter work days. Their initiative spurred the formation of similar orga-

nizations on other islands, as well as a Filipino union. The following year the Filipinos and the Japanese supported each other during a six-month strike on O'ahu, ignoring ethnic differences in favor of united strikes and unions. These early strikes won small victories against the plantation owners, but they did not establish strong, permanent labor unions.

World War II brought a temporary end to labor strife. Many plantation workers joined the military. Labor was in short supply as many small businesses sprung up to serve the thousands of servicemen stationed in the Islands. However, after the war ended in 1945, labor struggles resumed. Labor had new reasons to be optimistic. The 1935 federal Wagner Act had made it much easier to demand employer recognition of unions.

Above left: The headline of the August 4, 1938, Voice of Labor *protests the police brutality of the August 1 clash between police and strikers in Hilo remembered as the Hilo Massacre. Seventy police attacked two hundred unarmed demonstrators, fifty of whom were injured, some severely.* [Hawai'i State Archives]

Above right: The signs of these workers picketing reflect the issues of the time—including for police to stay neutral. Date unknown. [Bishop Museum]

Left: Sugar workers stage a sit-in while management, the man in a hat and wearing boots, accompanied by colleagues wearing white shirts and ties, addresses them. Date unknown. [Hawai'i State Archives]

Honitzen Company 299th Infantry-Honomu, Hawaii. Hilo Photo Works. Photo by June 27 1929

Sergeant Alex Akita of Honomū's National Guard unit, the 299th Infantry, sits in the front row, holding the unit plaque. Note the small cannon and water-cooled machine gun. After Pearl Harbor, Japanese Americans were asked to leave the Guard; many of them later found their way into military units such as the much-decorated Japanese-American 442nd Regimental Combat Team. 1929. [Yugawa Family Collection]

The attack on Pearl Harbor by Japanese forces on the morning of December 7, 1941, silenced the rhythms of the Big Island's sleepy plantations, which until then had been punctuated by the whistle of the mills. They were replaced with the stricter, more somber rules of martial law.

A Vulnerable Island

It was thought that the Big Island, in its poorly defended isolation, would be a sure target for a follow-up attack and could form an easily conquered strategic base for the enemy. The American military stormed into little towns, enforced nightly blackouts, appropriated radios and pickup trucks, built machine gun nests, and unrolled miles of barbed wire to protect the island's rugged shores against invasions. Māhukona in Kohala—an important sugar port—was closed. Farmers and ranchers were told to drive stakes into their lands to prevent the enemy from landing in planes. Men, women, and children had to tote around heavy gas masks. Liquor, rice, gasoline, and tires were rationed.

Hundreds of islanders were drafted or volunteered to fight in the war. To ensure a steady food supply, residents planted Victory Gardens with seeds provided by the government. Farmers who had not been selected for military duty planted larger crops to contribute to the Army's food center in Hilo. Communities organized their own battalions of Hawaii Rifles. Mothers whose own sons left for the war cared for the American soldiers who were stationed or trained on the Big Island. They did laundry, cooked meals, and heated bath water, offering a sense of home.

Nerves were taut. Three weeks after Pearl Harbor, a lone Japanese submarine fired at some oil storage tanks on a Hilo shore. Although it appeared to be an isolated incident, it fueled islanders' fears. Distrust grew.

After Pearl Harbor, Japanese everywhere in the United States became suspect. On the Mainland, the Japanese were sent to relocation camps without discernment, but in the islands this was not practical; more than one-third of Hawai'i's residents were of Japanese descent. Instead, the armed forces concentrated on anyone with influence or direct ties to Japan. They questioned *issei*, Shinto and Buddhist priests, language school teachers, outspoken leaders, and successful businessmen. The Japanese immigrants destroyed family photographs and memorabilia in an effort to remain free and safe.

About one hundred Japanese on the Big Island were interned on O'ahu or the Mainland. Despite the war, sugar production across the island continued as before. Women worked the plantations without the men. Schools closed earlier in the afternoons so that students could help in the fields.

Above left: Inspecting vegetable plots. Circa 1940s. [Bishop Museum]

Above: A hoe hana (weeding) crew at Kohala. Circa 1940s. [Bishop Museum]

Top right: Aluminum kitchen utensils were recycled as part of Kohala's civilian war effort. Circa 1942. [Bishop Museum]

VOLUNTEERS 2ND GROUP LOCAL BOARD 3 HONOKAA

Volunteer enlistees draped in lei. March 27, 1943. [Bishop Musem]

Japanese-American men who were already part of the American military when Pearl Harbor was attacked became as suspect as anyone else of Japanese descent. About seven weeks after December 7, they were segregated from their units and retrained as the 100th Battalion, to be sent to North Africa, then to Italy.

In Hawai'i, eligible civilian *nisei* were denied war participation altogether and were classified as enemy aliens. In January 1942, driven to prove their loyalty to America, a group of Big Island nisei joined others from the Islands to form the Varsity Victory Volunteers. One hundred seventy young Japanese Americans put down the schoolbooks that promised freedom from a future as plantation laborers, and chose picks and shovels instead. In their own way, they joined the Army stationed in the Islands—by building roads, bridges, and barracks.

On February 1, 1943, President Roosevelt allowed the formation of an all-nisei unit—the 442nd Battalion. From the most remote sugar towns on the Big Island, young men who had never left their plantation villages followed their friends to volunteer. Among them were the Varsity Victory Volunteers.

Throughout the Islands, a total of over 9,000 nisei came forward to join the 442nd, six times more than the number required Eventually 2,645 Japanese-American islanders were selected, two thirds of the entire battalion. Joining the 100th Battalion in Europe, they fought the war abroad and prejudice at home. Together, the units earned 9,468 Purple Hearts.

Nisei returning from the war were no longer willing to accept the old hierarchical plantation ways; they played a crucial role as Hawai'i moved from territorial status to statehood in 1959.

Left: A group of young men about to leave Kona to enter military service during WWII. Note the lei, farewell gifts from family and friends. Date unknown. [Kona Historical Society.]

Below left: Hilo Minute Men stringing barbed wire. Spring 1942. [Hawai'i State Archives]

Below right: Red Cross workers in front of what is now Parker School. Date unknown. [Pacific War Memorial Association]

163

WAIMEA'S CAMP TARAWA

In December 1943, Marines of the 2nd Division arrived in the town of Waimea. The Army forces had just left the Big Island; strategists judged that after the U.S. victory in the Battle of Midway, the threat of an immediate attack on the island had dissipated.

The 2nd Division had played a major role in the Pacific war. They had come straight from Tarawa Atoll in the Central Pacific Gilbert Islands. They were the survivors of one of the bloodiest battles in history; they were exhausted, feverish, and traumatized. They had come to rest and to recuperate—and also to train for future battles, possibly on Saipan or Tinian.

The Marines arrived with nothing more than the torn clothes on their backs. After a rough journey from Hilo, they found that transportation arrangements had broken down. They had to walk for miles to reach their temporary accommodations on the Parker Ranch. They soon found that the Parker Ranch camp lacked

This marker was erected at the entrance to Camp Tarawa in 1995. Camp Tarawa was located on the mauka and makai sides of the Upper Road to Kona as it emerges from the center of Waimea toward Waikoloa. [Pacific War Memorial Association]

basics such as food, drinking water, and blankets. Sleeping tents had yet to be set up. On their first day in Waimea, the men had to buy supplies at the little Hayashi Store—which sold out of goods—and finish setting up tents in biting wind and rain.

The Parker Ranch grounds were named Camp Tarawa. When, during the early summer of 1944, the 2nd Division left for destinations west, the 5th Division took its place days afterward.

Over the course of two years, nearly fifty thousand Marines trained at the camp. The sandy beaches of Hāpuna and Pololū became the sites for amphibious training. Battalions trained on the ranch lands up at Kahuā and ran their jeeps through unharvested sugar cane fields.

The Marines' presence changed the cattle town of Waimea, population four hundred, as well as surrounding plantation towns. The 2nd Division built a dam and a water reservoir, and expanded Waimea's limited electricity supply. They made ice cream for themselves and local children. Waimea's elementary school and little hotel were transformed into modern hospital facilities. Entertainers and hula dancers came to town.

Business around Waimea boomed. Intense friendships between Big Islanders and Marines were forged. Entrepreneurial cooks could hardly supply enough hamburgers. The 5th Division especially, less exhausted and traumatized than the 2nd had been, knew how to have a good time. In Honokaʻa (nicknamed Honey Cow), Paʻauilo, and as far away as Hāwī, North Kohala, commerce, bars, and prostitution thrived. Japanese women in those towns sewed kimonos that the Marines sent home as special gifts to mothers and wives. Waimea women knit warm sweaters for cold Waimea days and gave them to Marines. Parker Ranch cowboys staged rodeos. Families invited the Marines to home-cooked meals and to outings to favorite streams and waterfalls. Supposedly, several freshwater ponds took on the name Queen's Bath during those years, named for the real or imagined presence of girlfriends.

Right after Christmas 1944, the 5th Division Marines left. Daily they had climbed the steep hills surrounding Waimea. They were certainly prepared for a critical confrontation that might conclude the Pacific Campaign; they did not know that they would be the ones to raise the American flag on the summit of Mount Suribachi on Iwo Jima on February 23, 1945.

Afterwards, a few returned briefly to Camp Tarawa. Life in Waimea went back to the way it had been.

In a quiet event in 1982, a stone monument marking Camp Tarawa's main gate was unveiled; it had been donated by the Exchange Club of Waimea. In 1995, nearly fifty veterans returned for a special reunion with Waimea residents.

>X<>X<>X<>X<>X<

Above left: Headlines show the 5th Division's heavy casualties on Iwo Jima. [Pacific War Memorial Association]

Above right: Elsie's was one of the many stores that popped up in Kohala and Honoka'a to serve the Marines. Circa 1945. [Kona Historical Society]

Left: The Marine Band parades through town, possibly Main Street in Honoka'a. 1945. [Pacific War Memorial Association]

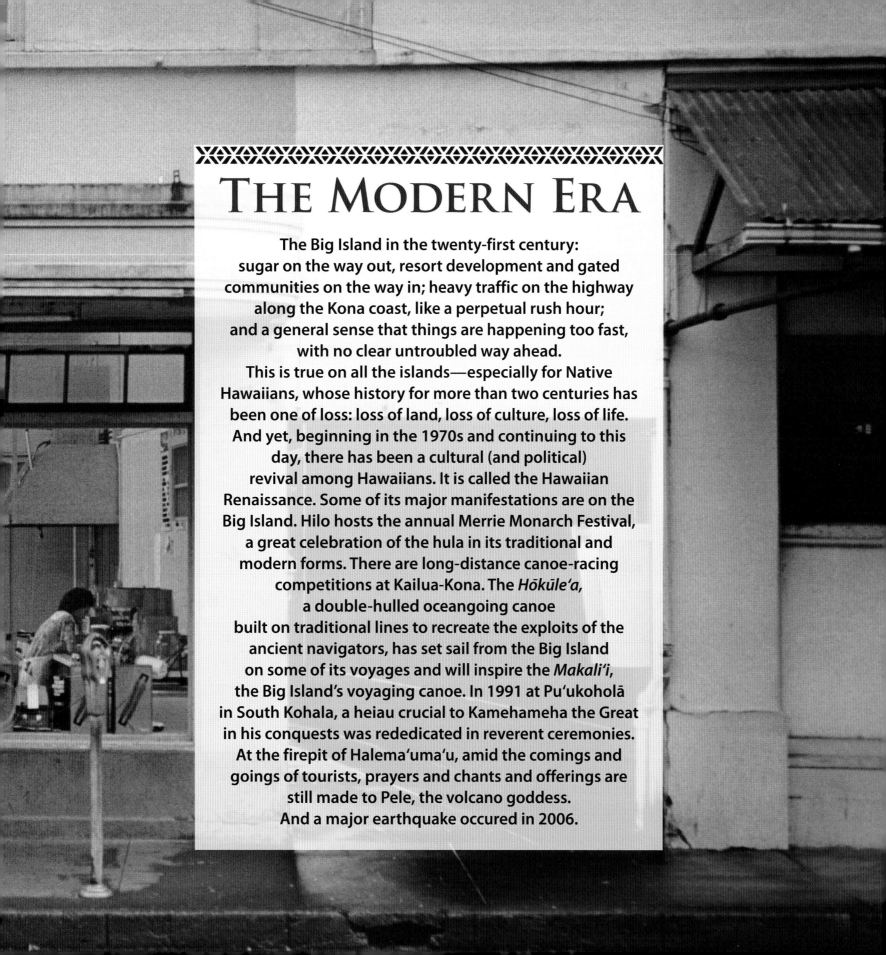

THE MODERN ERA

The Big Island in the twenty-first century:
sugar on the way out, resort development and gated
communities on the way in; heavy traffic on the highway
along the Kona coast, like a perpetual rush hour;
and a general sense that things are happening too fast,
with no clear untroubled way ahead.
This is true on all the islands—especially for Native
Hawaiians, whose history for more than two centuries has
been one of loss: loss of land, loss of culture, loss of life.
And yet, beginning in the 1970s and continuing to this
day, there has been a cultural (and political)
revival among Hawaiians. It is called the Hawaiian
Renaissance. Some of its major manifestations are on the
Big Island. Hilo hosts the annual Merrie Monarch Festival,
a great celebration of the hula in its traditional and
modern forms. There are long-distance canoe-racing
competitions at Kailua-Kona. The *Hōkūle'a*,
a double-hulled oceangoing canoe
built on traditional lines to recreate the exploits of the
ancient navigators, has set sail from the Big Island
on some of its voyages and will inspire the *Makali'i*,
the Big Island's voyaging canoe. In 1991 at Pu'ukoholā
in South Kohala, a heiau crucial to Kamehameha the Great
in his conquests was rededicated in reverent ceremonies.
At the firepit of Halema'uma'u, amid the comings and
goings of tourists, prayers and chants and offerings are
still made to Pele, the volcano goddess.
And a major earthquake occured in 2006.

NATURAL FORCES

Previous Pages: Like Edward Hopper's famous painting of customers in a diner (**Nighthawks**), this photograph of Eugene's Place in Hilo evokes a similar cinematic feeling through its viewpoint, lighting, and mood. The Mamo Theater building, location of Eugene's Place, was built about 1921. The theater was named Yura-Kwan until it was remodeled in 1937. It eventually became Ray's Diner. The last movie was shown at the Mamo in 1983. On April 15, 1995, the roof collapsed. The building was demolished and the site became a parking lot. Circa 1977. [Franco Salmoiraghi]

During the last days of March in 1868, both Mauna Loa and Kīlauea came to life with clouds of sulfuric smoke. Hundreds of tremors were felt in Ka'ū and Kona, shook the area around Kīlauea, and triggered a fifteen-mile lava flow from Moku'āweoweo Crater at the summit of Mauna Loa. Activity culminated with a 7.9-magnitude earthquake that destroyed large parts of Hilo, Puna, and Ka'ū. This earthquake was the strongest and most destructive in recorded Hawaiian history. The earth roiled and split. Stone churches crumbled. Thatch houses collapsed. The tops of cinder cones avalanched down and covered villages in ash. A human could not remain standing. In Ka'ū, a mudslide thirty feet thick and three miles long killed eighty-one people, and swept away horses, trees, cattle, houses, and sheep. The earthquake generated a tsunami that hit the Big Island's southeastern coast with a series of waves that reached a peak height of sixty-five feet. Another sixty-two people lost their lives as a result.

The 1946 and 1960 Tsunamis

Early in the morning of April 1, 1946, a deadly wave surged from an underwater earthquake off Alaska (twenty-three hundred miles away from Hawai'i), and raced at speeds of four to five hundred miles per hour to reach the islands shortly before 6:00 a.m. It slammed into Hilo, having claimed thirty-seven lives on Kaua'i, O'ahu, and Maui.

On the flat, low-lying point of Laupāhoehoe, an elementary school was preparing for the day. Teachers were still in their cottages when the first three waves rolled in. As each wave receded and the ocean pulled back, schools of fish were left behind, much to the excitement of children who had just arrived. Six more waves followed, some as high as thirty feet. They submerged the point, dragged children out to sea, and demolished the school and the cottages. Twenty-four people, among them sixteen children and four teachers, died.

Farther south, the waves mangled railroad trestles and destroyed the Hakalau Sugar Mill, the island's largest at the time. In Hilo, the tsunami wrecked the pier and the railroad station, swallowing a railroad engine, and tore through the breakwater, tossing five-ton boulders around. Bayfront stores and a Japanese settlement were erased. Another ninety-six people were killed.

In response to the disaster, the Territory developed a Tsunami Warning System. Hilo's bay-front area became a designated recreational area, not to be rebuilt. Two non-fatal tsunamis followed, in 1952 and 1957.

On May 22, 1960, sixty-six hundred miles away from Hawai'i, a magnitude 8.2 earthquake hit Chile, killing more than two-thousand people. It generated a set of giant waves that reached Hilo fifteen hours later. True to predictions that the tsunami would hit Hilo around midnight, at 12:46 a.m. the second of two waves reached as high as nine feet above normal, then receded. It seemed that the worst had passed. Residents returned to the shoreline. At 1:02 a.m., a third wave, thirty-five feet high, hit at a speed of thirty miles per hour. It flooded 580 acres, plunged the city into sudden darkness, and demolished 215 family homes and hundreds of businesses, and killed sixty-one people.

This time, Hilo created a green, protective buffer zone with gardens, golf greens, and lagoons along its oceanfront, with the Wailoa River State Recreation area at the center. To commemorate the Island's tsunami victims and to educate future generations, the Pacific Tsunami Museum opened in downtown Hilo in 1997. A clock in Waiākea, struck by a wave, remains a silent reminder of that fatal moment in time.

Tsunamis are especially prevalent in the Pacific Ocean, which contains more regions of volcanic activity than anywhere else on earth. When earthquakes occur under the sea bottom, they often cause the formation of fast-moving waves that travel rapidly outward. At sea, these waves are hardly distinguishable from normal ocean waves, but as they approach land, they can build up in shallower water, inundating coastal areas and washing away everything in their path. Hawai'i has often suffered devastation from tsunamis.

Above: This dramatic photograph was taken on April 1, 1946, as a powerful tsunami slammed into Hilo. In the early hours, the sea floor on the northern slope of the Aleutian Trench began to move, sending out tremors that lasted only a minute. Although the earthquake was recorded around the world and on seismographs at the University of Hawai'i and the Hawai'i Volcano Observatory, there was then no early warning system. Five hours and two thousand miles from the earthquake, the waters of Hilo Bay suddenly began to drain, as hundreds of residents watched in fascination. Moments later, a wave slammed into the town's waterfront with such power that buildings were smashed, railroads and bridges uprooted, and people sucked out to sea. Unaware that more waves were coming, shocked curiosity-seekers rushed to the shoreline. Another wave hit. A third and final wave sent residents running for their lives. At nearby Laupāhoehoe, a school class watched the receding ocean that preceded the immense wave, and a crowd ran out to collect exposed fish and shells. Sixteen children and four teachers were killed when the tsunami slammed into the unprotected village. The "April Fool's Day" disaster claimed 159 lives. Only 115 bodies were recovered. [Hawai'i State Archives]

Left: People are still in shock after the first two waves and are milling around Waiānuenue Street unaware the third and largest wave has just crossed Kamehameha Avenue, smashing a school bus and other structures into Hilo Drug store along the way. 1946. [Richard Otaki Collection]

169

Above: Hilo Bay exposed to the ocean floor as the first wave approached. In the distance is Wainaku Sugar Mill. 1946. [Richard Otaki Collection]

Right: The Wailuku River railroad bridge, twenty feet above sea level, was engulfed by the second wave, then taken out to sea. 1946. [Richard Otaki Collection]

This series of photos of the aftermath were taken by Richard Otaki, a freelance photographer hired by Hawaii Tribune Herald. 1946. [Richard Otaki Collection]

Top left: The long building at the mouth of Wailoa River was once Suisan Fishmarket.

Top right: Footprints are all that are visible along a barren Kamehameha Avenue. Today, only driveways that lead to nowhere remain in this inundation zone.

Above left: The old Hilo Theater is all that is left along the bay front.

Above right: The pine tree next to the Amfac building is now the location of Mo'ohea Park.

XXXXXXXXXXXXXXX
This house was pushed by 1960 tsunami
waves into the Waiolama Canal. Left
of the canal sits a heavily damaged
1957 Chevy. [Jack & Mary Ann Lynch
Collection]

✕◯✕◯✕◯✕◯✕◯✕◯✕◯✕◯✕

In the aftermath of the 1960 tsunami, people mill around Mamo and Keawe Streets. On the left is Elsie's, a popular eating place. Farther down Mamo Street, workers dismantle a building that was pushed into the street. Hilo was hardest hit by the tsunami, which did little damage to the rest of the Islands. [Jack & Mary Ann Lynch Collection]

173

A DISAPPEARING INDUSTRY

✕✕✕✕✕✕✕✕✕✕✕✕✕✕
Above: Herbicides here being mixed in the field, were first used in 1916 but were not used in the sugar cane fields until the 1940s. [David Weiss/Final Harvest]

For close to a hundred years, Hawai'i's sugar industry had managed to survive, even thrive, through good management and constantly investing in new equipment and technology. It had surmounted huge obstacles: huge obstacles: nineteenth-century American tariffs against foreign sugar; the McKinley Tariff Act of 1890, which reduced sugar imports; unstable prices, labor shortages, and foreign competition.

The Island sugar companies had had one great advantage: sugar cane could only be grown in tropical climates, and for many years, Hawai'i was the only American tropical territory within cheap, fast shipping distance of California and the rest of the West Coast. Both Louisiana and Florida grew cane, but their sugar had to be shipped west by rail across the continent. For a long time, transport by ship across the Pacific was actually faster and cheaper.

Eventually, this advantage eroded. Not only did ground transport improve, but new crops increasingly took the place of sugar cane. Sugar made from sugar beets (which can be grown in temperate climates)

was taking more and more of the sugar market. In the 1970s, chemists learned to transform cheap corn into high-fructose corn syrup, which is cheaper than sugar. Manufacturers of soda drinks and processed foods switched to HFCS and the market for cane sugar contracted even further.

As competition increased, the Island sugar companies faced increasing problems at home. Because of new U.S. immigration rules, they could no longer import cheap labor from China and Japan. They had to turn increasingly to Filipino workers. But workers were learning to organize for better wages and conditions. And in the postwar political climate, they were beginning to prevail.

The war brought a temporary halt to labor strife. But in the postwar years, struggle resumed. And the balance of political power had shifted. The earliest plantation workers were immigrants. They could not vote. Their children, born in Hawai'i under the American flag, were citizens. They could and did vote, and they voted Democratic. Hawai'i became a solidly Democratic state. The Democratic party was much friendlier to labor than the old pre-war Republican regime. In 1946, Big Island laborers joined in a massive 79-day Territory-wide strike organized by the International Longshoremen's and Warehousemen's Union (ILWU). Most historians believe that it was this strike, which crippled the Island economy, that truly marked the rise of labor power.

While wages rose, by consolidating and mechanizing the plantations were able to cut labor costs and still be profitable. When consolidation and mechanization could go no further, sugar plantations began to close down.

Kohala's sugar quality had long been questionable, due to its trade winds, which sucked moisture and sweetness away. There was no funding to purchase or maintain new equipment. The opening of Kawaihae Harbor in 1959 and a coastal highway in 1968 did little to help. In 1971, Castle & Cooke announced the closure of Kohala Sugar Plantation, ending five hundred jobs. Sugar in Kohala finished in 1975. The opening of the Mauna Kea tourist resort provided 250 jobs, but Kohala entered a depression that lasted until the 1990s.

In Hilo and Hāmākua, two tsunamis had shaken the confidence of the plantations. New pollution laws and efforts to control an excess of weeds proved costly. Puna Sugar Company closed its doors in 1984.

Hāmākua Sugar Company, which had once been the second largest in the state, closed in 1993, leaving more than six hundred workers without work. That same year C. Brewer's Mauna Kea Agribusiness Company, along with Hilo Coast Processing Company, announced they would shut down after the autumn harvest, leaving another six hundred without jobs.

In 1995 the small Ka'ū Agribusiness Company—Ka'ū's largest single employer, closed as well.

Former cane fields were bought up by private land investment corporations, to be used for commercial development, housing, and small agricultural enterprises. Some former sugar workers found resort employment—one- and two-hour commutes away. The Big Island survived the death of Big Sugar, but plantation communities and thriving sugar towns are now only memories.

Above: Luna, or foremen, rode on horseback and were in charge of the work crews. Date unknown. [David Weiss/Final Harvest]

Far Left: E.C. Culver (seated) was a chief chemist for several Hāmākua Coast factories. Circa 1940. [David Weiss/Final Harvest]

Left: Pau hana (finished work), sugar workers head home. Date unknown. [Lyman House Memorial Museum]

In the 1970s and '80s, sugar plantations all over the Islands were closing. They could no longer compete with Mainland sugar beets, or with sugar cane grown in countries with cheap labor and lower transportation costs. The Hāmākua Sugar Company, owned by local company Theo Davies, struggled on. Hawai'i State authorities invested $10 million, hoping to keep it, and the hundreds of jobs it supported alive. Unions made concessions. For a brief time, prospects looked bright enough that investor Francis Morgan took a gamble. He bought the plantation in 1984, believing that he could turn the business around. His efforts were unsuccessful, and the company declared bankruptcy in 1993. Its last day of operation was September 30, 1994.

This was a major blow to the Hāmākua coast. Generations of workers had worked for the company. Thanks to the unions, plantation life had become increasingly well-paid, even pleasant. One worker said, "At one point I just sat on the steps, and I just listened to the mill, and then I finally felt what the workers were talking about. Like the mill was tired, like it was time, like it was dying. And I could actually feel all of that. The plantation took care of us. The plantation was everybody's mom over here. They held us. I mean, you had plantation life, and then you get the real world. And we were so sheltered. . .I don't think the hurt ever going go away." [University of Hawai'i Center for Oral History]

Above right: Personnel of the main automotive repair shop at Pa'auilo. 1994. [David Weiss/Final Harvest]

Right: Supervisors with two of the three harvesting groups and the road construction group. 1994. [David Weiss/Final Harvest]

✕✕✕✕✕✕✕✕✕✕✕✕✕✕

Left: A cane haul truck drives through the main street of Pāhoa Town to deliver its load of harvested sugar cane to the Kea'au Sugar Mill. Pāhoa was once a logging and sawmill town, and later prospered because of the sugar industry. The street is narrow and the wooden boardwalks are from another era. Puna Sugar Company was several miles away in Kea'au and their fields extended past Pāhoa. After the mill was closed in 1984, the sugar lands were subdivided and people began homesteading in the area of relatively cheap land. 1975. [Franco Salmoiraghi]

Below left: Hula girls who volunteered to dance as a gesture of aloha bid farwell to Hāmākua Sugar. 1994. [David Weiss/Final Harvest]

KA'U SUGAR

Below left: Ledger books in the records room of Ka'u Sugar Company in Pāhala. The records room was the sugar plantation's archive of current accounts, and its history. The surviving ledgers provide detailed insights into plantation life. 1998. [Franco Salmoiraghi]

Below right: List of names in a Ka'u Sugar record book. Every plantation had its own system of record keeping. The scribes of the ledgers had impeccably legible handwriting. 1998. [Franco Salmoiraghi]

On March 27, 1996, Ka'u Sugar Company processed its last harvest from sugar cane fields above Pāhala Town. The Ka'ū mill was the last of thirteen Big Island sugar companies that had been in operation for over 125 years. From a population of several thousand during sugar's boom times, the town's population dwindled; only about one thousand residents remain.

For centuries, the introduction of new plants by the Polynesians and Europeans had altered the landscape of Hawai'i. Not many years ago, thousands of acres of sugar cane were growing, adding a lush greenness to much of the Big Island, and often displacing native plant species.

With the mill closing, the town of Pāhala became very quiet. The mill was part of the town and its presence was constantly felt through the sound of its hum and mechanical vibration. Today, there is no longer the distinctive rumble of cane trucks downshifting as they roll through town into the mill to unload their haul of cane grown at higher elevations.

Even before the mill closed, it was in severe disrepair and felt as if it were already abandoned. Cobwebs, dust, and spiders filled spaces in the huge mill structures. Yet, even after demolition, the distinctive sugar mill smells have lingered. The acrid mix of sugar juices, molasses, dirt, grease, machinery, dust, and ash permeates the ground and the air.

After the closing of the mill and during demolition, dust blew through the empty mill and the shafts of sunlight made the dark inner spaces of the factory building visible, like the ruins of an industrial cathedral—rust and deterioration were everywhere. Plants and weeds grew out of cracks, from accumulations of mud, grease, and bagasse, left after extracting sugar from the cane. Much had been stripped from the mill: tools, lockers, lathes, and furniture. Only seemingly useless machinery and walk-ramps remained.

The mill equipment was sold to a company in Ecuador, which brought in Mexican laborers. With cutting torches the mill was stripped of its remaining usable parts and shipped to South America. The buildings were bulldozed. The metal was cut into pieces with huge scissor-like machines and hauled by truck to the Hilo Municipal Dump, a pile of scrap waiting to be sent to metal recycling plants in Honolulu and elsewhere.

Ka'u Sugar was gone. Only a bare field remains where the mill once stood. Pāhala Town survives as a living community, but without the mill, the Pāhala Theater, the camaraderie of a work place, and all the other interwoven pieces of the past, it is a very different place.

— *Franco Salmoiraghi*

Below left: A plantation-style house, Pāhala Town. 1996. [Franco Salmoiraghi]

Below right: Wood Valley Sugar Camp store, located in the former sugar fields on the slopes of Mauna Loa, above Pāhala. 1972. [Franco Salmoiraghi]

Above: The mill-yard crane loads cane for the mill feeder table for washing and crushing. 1996. [Franco Salmoiraghi]

Above right: During the last few days at Ka'u Sugar operations, cane-haul trucks waited to be unloaded at the mill. 1996. [Franco Salmoiraghi]

Right: At dusk, steam glows in the bright lights of the Ka'u Sugar Mill cleaning plant. With belts and wheels loudly turning and vibrating, and as lights filtered through steam, the transition from day to night was visually stunning. 1996. [Franco Salmoiraghi]

Left: Workers wait in front of the plant during closing day ceremonies. March 27, 1996. [Franco Salmoiraghi]

Below left: Pāhala ladies at the closing ceremony in the mill yard. Left to right: Mutsuyo Kai, Irene Takahara, and Hinae Okinaka. March 27, 1996. [Franco Salmoiraghi]

Below right: During the changing of the shift, workers gather to talk story at the supervisor's cottage at the entrance to the mill yard. Left to right: Donald Lorenzo, harvesting supervisor; Rudy Lazo, mill yard crane operator; Agustin Madriaga, truck driver; Amante Aurellio, truck driver, and Joseph Pedro, harvesting chief coordinator. 1996. [Franco Salmoiraghi]

Last run. Cane truck and driver Isidro Saribay before beginning the descent from the fields above Pāhala. March 27, 1996. [Franco Salmoiraghi]

Aloha 'Oe. A convoy of cane-haul trucks loaded with the last harvest from the upper fields moved through town in a closing day parade on their way to deposit their last load of cane at the processing mill. The drivers decorated their trucks with flowers and banners to say aloha to their work, their livelihood, and the only lifestyle many of them knew. March 27, 1996. [Franco Salmoiraghi]

KALAPANA—A LOOK BACK IN TIME

In an isolated coastal area in the Puna District of the Big Island, a fishing village known as Kalapana existed for centuries. Here, on ancient land sacred to Pele, goddess of the volcanoes, the Hawaiian people kept the old ways. They lived subsistence-style, with no electricity or running water, in simple homes in Kalapana, Kaimū, and Kapaʻahu. They harvested the land and the ocean, raised animals, spoke Hawaiian, and honored their traditions, ancestors, and gods. Kūpuna—the elders—were treated with respect, and the ʻohana—the family unit—was strong. When I visited this tightly knit community in 1971, it was legendary as one of the last outposts of old-time Hawaiʻi.

Yet change was in the air. Younger generations were moving away and subdivisions moving in. Proposed development for the beloved Kaimū Black Sand Beach threatened the local lifestyle. Native Hawaiian activism and what would later be called "The First Hawaiian Renaissance" were in the early stages. The kūpuna said Pele would come and "clean house" when change became too great, but they knew it was up to them to pass on their values and traditions. In this uncertain climate, the kūpuna welcomed me, believing the photographs I wanted to make of their daily lives would be a legacy to future generations. The images here, made between 1971 and 1975, resulted from our collaborations.

During the 1980s and in 1990, Kīlauea's flows covered Kalapana in molten lava, destroying most of the homes. In 1991, the state authorized a new village for displaced Hawaiians at Kīkala-Keōkea, on the coast three miles northeast of Kalapana. The forty-eight village residents holding leases wait for the state to complete infrastructure. Where the lava flowed, other ʻohana located their property and are building anew. In the future, the Kalapana Community Association hopes to establish a living museum to share and celebrate Kalapana's rich culture and history. The story continues.

—*Mary Ann Lynch*

Many Hands. *Making kūlolo, a Hawaiian pudding, was an all-day communal activity. Here, shredded coconut wrapped in burlap is hand-twisted to make coconut milk. This will be combined with grated taro and brown sugar, wrapped in kī leaves, and cooked in the imu, a Hawaiian underground oven. [Mary Ann Lynch]*

184

People of the Rock. *Left: Mary Kahilihiwa stands with her niece Stacey Roberts. Like many Hawaiian homes, Mary's was built on lava rock. Hawaiian families were very large, and children were often raised by their grandparents or other elders, in a custom called hānai. [Mary Ann Lynch]*

Horseman. *Below left: Samson Ka'awaloa was a horseman from his youth. Later he became a horse ranger for Hawaiian Volcanoes National Park. He lives in the Pāhoa area, where many Hawaiian residents of Kalapana relocated. [Mary Ann Lynch]*

Uncle Oulu's Best Friend. *Below right: "Girly-Boy," Samuel Oulu Konanui's horse, freely wandered around his yard in Kapa'ahu. "She is the girl and I am the boy," he said. "That's why I named her Girly-Boy." [Mary Ann Lynch]*

A Good Day's Hunt. *Above left:Abraham Kaapana carries one of two wild pigs that will be taken home and prepared for cooking. [Mary Ann Lynch]*

Backyard Baking. *Above right: Daisy Pai checks the imu where kūlolo is cooking. Traditionally, everything from fresh pig and fish to breadfruit and taro was cooked in lava rock ovens such as this one. [Mary Ann Lynch]*

Hawaiian Genealogy. *Annie Quihano looks up an ancestor in the family genealogy. Hawaiian family reunions bring hundreds of people together for days and nights of music and hula, talking story, and updating genealogies. By passing on their culture, history, and land rights, Native Hawaiians— Hawai'i's indigenous people—have kept their community alive socially and politically, and their reverence for the land at the heart of the state. [Mary Ann Lynch]*

"Livin' On Easy." *Left: Robert Keliihoomalu and Gabriel Kealoha "kick back" in the good old days. Uncle Robert's house in Kaimū was one of the few spared during the 1990 eruptions. He is active in the Hawaiian sovereignty movement. [Mary Ann Lynch]*

School Days. *Below: The Hauanio boys in the old Kalapana schoolhouse. At the time it closed in the 1960s, there was one class, with students from kindergarten to sixth grade, and one teacher, who was also the principal. [Mary Ann Lynch]*

Home Entertainment.
Left: Abe Kaapana plays the autoharp while others skin the pigs from the day's hunt. Kalapana families produced many of Hawai'i's leading musicians, including Abe's twin brothers Led and Ned Kaapana, and Dennis Pavao, who formed the renowned trio Hui 'Ohana in their teens. [Mary Ann Lynch]

187

Home Sweet Home. *Above left: Samuel Oulu Konanui was known as a healer, master storyteller, and "living book." He generously shared his time and knowledge with me, often saying, "With you, people are going to see what this Kalapana was all about." After his house burned down in 1971, he moved into his shed, which he called "my new Home Sweet Home." [Mary Ann Lynch]*

Nature's Gifts. *Above right: Maria Roberts uses a machete to open a coconut taken from a tree in front of her home. Kalapana families continue to teach National Park workshops on native plants and materials and to work as cultural interpreters. [Mary Ann Lynch]*

Ocean Lifeline. *Right: Sus Matsuo has just scaled the cliffs, returning from picking 'opihi from wave-battered rocks below. 'Opihi, a small salty limpet generally eaten raw, is a delicacy prized by Hawaiians. Sus's partner, Harry Nuuanu, is pulling up the thick rope that had connected the men. [Mary Ann Lynch]*

Going Home. *Left: Boys on bikes head home beneath clear Kalapana skies and swaying palms. Though Pele's flows covered this landscape, new land was formed in its place. Kalapana's story continues, in the hearts, minds, and futures of its people. [Mary Ann Lynch]*

Master Weaver. *Below left: Annie Quihano holds one of her intricately woven lauhala hats, made from the leaves of the hala (pandanus) tree. Annie had seven different patterns of her own design, and there was a waiting list for them all. Gathering and preparing the materials was a family affair. [Mary Ann Lynch]*

Through the Years. *Below: Daisy Pai and Maria Roberts, longtime friends, neighbors, and first cousins, at Daisy's house. [Mary Ann Lynch]*

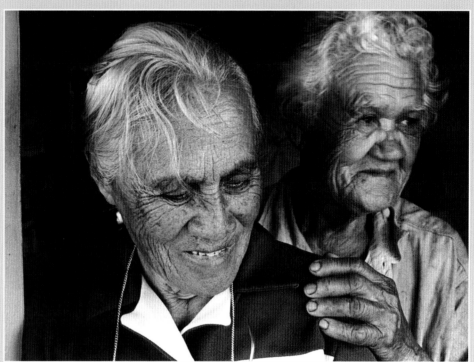

THE HULA

XXXXXXXXXXXXXXX

A hula group at the old Beamer home in Hilo, "Hale Hiku." Isabella Kalili Desha with gourd rattle (fourth from left). Baby Beamer (in front) stands next to famed chanter Kuluwaimaka (kneeling with gourd). 1928. [Baker-Van Dyke Collection]

Hula is an ancient Hawaiian art form that combines mele (chanted poetry or song) and dance. In pre-contact Hawai'i, hula was sometimes a mere amusement, but sometimes very serious business indeed. The sacred hula had to be performed without any mistakes, which were unlucky omens and possibly offenses against the gods.

The first Westerners who came to Hawai'i were much impressed by the grace and precision of the hula, but they were of two minds about some of the content, which could be very sexually explicit. The missionaries were shocked. They succeeded in banning public performance of hula, save in a few waterfront taverns that paid for licenses.

Hula went underground. It was taught in private, performed only when safe. But by the 1870s, the Hawaiian monarchy had distanced itself from its missionary mentors and the hula was rehabilitated. In the late 1870s, King David Kalākaua openly patronized the hula. Several hula troupes performed at his coronation, and important Western visitors were treated to command performances.

Hula changed over the course of the nineteenth century. Serious kumu hula, hula masters, continued to teach the hula kahiko, the old-style hula accompanied only by chanting and percussion instruments. But they also created a new kind of hula, then called hula ku'i, that was danced to Western-style music by dancers in Western-style dress. Hula ku'i, now called hula 'auana, was typically graceful rather than powerful, and flirtatious rather than overtly sexual. When tourists came to the Islands, this was the hula they wanted to see. A thinned-down, sweet, and commer-

cialized version of the hula ku'i, performed by pretty girls in cellophane grass skirts, became popular with visitors. The hula had been debased and commercialized.

Native Hawaiians pushed back against this commercialization. The Hawaiian Renaissance of the 1970s and later underlined this trend. Hula became respectable, and hula kahiko was newly popular. There were more hālau hula (hula troupes), more contests, more books, and more exposure. Hula is increasingly popular outside the Islands, and troupes come from as far away as Japan or Texas to participate in local contests.

The Big Island has played a large role in the revival of the hula. Some of the Islands' most respected dancers, such as 'Iolani Luahine, have lived and taught on the Big Island. The Big Island was the first to hold a public hula festival, the Merrie Monarch. The first Merrie Monarch was held in 1963. It was sponsored by the Big Island Chamber of Commerce and named in honor of King Kalākaua. By the 1980s, the festival had grown into a week-long event, held in the week following Easter Sunday. It has become the state's top hula competition, attracting thousands of spectators and drawing hālau hula from around the world.

Above left: This photograph of Maggie Sniffen, student at Kohala Seminary, has become an icon for Hawai'i. Circa 1912. [Baker-Van Dyke Collection]

Above right: 'Iolani Luahine was one of Hawai'i's famed hula dancers and chanters, one who kept the ancient spirit alive with her unparalleled artistry. She could transform any music into a hula, delighting tourists with her kolohe, or mischievous, moves, or entrancing kama'āina with the authority she radiated when dancing kahiko, the style of old. Born as Harriet Lanihau Makekau in the village of Nāpo'opoo, she was hanaied, or adopted, by her great aunt, Keahi Luahine, who had been a dancer in the court of King Kalākaua. At the age of four, she was dedicated to Laka, the goddess of hula, and was given the name 'Iolani Luahine by her aunt. In 1940 at the age of twenty-five, already skilled in the hula kahiko, she performed in Washington, D.C., at the National Ford Festival of Dance. After the death of her aunt, she perfected her chants and style under the tutelage of the incomparable Mary Kawena Pukui. Her intense, inspired movements and hypnotic eyes left those who watched her dance with the distinct feeling that they had traversed time, place, and culture. Her mesmerizing appearance in 1970 at Kanikapila, the first annual Hawaiian music festival hosted at the University of Hawai'i, was a revelation to spectators who had seen only commercialized tourist hula. When 'Iolani Luahine died in 1978, the Islands were deprived of one of the true devotees of Laka. "When 'Iolani dances," as one admiring reviewer wrote, "you feel thousands of years of dancing ancestors concentrated in this one body... dancing for her gods and they through her." Date unknown. [Kona Historical Society.]

The pride and power of the Hawaiian heritage has in recent years found a new meaning in the celebration of the Merrie Monarch Festival. For the Hawaiian and Hawaiian-at-heart, no festival compares to the annual Merrie Monarch Hula Festival, where both men's and women's hālau compete in ancient and modern dancing styles. The first Merrie Monarch Festival was held in 1963 in Hilo, as a celebration of hula in honor of King Kalākaua (nicknamed the "Merrie Monarch"), who was instrumental in restoring this art form to prominence in the late nineteenth century. The idea for a statewide hula competition originated from Hilo residents George Naope and Gene Wilheim, who conceived the festival as a way to draw international attention to hula and Hilo town. By 1971, the competition was drawing hālau from around the state who came to dance and be judged on movement, costume, adornments, style, stance, and manner. The annual event, at the Edith Kana'ole Stadium, is now televised state-wide. Above: Nina Maxwell's Pukalani hālau hula performs during the 1985 festival. [Boone Morrison]

The men of Johnny Lum Ho's hālau, Ka Ua Lehua, dance at the 1983 competitions. [Boone Morrison]

PUʻUKOHOLĀ HEIAU AND HOʻOKUʻIKAHI

Sam Kaʻai watches the preparations for Hōkūleʻa's departure from the cliffs at Kahukupoko, Ka Lae (South Point), Kaʻū. In August 1991, Keoua Kūʻahuʻula's descendants retraced their ancestor's route to Puʻukoholā. [Franco Salmoiraghi]

In 1791, the ambitious warrior chief Kamehameha was seeking supremacy over his first cousin Keoua Kūʻahuʻula of Kaʻū District as well as over other rivals on other islands for control of Hawaiʻi Island.

Upon the advice of a renowned kahuna (high priest), Kamehameha restored and re-dedicated the imposing heiau of Puʻukoholā to his war god, Kūkāʻilimoku. The dedication was rendered ritually successful by the slaughter and sacrifice of High Chief Keoua Kūʻahuʻula and his entire canoe load of supporters—highborn chiefs from the Kaʻū District.

In 1989, Sam Kaʻai of Maui began planning for a Hoʻokuʻikahi (unification ceremony) at Puʻukoholā Heiau in South Kohala for the upcoming two-hundredth anniversary of Kamehameha's dedication of his "temple of state" in Kawaihae, Hawaiʻi. After nearly two centuries, resentment against Kamehameha still smoldered. A bicentenary observance, therefore, could not be just a costumed pageant, but would also have to address the process of healing historic wounds.

Under Sam Kaʻai's inspired leadership, participants and volunteers came forth to help make weapons, military and ceremonial garb and paraphernalia, as well as to train as chiefs, warriors, and chanters, so as to make this historical observance a success.

With delegations, participants, and observers from Tahiti, Rapa Nui (Easter Island), Sāmoa, and Aotearoa (New Zealand), as well as hundreds of Native Hawaiians, the gathering, tributes, and meeting of minds, hearts, and spirits gave indication that on the weekend of August 16–17, 1991, a reconciliation, and a spiritual unification of Hawaiians, did in fact take place.

— *Kalani Meinecke*

On their journey from Ka'ū to Pu'ukoholā, the descendants of Keoua Kū'ahu'ula and his escorts landed at what is now Pu'uhonua O Hōnaunau National Historical Park. There, they made prayers and offerings where the sacred bones of high chiefs once lay in the Royal Mausoleum, Hale o Keawe. [Franco Salmoiraghi]

Right: The descendants of Keoua Kū'ahu'ula and Kamehameha proceed together to take part in ceremonies at the heiau. [Franco Salmoiraghi]

Below right: John Keolamaka'āinana Lake directs members of his hālau at Pu'ukoholā. "Reconciliation between the people of Ka'ū and Kohala became an open invitation to all Hawaiians to participate in a solemn occasion requiring serious practice, dedication, pule (prayer) without censure, attention to authentic learning and protocol, and faith in our ancestors to guide the process."
—John Keolamaka'āinana Lake [Franco Salmoiraghi]

Left: Nā Koa (the warriors) at Puʻukoholā inspected by Sam Kaʻai, at left, wearing a mahiole (helmet; a a symbol of a warrior chief) during a rehearsal for the ceremony. "It's not about being war-like; Nā Koa is about being courageous enough to look at your spirit."
—Sam Kaʻai
[Franco Salmoiraghi]

Below left: Hoʻokuʻikahi Ceremony at Puʻukoholā, Kawaihae. "Puʻukoholā is a temple of state. Our nation was built here. This is where Kamehameha started his campaign for sovereignty. Two hundred years later, we have come back to Puʻukoholā. It gives us an identity—a cultural, historical, politcal, economic, and social foundation."
—John Keolamakaʻāinana Lake
[Franco Salmoiraghi]

(Quotations adapted from the film Hoʻokuʻikahi: To Unify As One, written by Meleanna Aluli Meyer with John Keolamakaʻāinana Lake, and published with a photographic essay by Franco Salmoiraghi in the book Maps of Reconciliation, the Winter 2007 (19:2) issue of Mānoa.)

THE LAST PEOPLE OF WAIPI'O

Waipi'o Valley is one of a series of valleys, in an area once accessible only by foot or horseback. The nearly perpendicular cliffs range in heights from one thousand feet at the valley's mouth to three thousand feet at its head. For centuries, the valley floor has been used as a principal center of taro cultivation. There is a poetic reference to the valley as *Waipi'o Mano Wai*, meaning, "Waipi'o, source of water and life".

In her book *Na Kua'aina—Living Hawaiian Culture*, Davianna Pomaika'i McGregor refers to Waipi'o Valley as a cultural *kipuka*, an isolated place that remained a traditional center of spiritual power. "The *kua'aina*, the remnants of native people who lived in the valley until the 1980s, were among those few people in Hawai'i who actively lived Hawaiian culture and kept the spirit of the land alive. They remained in rural areas; took care of the *kūpuna* (elders); continued to speak Hawaiian; toiled in taro patches, and took what is precious and sacred in Native Hawaiian culture into their care."

In 1946, a fifty-foot tidal wave destroyed most of the homes and taro patches left in Waipi'o, leaving many of the last residents to move to the topside village of Kukuihaele to live closer to modern conveniences. Without a living, working population to maintain the streams and *lo'i* (irrigated terraces), flooding became a devastating problem for the remaining farmers and residents.

In 1954, the Lennox Report to the trustees of Bishop Estate estimated that thirty to forty people were living in Waipi'o. It remained a nearly inaccessible place until the early 1960s, when a very steep four-wheel-drive-only road was constructed, following an ancient footpath. This allowed part-time residents and farmers easier access between their taro fields and the market. Two oral history projects documented the history and culture of Waipi'o in the mid-1970s, which was a time of pivotal change. Many of these photographs were made during that time, when there were approximately twenty full-time residents still living in the valley. Only a few have lived there since birth.

—*Franco Salmoiraghi*

Fields of laupa'e kalo (young taro) grow in the flat areas of the valley floor where taro cultivation is now a mostly commercial activity and large taro patches, have replaced the smaller traditional loi of earlier times. Growing taro also remains a cultural opportunity for younger generations of Hawaiians who visit Waipi'o for inspiration and education. 1985. [Franco Salmoiraghi]

Left: Fannie (Hauanio) and Romualdo Duldulao at the entrance to their Waipi'o taro farm. Fannie was born in Waipi'o in 1911 and lived her entire life in the valley and topside in Kukuihaele. She farmed taro for more than forty-five years. 1978. [Franco Salmoiraghi]

Below left: Lanny Takahashi leads his mules loaded with bags of taro across Wailoa Stream. Onto a waiting truck, the taro was loaded and hauled up the cliff to be sold. Lanny, a carpenter, came to the valley in 1976 to help a friend build a house, stayed on, and became a part-time taro farmer. 1978. [Franco Salmoiraghi]

Right: Roy Toko and his sons Alston, Ellaham, and Naaman at their house in the Waipi'o topside community of Kukuihaele, preparing for a weekend trip to their farm in the valley. Roy was born in Kukuihaele to a Filipino/Chinese/Japanese/Hawaiian family. His maternal great-grandfather was among the gannenmono, who in 1868 became the first Japanese immigrant workers to arrive in Hawai'i. 1974. [Franco Salmoiraghi]

Below right: Talking story at the taro field shack of Roy and Gladys (Hauanio) Toko. 1974. [Franco Salmoiraghi]

Left: In the 1970s, hippies began drifting into Waipi'o and were hired as taro pullers by the farmers, who were short of helping hands. Lance Gravett (second from left) and Cheryl Peterson (right) enjoy a pau hana (after work) beer with friends and fellow workers, next to their home in the valley. [Franco Salmoiraghi]

Below left: The Samuel Mock Chew family on the steps of their former home. Sam Mock Chew, born in Waipi'o in 1924, was a descendant of Hawaiian and Chinese farmers. Growing up, he worked for his father, who was one of the big taro farmers in the valley. The old family home was destroyed by a tsunami in 1946, but the site was still used by the family to gather after working in the fields. Front row: Ronald and Cynthia (Mock Chew) Kanekoa. Back row: Dennis Mock Chew with Jayson Kanekoa (son of Ronald and Cynthia), Hazel Mock Chew, Sam Mock Chew, and Lyle Mock Chew. 1974. [Franco Salmoiraghi]

Hi'ilawe is the tallest waterfall in Hawai'i. With a vertical drop of more than one thousand feet—the boy crossing the stream is just inches away from the edge—hiking the cliffs of Waipi'o is a daring adventure. The ocean side of Waipi'o Valley is visible in the background. In 2004, the State Water Commission confirmed a decision to fully restore flows that had been diverted for many years to three streams that feed the twin falls of Hi'ilawe and Hakalaoa, which converge in a huge plunge pool at the bottom of the pali (cliff). There, they form Hi'ilawe Stream, one of two primary waterways that flow through Waipi'o and into the ocean. The restoration culminated years of effort by the Waipi'o Valley Community Association and others, to stop the wasting of water by Lalakea Ditch, which was last used by Hāmākua Sugar Company in 1989. The company had begun diverting the streams in the early 1900s for sugar cane irrigation and processing. 1974. [Franco Salmoiraghi]

202

Far left: Sam Liʻa Kalainaina at his top-side home in Kukuihaele. Sam Liʻa, born in 1881, was a songwriter of a bygone era. Hawaiian musician Eddie Kamae met Sam in 1971 while searching for lyrics to an old song, and Sam became the subject of Kamae's first documentary, Liʻa: The Legacy of a Hawaiian Man. The film celebrates the music and spirit of the revered Big Island performer and composer, who died in 1975, and whose life was shaped and nourished by Waipiʻo Valley. His songwriter father, Sam Liʻa Kalainaina, Sr, created the well-known Hawaiian classic, Hiʻilawe—a song about two lovers and named after Waipiʻo's spectacular double waterfall. 1974. [Franco Salmoiraghi]

Left: Ginji Araki going fishing in Waipiʻo Valley. Until his death at age 92, Araki-san had lived in Waipiʻo for more than forty years and built the famous five-room "no-name" hotel there. He spoke a combination of Japanese, Hawaiian, pidgin, and English, and was known for his sake drinking. He said, "No moh sake, no moh life." 1974. [Franco Salmoiraghi]

Below left: Fishermen launching the Moana Rae from Wailoa stream into the ocean at Waipiʻo Bay. The canoe was one of the last modern and unique Waipiʻo-style motorized canoes in use for ocean fishing. Left to right: Samuel Mock Chew (white hat); Newton Toko (behind canoe front on left); Victor "Polo" Hauanio (in canoe in white tee shirt); Jayson Mock Chew (right front on ama (outrigger float)); Naaman Toko (back right in front of "Rae"). Fourth of July, 1974. [Franco Salmoiraghi]

RESORT DEVELOPMENT

Duke Kahanamoku, famed surfer and Olympic swimming champion (right) with Francis Hyde I'i Brown (left) at Brown's Keawaiki estate. Francis was the son of Charles Augustus Brown, a Massachusetts businessman who settled in Honolulu and married Irene Kahalelaukoa I'i in 1886. Their son Francis was brought up in the best Honolulu circles. In the 1930s, he moved to the Big Island and began buying land near Kalahuipua'a, which was eventually turned into resort developments. He was an avid sportsman. [Bishop Museum]

In pre-contact times, the Kohala coast north of Kailua-Kona had been dotted with fishing villages and fish ponds; the offshore fishing was good. The area was dry, but the fishermen could easily trade for produce from wetter regions. By the early 1900s, few villagers remained; only wild goats and cattle clambered over the lava-strewn land, nibbling on the pods of thorny kiawe trees. In the 1960s, the Kohala coast began its transformation into a tourist resort destination.

The first guest lodgings to open, in 1964 at Ka'ūpūlehu in North Kona, were the concept of a wealthy yachtsman, Johnno Jackson, who had arrived in his private schooner and taken a fancy to the area's white sand beaches and calm bays. His recreation of an ancient Hawaiian village was a near-impossible undertaking. In order to build the Polynesian-style cottages, he had to first build a twenty-six hundred-foot aircraft landing strip and a power plant, as well as dig a well. Construction materials had to be flown in by plane. Two years later he sold the complex, which was renamed Kona Village Resort.

Laurance S. Rockefeller, of the wealthy Rockefeller family, also visited the island and envisioned a large hotel at pristine Kauna'oa Bay at the north end of the Kohala coast. In 1960, he leased land from Parker Ranch. The Big Island's first destination resort was built at a cost of $15 million. It included 154 rooms, Asian and Pacific Island art collections, thirty acres of manicured grounds, and a secluded beach. A $2 million golf course, designed by Robert Trent Jones, Sr., saw its first tee-off in July 1965, six months before the grand opening of Rockefeller's Mauna Kea Beach Hotel.

The opening of Queen Ka'ahumanu Highway in 1975 allowed developers to turn the shoreline between Ka'ūpūlehu and Kauna'oa into a string of luxury resorts, condominiums, championship golf courses, and luxurious private homes. Now some 40 percent of the Big Island's ten thousand hotel rooms are on the Kohala coast. Nearby communities, such as Waimea, Waikoloa, and Hāwī and Kapa'au in North Kohala, offer not just additional accommodations, such as bed and breakfasts, but tourist activities, retail stores, and restaurants. Property values on the once-arid Kohala coast soared as tourists flocked to the Big Island.

Recently, in 2008 and 2009, the worldwide economic downturn has affected the Kohala coast. Hotel vacancy rates have risen and some hotel workers have been let go. New construction has faltered, and property values have stagnated.

Left: Hilton Hotel Corporation executives. February 1, 1966. [Kona Historical Society]

Below left: Duke Kahanamoku congratulates a fisherman on his catch at the second Hawaiian International Billfish Tournament. 1961. [Kona Historical Society]

Below right: Construction of the Mauna Kea Beach Hotel. 1967. [Kona Historical Society]

ON THE ROAD

Franco Salmoiraghi photographed the Big Island's country and small-town life over a period of twenty-five years, from the 1960s to the 1990s. His work documents nature and humanity, places and people, capturing what has changed and what has remained, much that has vanished and much that is timeless.

A dilapidated storefront and a pristine '57 Chevy contrast with each other in this street scene of a nearly abandoned Hāmākua coast sugar town. 1975. [Franco Salmoiraghi]

My Big Island photographic journey began with two trips in 1968. I was in my twenties and had moved to Honolulu from the Mainland a few months before.

The first visit was a typical tourist trek—exploring from Hilo to Volcano and viewing Waipi'o Valley from the lookout. The second visit was as a photographer for an archaeological expedition surveying the South Kohala coastline, before the building of the Queen Ka'ahumanu Highway and new Kona airport. We helicoptered into an unpopulated and barren environment of lava, ocean, and unrelenting sunlight. For me, it was an unforgettable experience.

Once you begin to move about in the immensity of the Big Island, walking, driving, or flying through the changing elements of weather, altitude, and geography, there is an immediate realization that you have entered an enchanted place, where the material world and the world of the spirit co-exist. There are experiences of unexplained phenomena that make you feel as if magic is resonating in the air and light.

You are in the home of Pele, the goddess of fire, Poli'ahu, the goddess of mist, snow and ice, and other Hawaiian deities and their human descendants. Miles of road; landscapes with immense vistas of mountains and ocean; rain forests and deserts; geographic zones that make using a map both necessary and fascinating; and exceptionally strong fault lines of magnetic energy and unstable geology as you pass through micro-climates that give rise to visions and surprises. This is the Big Island....

In 1973, I moved from Honolulu to the Big Island and lived there for twelve years: in Āhualoa, an old sugar plantation house in Hilo, Volcano Village, and then Waiākea Uka. Four very different landscapes.

Hilo and the Big Island were vastly different from Honolulu in the 1970's—hundreds of miles and many cultural zones away. It was, and in many ways still is, a place outside of modern big-city time, simultaneously exotic and familiar.

Familiarity for me came from the people who worked the land, sugar fields, mills, and small-town stores. Like my own Italian immigrant grandparents who came to southern Illinois to work the coal mines, these Big Island people lived simple lives, often growing and gathering their own food. I was captivated and began making longer and longer expeditions to photograph my encounters with this new culture and geography.

During this time, my obsession was to drive randomly around, meet people, and see everything—to find and photograph the soul of the Big Island. My photographs accumulated to thousands of negatives and became an archive. This selection is a small vignette from that time.

—*Franco Salmoiraghi*

Above left: Walking through Pāhoa town on a summer day, I spoke briefly with these two men in a garage. The dog wandered over just in time to get in the photograph. Pāhoa was once a logging and sawmill town, and later a booming sugar town. After Puna Sugar Company closed its Keaʻau operations in 1984, the sugar lands were replaced with affordable subdivisions. Pāhoa's population is about one thousand and its shops and restaurants now serve a larger outlying population. 1975. [Franco Salmoiraghi]

Far left: From Hilo it is a seventy-mile drive to the nearest white sand beach and warm ocean water. One day while swimming at Spencer Beach Park near Puakō, I photographed these sisters, Doreen and Angie Ahia, against one of the large kiawe trees growing along the coast. 1975. [Franco Salmoiraghi]

Left: On a bench in front of a Pāhoa grocery store, this obasan sits wearing her rubber kamaboko slippers. Japanese wooden geta footwear evolved into rubber slippers and continued to change over the years. In the mid-1970s, the thick-soled kamaboko (fishcake) style made its appearance. The time period in which a photograph was made can often be estimated from the type of footwear seen in the picture. 1975. [Franco Salmoiraghi]

207

Right: Historic Honoka'a is the main commercial and shopping area between Hilo and Waimea. Its economy was based on the success of the Hāmākua Sugar Company from 1873 to its closing in 1994. The pool hall was a popular hangout. 1975. [Franco Salmoiraghi]

Below right: Bailey Matsuda, Bill Brooks, Ian McKay, and friend Bonnie in their sugar shack home above Hilo. The three local guys' band, Rosewood, played a soft mellow '70s-style music. In the twenty-first century, Bailey teaches music, Bill is an environmental architect, and Ian is a teacher and traveler. 1972. [Franco Salmoiraghi]

Below far right: There was once a fairly large population of single men living in Hilo's Mamo Street area. The rooming houses, theater, diners, and several bars provided a place for entertainment and camaraderie, particularly in front of the Mamo Pool Hall, which was the center of the neighborhood. 1975. [Franco Salmoiraghi]

208

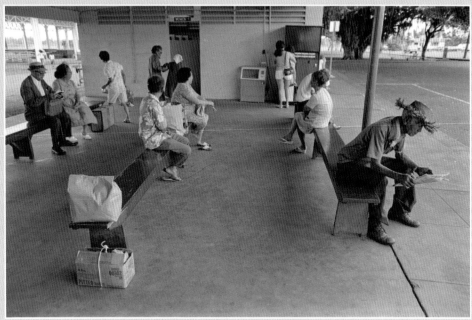

Left: Saturday afternoon in front of the Pahala Theater. 1972

Above right: Luther Kahekili Makekau, here reading a newspaper at Mo'oheau Park Bus Station in Hilo, was the subject of Eddie Kamae's 1997 documentary film Luther Kahekili Makekau: A One Kine Hawaiian Man. *Kamae wrote that his film pays tribute to the untamed spirit of a colorful and controversial Hawaiian. Known throughout the Islands, Makekau was part philosopher and part outlaw, a chanter and a singer, a fighter and a lover, a cattle rustler, a rebel, and a poet. Born on Maui in 1890 during the reign of King Kalākaua, he lived nearly a hundred years, shaped by a century of turbulent cultural change. 1976. [Franco Salmoiraghi]*

Left: In November 1975, a 7.2-magnitude earthquake caused the Kalapana area to sink several feet. Later, the area was covered in a series of lava flows and is now remembered as a place that no longer exists. In this photograph, made shortly before the destruction, Ted Limpahan of Pāhoa swims in the historic Queen's Bath. 1975. [Franco Salmoiraghi]

Right: This Fourth of July celebration at Nāʻālehu County Park in 1976 included a demolition derby. A group of cars line up and begin ramming each other until only one car is left running and is declared the winner. Nāʻālehu, a small town of about nine hundred people, is called the southernmost town in the United States. It is near South Point—Ka Lae, as the Hawaiians call that part of the island of Hawaiʻi. Archaeological excavations have shown that the area was inhabited by A.D. 750.

Above far right: A man waters his yard plants in Pāpaʻaloa Village, a remnant of one of the many plantation villages and camps that once thrived along the Hāmākua Coast. The village of approximately five hundred people is located between Laupāhoehoe and Honokaʻa. 1975. [Franco Salmoiraghi]

Below right: (from left) Rodney Medeiros, Roman Molina, Gerry Palermo (in back), Domingo Molina, and Francisco Arnon, at Arnon's home in Waiākea Uka. They slaughtered the pig for the wedding celebration of his granddaughter, Pua Auyong, the following day at the family home. 1976. [Franco Salmoiraghi]

Below far right: Man with two boys at a Miloliʻi fishing village home on the South Kona Coast. 1976. [Franco Salmoiraghi]

Above left: Agapito Billaber and Maria Baclay dancing at a backyard barrio festival celebration at the home of Francisco Arnon, above Hilo. The celebration was for the Feast of the Assumption of the Blessed Virgin Mary on August 15. This barrio festival tradition had been carried over from the family barrio of Dauis, Bahol Island, in Central Visayas, Philippines, and was practiced in Hilo for over sixty years. Birhen Dela Asuncion is the patron saint, and the celebration was preceded by a novena of rosary devotions, culminating in a very popular party. 1976. [Franco Salmoiraghi]

Below: I was driving on the misty back roads above Āhualoa in the Hāmākua Hawaiian Homes Lands when I heard shouts in the ghostly stillness. I found this group—James Lindsey, friends and family—having lunch along the roadside after working with their herd of cattle. From a portable tape recorder came the music of Gabby Pahinui, Sunday Manoa, and others. 1974. [Franco Salmoiraghi]

Left: Yutaka Kimura (1905–2003), former Parker Ranch chief cowboy, at the Mana Corral in Waimea. Yutaka, known as "Chief," was a herdsman and director of cattle genetics and breeding, working to improve Parker Ranch's line of Herefords for forty-nine years. He was inducted into the Paniolo Hall of Fame for keeping Hawai'i's paniolo heritage alive and making paniolo culture legendary. His life was the subject of a book, Parker Ranch Paniolo: Yutaka Kimura by Jiro Nakano. 1985. [Franco Salmoiraghi]

HAWAIIAN WAYS: THE TRADITION CONTINUES

Of all the recent manifestations of the
Hawaiian Renaissance, no one event
has had a more dramatic effect than
the 1976 voyage of the Hōkūle'a, a
sixty-foot-long replica of the ancient
double-hulled migration canoe that
brought the first Polynesians to Hawai'i
a thousand years ago. One of the
members of the early Hōkūle'a voyages was Clay Bertelmann, a cowboy
at Parker Ranch in Waimea. In 1993,
Bertelmann founded Na Kalai Wa'a
Moku o Hawai'i, a Big Island voyaging
program. Along with Mau Piailug, the
Micronesian navigator who mentored
the crew of the Hōkūle'a, Bertelmann
built the Big Island's own voyaging
canoe, the fifty-four-foot Makali'i,
whose maiden voyage came in February,
1995. The Makali'i voyaging program
continues as one of the island's most
important platforms to reconnect
Hawaiian youths with their heritage,
roots, and traditions. After Bertelmann's
death in January, 2004, the voyaging
'ohana pledged to build a voyaging
canoe for Mau Piailug and the people
of Micronesia as a symbol of gratitude
and unity. The Alingano Maisu was built
in Kawaihae and given to Mau in 2007.
Today, Na Kalai Wa'a continues its educational and cultural programs from its
home in Māhukona. [Alexis Higdon]

Early in the twentieth century, it would have been reasonable to predict that the Hawaiian culture would continue to weaken and fade—victim of modernization and Americanization. All the more so when in 1959 Hawai'i became the Fiftieth State, finally politically integrated into the union. Citizens of Hawai'i were now, by definition, fully citizens of the United States. And the economy of Hawai'i was inextricably connected with the American economy: in the second half of the century, Hawai'i grew ever more dependent upon dollars from tourism and military spending, massive inputs from outside. The big world was dominating the little world of the Islands as never before. In such a world—urbanized, developed, Americanized—what might "being Hawaiian" mean? What could it possibly amount to anymore?

Against all expectations—against all odds—there emerged a movement that was soon called the Hawaiian Renaissance. The Renaissance, which took root in the 1970s and flowered in the decades that followed, was expressed culturally in a renewed interest in Hawaiian traditions, including hula, music, history, literature, and crafts; politically, in demands for economic and social changes to correct past historical injustices; and socially, in renewed pride in being Hawaiian.

One of the great symbols of the Hawaiian Renaissance was *Hōkūle'a*, a big double-hulled oceangoing voyaging canoe, a reconstruction of the kind of vessel in which the ancient Polynesians had sailed to Hawai'i. Aboard *Hōkūle'a*, in a series of voyages across the Pacific, modern-day Hawaiians recreated and demonstrated the superb navigational skills of their ancestors, rekindling a deep sense of Hawaiian pride.

By the late 1980s, the political side of the Hawaiian Renaissance had developed into a movement for sovereignty—the return of Hawai'i to political independence from the United States. In a real sense, this was a revolutionary idea. In 1993, the hundredth anniversary of the overthrow of the Hawaiian kingdom by American revolutionaries, thousands of Native Hawaiians marched through the streets of Honolulu in one of the biggest political demonstrations in Hawaiian history, chanting for sovereignty. The question of the right relation between the Hawaiian people and the lands of Hawai'i and the government of the United States remains contested terrain—a matter of continuous debate, unresolved.

On the Big Island the sovereignty movement has had real longterm issues to deal with.

As on all islands, Hawaiians ranked at the bottom among all ethnic groups on basic measures of quality of life and "success" as measured in mainstream terms—health, education, income, social status. There were specific Big Island issues of great concern to Hawaiians. Over the years, subdivisions, roads, and resort development had taken away shoreline access and gathering fields. Gates and "No Trespassing" signs blocked old trails. Title to many kuleana lands, once in the hands of Hawaiian families, had become obscured or lost entirely. The lands of the Big Island were no longer the 'āina of old. The ground on which twenty-first-century Hawaiians stood kept shifting under their feet.

Hōkūle'a had demonstrated the capability of Hawaiians to navigate the ocean. On land, on the Big Island, from the mountains to the sea, there was a matching challenge—how to draw strength from tradition and direct it to navigate the future. With different thoughts about what restoration and restitution meant, Native Hawaiians in one way or another began searching to reclaim their legacy and rights.

Fifty-eight men's paddling crews start the eighteen-mile Queen Lili'uokalani Long Distance Canoe Race. The course runs from Hōnaunau to Kailua Bay. Date unknown. [Kona Historical Society]

Above: Members of the Kai Opua Canoe Club pose in front of the reconstructed Ahu'ena Heiau in Kailua-Kona. Date unknown. [Kona Historical Society.]

Right: Hawaiian canoe-building skills were put to use in building the twenty-six-foot-long Mauloa, a wa'a kaukahi (coastal canoe). Micronesian navigator Mau Piailug led a Hawaiian team in carving the Mauloa with traditional and locally made adzes from a single koa tree. It was caulked with breadfruit sap, lashed with coconut cordage, and fitted with a lauhala sail. Mauloa means "perpetuation." The tree-harvesting ceremony was held on Bishop Estate ranch lands, above Hawai'i Volcanoes National Park. March 1992. [Franco Salmoiraghi]

214

✕✕✕✕✕✕✕✕✕✕✕✕✕✕✕✕✕

Above: The Kamehameha Day Parade passes in front of the Ocean View Inn. Then as now, the parade was eagerly anticipated and drew large crowds. Date unknown. [Kona Historical Society]

Below left: Ben Heloka carries the opening banner of the 1968 Kamehameha Day Parade. He is wearing an akulikuli or maile lei; his horse is adorned with a lehua liko lei. [Kona Historical Society]

Below right: A chanter in front of Hulihe'e Palace. 1991. [Kona Historical Society]

In the 1980s Native Hawaiians raised a battle cry against the State of Hawai'i over geothermal development in the rainforest on the slopes of Kilauea, and began a successful struggle to preserve the land and their gathering rights for the products of the forest. Plans for a geothermal power plant and wells were shut down with a civil disobedience campaign launched by the Pele Defense Fund, associated with the Protect Kaho'olawe 'Ohana.

Right: Pua Kanahele chants and leads the first protest march at Wao Kele O Puna, the drilling site of the geothermal test well. October 1989. [Franco Salmoiraghi]

Below right: A confrontation in March 1990 brought fifteen hundred protesters to the forest and led to the arrest of 141 people. In 2001, Campbell Estate put the land up for sale, and Hawai'i Senators Daniel Inouye and Daniel Akaka pressured the U.S. Forest Service to commit $3.35 million to protect forests of cultural significance. Eventually, the Trust for Public Land, under their Tribal and Native Lands Program, paid the remainder of the $3.65 million to purchase nearly twenty-six thousand acres of Wao Kele O Puna. It was signed over to the Office of Hawaiian Affairs for managing Native Hawaiian lands in trust. [Franco Salmoiraghi]

Left: Mililani Trask speaking before the big march. March 25, 1990. [Franco Salmoiraghi]

Below left: Aunty Edith Kanakaole and her group perform at an Imua "Save Our Surf" rally on the University of Hawai'i Hilo campus in 1971. SOS won its struggle to protect the historic surfing and fishing area at Kaimū Black Sand Beach in the Puna District. Aunty Edith's mother (Mary Kanaele), who taught her hula in the tradition of Pele, was from Puna. [Mary Ann Lynch].

MILOLI'I: A MOST HAWAIIAN PLACE

Drying Nets at Sunset. 'Ōpelu (mackerel scad) season and nets drying at sunset—a scene that might have looked the same a hundred years ago. 1982. [Boone Morrison]

These images, photographed between 1971 and the present, document life in Miloli'i, on the Big Island. I lived for long periods in this remote place, periods interspersed with returns to my home in Volcano. Diana Aki kindly allowed me to park my van in her yard and camp there; she treated me like family, for which I will always be grateful.

Miloli'i is a straggling village on the southwestern coast of the Big Island; a sign outside the community center boasts that it is "the last Hawaiian fishing village." Houses are lined up along the road, next to a dry black lava coast, just south of a 1926 lava flow from Mauna Loa. Many of the houses have no running water, electricity, or telephone. The paved road, and utilities, came here late or not at all. There is a small beach park near the ocean, with a paved parking lot.

For many years, the village was left to itself. Life centered on fishing for the 'ahi, or yellow fin tuna, that were found just offshore. The fishermen left before first light to reach the fishing grounds at dawn. They fished from plywood canoes, with nothing more than a hand line, and regularly brought in fish weighing 150 pounds or more.

Afternoons were spent hauling the catch to Kona, the nearest market, and shopping for fuel, ice, and other supplies. Anyone returning from the "outside" would bring back containers filled with fresh water, otherwise scarce on that dry coast. That was life.

Of the population of 125 or so, all were full or part Hawaiian. The kūpuna, or elders, spoke Hawaiian to each other. In the 1970s, it was as close to the old ways as one could live in modern Hawai'i.

In recent times, as Miloli'i's reputation for being an "untouched Hawaiian paradise" has spread, tourism has come to the village. But the small village store is still open and fishing is still a way of life, although some folks work "outside" when the 'ahi aren't running. The community has even built a traditional hālau, or boat shed.

—*Boone Morrison*

Miloliʻi Village from the Air.
Left: Miloliʻi is only one third of a mile in length. It is located at the end of an eight-mile winding narrow road, originally a donkey trail. The road is now paved but it remains a challenge for inexperienced drivers. 1984. [Boone Morrison]

Hauʻoli Kamanao Church. Above: This former Congregational church is now a non-denominational house of worship used by visiting ministers from several Christian denominations. 1979. [Boone Morrison]

The Main Beach. Left: The Main Beach is still the center of village life. Note the fiberglass skiff anchored there. From the 1930s onwards, local fishermen used inexpensive homemade plywood canoes, known as ʻōpelu canoes, which replaced Hawaiian-style dugout canoes. In turn, these canoes were gone by 1990, replaced by fiberglass boats. 1974. [Boone Morrison]

219

Takatu and his 500-pound Marlin at Miloli'i Boat Landing. *Above left: A cherished memory: Takatu displaying the enormous fish he took all by himself, from a fifteen-foot open skiff, on a hand line. The fish was too large to haul into the boat, so he towed the fish to shore. Takatu, a renowned fisherman, was later lost at sea. 1984. [Boone Morrison]*

Eugene Kaupiko at the Miloli'i Grocery. *Above right: This store has been a village fixture for decades. It belonged to the late Eugene Kaupiko and is now run by his son, Willy Kaupiko. It has changed little; only some of the brand names are different. 1981. [Boone Morrison]*

Plumeria Flowers. *Right: These children perched in a large plumeria tree to listen to Diana Aki and friends play music on her lānai. 1977. [Boone Morrison]*

Papa Jessie Sewing Net. *Above left: The late Papa Jessie was at least eighty years old when this photograph was taken. His eyesight was failing and he worked largely by feel, but his nets were still regarded as the best on the Kona coast. 1976. [Boone Morrison]*

Mr. Aki at Home. *Above right: At dusk, the late Benjamin Aki, a retired fisherman, would light a kerosene lamp and make a cup of coffee in his kitchen, the center of his home. 1976. [Boone Morrison]*

Diana Aki. *Far left: A photograph of a young Diana. She would go on to become a Na Hōkū- award-winning singer, a respected kupuna, and the guardian of the music of Miloli'i. 1983. [Boone Morrison]*

Sleeping Children. *Left: Several of Diana Aki's many children asleep on a pūne'e. The family enjoys the luxury of electric light—as long as the gasoline lasts. 1977. [Boone Morrison]*

HAWAI'I ISLAND LOOKING FORWARD

⊠⊠⊠⊠⊠⊠⊠⊠⊠⊠⊠⊠

Above left: After the 1960 tsunami badly damaged Hilo and its economy, the Big Island Chamber of Commerce was forced to explore new industries for the island. They turned to a team of astronomers who submitted proposals to NASA that outlined Mauna Kea's exceptional qualities as the highest point in the Pacific. The University of Hawai'i received a NASA grant and began its Institute for Astronomy, installing Mauna Kea's first large telescope, with an eighty-eight-inch aperture, in 1970. The complex now consists of thirteen telescopes employing more than five hundred people. Together they contribute nearly $60 million annually to the island's economy, nearly $92 million when adjusted for spillover effects. In 2013, a new thirty-meter telescope project received permission to build a telescope known as the TMT. It may one day trace objects that formed 13 billion years back in time. In 2015, when construction began, however, opposing parties brought construction to a halt in efforts to protect Mauna Kea's sacred and environmentally fragile nature. Efforts are under way to reconcile culture and science. [Kucera Design]

Above right: The windmills in North Kohala are a sign of the Big Island's future as a world leader in wind power energy. Plans for new wind farms are underway. 2009. [Kucera Design]

Look up into the night skies over the Big Island, and you will see the same stars that guided the ancient Polynesian navigators to Hawai'i.

The Hawaiians of old read those stars, gave them names, and drew essential sustaining knowledge from their presence and their movements. Gods lived in the heavens, and the summit of Mauna Kea was the home of the ancient deities, the sky father and the earth mother, who brought forth the Hawaiian people.

Now, on the scale of the twenty-first century, Mauna Kea is regarded simply as the highest mountain on the Big Island. Indeed, from its oceanic base at 3,280 fathoms to its topmost point in crystal-clear cold air at 13,796 feet above sea level, it is the highest mountain in the world, at 33,476 feet. The summit is the site of the biggest array of powerful telescopes on the globe, telescopes studying stars and galaxies and black holes scattered throughout the immensity of space.

At the peak of Mauna Kea, modern science and traditional Hawaiian culture converge on a single point—and it is a sharp, painful point, as witnessed in the difficult conversation around the Thirty-Meter-Telescope, which in 2015 encountered fierce opposition when its construction began. For science, the observatories are an inexhaustible source of knowledge—knowledge ever-expanding, ever-changing, reaching across billions of light years, infinite. For Hawaiian traditionalists, the sources of human knowledge are different—rooted in place, unchanging, eternal, sacred—and the observatories are a desecration.

There is another Big Island scientific observatory, this one on the rim of the caldera of Kīlauea, arguably the world's most continuously active volcano. Not far away is a hotel, serving tourists.

Both the observatory and the hotel exist in the domain of the goddess Pele. When Pele stamps her foot, the earth rumbles and quakes and heaves; Pele's moods are measured on the Richter scale. At her command, Kīlauea spews red-hot lava. Pele can take out subdivisions without drawing breath; she has done it in the past.

All of which is to say that on the Big Island many worlds co-exist. Some manifestations are not subject to scientific explanation. Every so often, at night, on a lonely winding stretch of Big Island back road, the figure of a woman will suddenly appear in the car headlights. Sometimes she is young and beautiful. Sometimes she is old and hideously ugly. She is Pele...

ELLISON S ONIZUKA (1946-1986)

Ellison S. Onizuka was the first Asian-American and the first Hawai'i resident to fly in the United States' manned space program. "Just" a coffee-country boy from mauka Kona, he was selected in 1978 as one of thirty-five final candidates out of more than eight thousand applicants to the NASA space program. In January, 1985, he flew on the space shuttle *Discovery*, a three-day classified Department of Defense mission. His second mission came on January 28, 1986, aboard the space shuttle *Challenger*. In a major malfunction after liftoff, the *Challenger* exploded, taking the lives of all seven space explorers on board. In Onizuka's honor, the astronomers' facilities on Mauna Kea at the 9,300-foot level have been renamed The Onizuka Center for International Astronomy. At the Kona International Airport, an interactive museum, the Astronaut Ellison S. Onizuka Space Center, offers children of all ages a history of the space program and a hands-on experience of educational exhibits. [NASA]

In 1933, Masamitsu Onizuka and his wife, Mitsue, opened the M. Onizuka Store in north Kona. It carried local necessities such as shoyu, Saloon Pilot crackers, rice, salted codfish, and candies, and was a popular and convenient stop for shopping. The store became more well known after their son, Ellison, became Hawai'i's first astronaut. Mrs. Onizuka continued to run the store after her husband's and son's deaths, until the day she died at the age of seventy-six in 1990. 1986. [Noel Black]

The lava flats of Pele cover thousands of acres. In the 1960s, American astronauts preparing for the first lunar landing trained on this terrain, the closest thing on earth to a moonscape. In 1986, an astronaut who was born and raised on the Big Island died in the *Challenger* disaster. At the 9,300-foot level of Mauna Kea is a scientific memorial in his name: the Onizuka Center for International Astronomy. At Kona International Airport, the tourist gateway to the Big Island, is an interactive museum, the Astronaut Ellison S. Onizuka Space Center. And now there is twenty-first-century talk of "space tourism" from a Hawai'i base.

Pele's lava flats are black and barren. The Big Island has lush forests too, where Hawaiians have always gone—and still go—to gather native medicinal plants. Kāhuna lapa'au, traditional healers of body and mind and spirit, still practice their arts. Other healers have different visions: in the mid-1990s, Dr. Earl Bakken, the inventor of the pacemaker, living in retirement on the Big Island, was moved to envision a center for healing where ancient Hawaiian medicine and modern technology could be brought together: high touch and high tech. At five-star resorts on the Kona Coast, one of the offerings at the hotel spas is a tourist version of lomilomi, the traditional Hawaiian massage.

High tech, high touch, high price—all these versions of how to attain health and enjoy it…and meanwhile, in the day-by-day world of the Big Island, in the towns, in the country, in the workplace, and in the cars that jam the highways, are scores of thousands of ordinary people who have serious worries about health care payments—and thousands who have no health care coverage at all.

This is the twenty-first century. In all kinds of ways, the Big Island is inextricably tied to the big world. And not just in regard to health care. Employment. Market competitiveness. Population growth. Land use. Infrastructure. Sustainability. Diversity. Food. Water. Energy. Invasive alien species. Natural disasters. Global warming. All these major big-world issues affect the Big Island, and Hawai'i generally, as they do every other place on earth.

On the Big Island, the rate of change and the directions of change make life more complex than it has ever been. Sugar is gone, tourism is fickle—no more banking on a single industry. Can other things take up the economic slack? Diversified agriculture? In the state of Hawai'i there are about fifty-five hundred farms; more than thirty-three thousand are on the Big Island. What about getting off fossil fuels? The Big Island has possibilities and startups in biofuels, wind farms, solar energy, geothermal and oceanic thermal energy—but nothing like self-sufficiency in sight.

And there is nothing like social stability. Traditional Hawaiian culture survives, and in some respects thrives, but not in the mainstream. The old plantation-town mixed plate of intermingled immigrant cultures is a thing of the past. People do not stay in one place the way they used to. Emigration is big on the Big Island.

Immigration is big too, mostly from the Mainland—and with it has come a new kind of society, grafted onto old places, displacing old ways: the gated community. So what is community anymore?

Almost every week on the Big Island there is a celebration, a commemoration, a festival, or a pageant that honors a tradition. Which of these will continue? Which will pass and be forgotten?

Will the past give strength to face the future? In a *Big Island Journey* fifty years from now, where will the tracks of time have led? What visions will the pictures show, what stories will the words tell? The book of Big Island life is never closed....

The 2006 earthquake was a reminder of the vulnerability of the Big Island to the forces of Mother Nature. Fortunately, the overall damage was not severe. The Big Island remains an isolated mass of land in the cradle of the world's biggest ocean, subject to lava flows that destroy homes and property, hurricanes, tsunamis, and earthquakes. 2006. [Kucera Design]

Today, the Big Island looks back to a past rich in history. Reminders are everywhere—in petroglyphs, heiau, old churches, abandoned sugar mills, old towns, and commemorations such as the Kamehameha Day Celebration which is attended by all, regardless of heritage. The island also looks to the future as it seeks new ways to sustain itself economically, whether from astronomy, wind power, growing exotic produce, or expanding cultural tourism. 2009. [Kucera Design]

GLOSSARY OF HAWAIIAN WORDS AND PLACE NAMES

ahupua'a:
land of a community usually extending from the uplands to the ocean. Such a division included fishing settlements, forests, and farm lands.

'āina:
land.

ali'i:
chief. Also, royalty.

'auwai:
ditch or canal.

bango number:
identification number and symbol stamped on copper tag given to immigration laborers.

hala:
pandanus tree.

hana:
work, labor.

hānai:
foster or adopted child.

haole:
foreigner; Caucasian.

heiau:
religious place, shrine, temple.

'ili:
land section within an ahupua'a, often prime agricultural land.

'iliahi:
Hawaiian sandalwood.

kahuna:
expert in a specific subject, priest.

kālaimoku:
advisor, prime minister.

kalo:
taro, one of the plants brought by Hawai'i's first settlers, valued for its starchy root.

kapa:
bark cloth traditionally made from paper mulberry or mamaki trees.

kapu:
taboo, prohibition.

kaukau:
food.

kauwā:
outcast.

keiki:
child, offspring.

kīpuka:
calm place in a high sea, an opening in a forest; also, a clear place or oasis within a lava bed, often filled with vegetation.

kō:
sugarcane.

ko'olau:
windward side of the Hawaiian islands.

kona:
leeward side of the Hawaiian islands; a leeward wind.

konohiki:
headman of an ahupua'a (local official), or head man working for a king (royal official).

kula:
open country; pasture; specifically dryland areas of shrub and grass or dryland farming areas.

kuleana:
lands awarded to commoners during the Mahele in the late 1840s, usually house plots and farm parcels.

kupuna:
grandparent, ancestor.

lo'i:
irrigated field, usually for taro.

luakini:
Hawaiian temple where human sacrifices were offered.

lū'au:
current term for Hawaiian feast. The name comes from a dish of young taro tops and coconut cream often served at feasts. The older term for feast is 'aha'āina.

luna:
boss, foreman.

Mahele:
government program of the late 1840s, which replaced the traditional feudal land tenure with Western-style fee simple tenure. The land was divided between the king, chiefs, and commoners, with the commoners getting by far the smallest share.

maka'āinana:
in traditional Hawaiian culture, a commoner, as opposed to an ali'i, or chief.

Makahiki:
a traditional Hawaiian festival period that lasted from the middle of October through January. During this time, Lono, the god of farmers, took precedence over Kū, the war god; warfare ceased and the people could engage in games and sports.

makai:
toward the ocean.

mana:
divine or spiritual power, life force.

mauka:
toward the mountain.

menehune:
a legendary race of small people said to live up in the hills and to sometimes help chiefs build fishponds and heiau.

'ohana:
family, extended family.

'ōkolehau:
liquor distilled from the ti root.

pā'ina:
small dinner party or meal.

pali:
slope, cliff, mountain side.

pau:
finished, all done.

pili:
native grass used for thatching.

poi:
cooked taro corms pounded into a paste and thinned with water.

pu'u:
small hill or cinder cone.

pu'uhonua:
place of refuge.

wai:
water, liquid (other than sea water).

Place Names

Hāmākua:
District in northeast Hawai'i. Meaning not defined.

Hilo:
District, ancient surfing area, and town in east Hawai'i. Perhaps named for the first night of the new moon.

Hualālai:
Volcano in North Kona. It last erupted in 1801; meaning not defined.

Kailua:
Village, bay, and ancient surfing area in Kona. The name means "two seas" or, in this case, "two currents."

Ka'ū:
District and desert in south Hawai'i; an ancient name found with slight variations elsewhere in Polynesia.

Kawaihae:
Village and bay in leeward Kohala. The name means "water of wrath." It is said that people fought bitterly for water from the one available pool.

Kīlauea:
Hawai'i's most active volcano, on the slopes of Mauna Loa in Puna. Name can be loosely translated as "spewing, spreading."

Kohala:
District in northwest Hawai'i.

| | Meaning not defined. | | for the Hawaiian long spear. | Waipiʻo: | Large valley in Hāmākua. The name means "curved water" and possibly refers to its many waterfalls. |

Kona: Leeward district in west Hawaiʻi, named for the leeward winds.

Laupāhoehoe: Land section and village in Hāmākua in east Hawaiʻi. The name means "smooth lava leaf."

Mauna Kea: Highest mountain in Hawaiʻi; often snowcapped. The name means "White Mountain."

Mauna Loa: Active volcano; possibly the largest volcanic mass in the Pacific. Its name means "Long Mountain."

Pololū: Large valley in Kohala, named

Puna: District in southeast Hawaiʻi. The meaning of the name is unclear; the area was possibly named for a spring.

Waikoloa: Land section at Puakō and Waikiʻi, west Hawaiʻi. The name means "duck water."

Waimea: Village and land division in upcountry Kohala, named for the reddish water that used to flow through with eroded red soil.

BIBLIOGRAPHY

Barrot, Théodore Adolphe. *Unless Haste Is Made.* Honolulu: Press Pacifica, 1978.

Bates, George W. *Sandwich Island Notes by a Haole.* New York: Harper & Brothers, 1854.

Beechert, Edward D. *Working in Hawaii: A Labor History.* Honolulu: University of Hawaiʻi Press, 1985.

Bergin, Dr. Billy. *Loyal to the Land, The Legendary Parker Ranch, 750–1950.* Honolulu: University of Hawaiʻi Press, 2004.

Bird, Isabella L. *Six Months in the Sandwich Islands: Among Hawaiʻi's Palm Groves, Coral Reefs, and Volcanoes.* Honolulu: Mutual Publishing, 1998.

Blickhahn, Harry Miller. *Uncle George of Kilauea, The Story of George Lycurgus.* Volcano: Volcano House, Hawaiʻi National Park, 1961.

Bouvet, P. Ernest *The Final Harvest: The Hamakua Sugar Company, 1869–1994.* Hong Kong: P. E. Bouvet, 2001.

Brennan, Joseph. *The Parker Ranch of Hawaiʻi: The Saga of a Ranch and a Dynasty.* Honolulu: Mutual Publishing, 1974.

Burchardt, Joan. *Little Britain, Letters from the Hawaiian Kingdom.* United Kingdom: Joan Burchardt, 2002.

Cahil, Emmett. *The Life and Times of John Young.* Honolulu: Island Heritage, 1999.

Char, Tin-Yuke and Jane Char Wai. *Chinese Historic Sites and Pioneer Families of the Island of Hawaii.* Honolulu: University of Hawaiʻi Press, 1983.

Clark, John R. K. *Beaches of the Big Island.* Honolulu: University of Hawaiʻi Press, 1985.

Condé, J. C. Narrow *Gauge in a Kingdom: The Hawaiian Railroad Company, 1878-1897.* Felton, California: Glenwood Publishing, 1971.

————*Sugar Trains: Narrow Gauge Rails of Hawaii.* Felton, California: Glenwood Publishing, 1973.

Cordy, Ross. *Exalted Sits the Chief.* Honolulu: Mutual Publishing, 2000.

Cowan-Smith Virginia; Stone, Bonnie. *Aloha Cowboy.* Honolulu: University of Hawaiʻi Press, 1988.

Craighill, E.S. and Mary Kawena Pukui. *The Polynesian Family System in Kaʻu, Hawaiʻi.* Honolulu: Mutual Publishing, 1998.

Daws, Gavan. *Shoal of Time: A History of the Hawaiian Islands.* New York, Macmillan, 1968.

Desha, Stephen L. *Kamehameha and his Warrior Kekūhaupiʻo.* Honolulu: Kamehameha Schools Press, 2000.

Dorrance, William H. and Francis S. Morgan. *Sugar Islands, The 165-Year Story of Sugar in Hawaii.* Honolulu: Mutual Publishing, 2000.

Dudley, Walt and Scott C. S. Stone. *The Tsunami of 1946 and 1960 and the Devastation of Hilo Town.* Hilo: Pacific Tsunami Museum, 2000.

Ellis, William. *Journal of William Ellis, A Narrative of an 1823 Tour Through Hawaiʻi with Remarks on the History, Traditions, Manners, Customs and Language of the Inhabitants of the Sandwich Islands.* Honolulu: Mutual Publishing, 2004.

Feher, Joseph. *Hawaii: A Pictorial History.* Honolulu: Bishop Museum Press, 1969.

BIBLIOGRAPHY (CONTINUED)

Grant, Glen and Bennett Hymer. *Hawai'i Looking Back: An Illustrated History of the Islands.* Honolulu: Mutual Publishing, 2000.

Grant, Glen. *Hawai'i the Big Island: A Visit to a Realm of Beauty, History and Fire.* Honolulu: Mutual Publishing, 1988.

Greenwell, James M. *One to Eighty-One ... My Personal Story.* Hilo: James M. Greenwell, 1997.

Kamakau, Samuel M. *Ka Poe Kahiko: The People of Old.* Honolulu: Bishop Museum Press, 1964.

Kane, Herb Kawainui. *Ancient Hawai'i.* Captain Cook, Hawai'i: The Kawainui Press, 1997.

———*Voyagers.* Bellevue, Washington: WhaleSong, Incorporated, 1991.

Kelly, Marion, et al. *Hilo Bay: A Chronological History.* Honolulu: Bernice P. Bishop Museum, 1981.

Kimura, Yukiko. *Issei, Japanese Immigrants in Hawaii.* Honolulu: University of Hawai'i Press, 1988.

Kinro, Gerald Y. *A Cup of Aloha: The Kona Coffee Epic.* Honolulu: University of Hawaii Press, 2003.

Kona Historical Society. *A Guide to Old Kona.* Kailua-Kona: Kona Historical Society, 1998.

Kotani, Roland. *The Japanese in Hawaii: A Century of Struggle.* Honolulu: The Hawaii Hochi, Ltd., 1985.

Kurisu, Yasushi "Scotch." *Sugar Town: Hawaii Plantation Days Remembered.* Honolulu: Watermark Publishing, 1995.

Kwiatkowski, P.F. *Na Ki'i Pohaku: A Hawaiian Petroglyph Primer.* Honolulu: Ku Pa'a Incorporated, 1991.

Lee, Dr. Samuel S. O. and 75th Anniversary of Korean Immigration Committee. *75th Anniversary of Korean Immigration to Hawaii, 1903-1978.* Honolulu: 75th Anniversary of Korean Immigration Committee, 1978.

Lind, Andrew W. *Hawaii's People.* Honolulu: University Press of Hawai'i, 1955.

Lyman, Sarah. *Sarah Joiner Lyman of Hawai'i—Her Own Story.* Hilo: Lyman House Memorial Museum, 1970.

Mauna Lani Resort. *View Into the Past: Mauna Lani Resort at Kalāhuipua'a.* Kohala: Mauna Lani Resort, 2003.

Moore, Susanna. *I Myself Have Seen It: The Myth of Hawaii.* Washington, D.C.: National Geographic Society, 2003.

Murray-Oliver, Anthony. *Captain Cook's Hawai'i: As Seen By His Artists.* Wellington, New Zealand: Milwood Press,1975.

Oaks, Robert F. *Hawaii: A History of the Big Island.* Charleston, SC: Arcadia Publishing, 2003.

Ogawa, Dennis M. et al. *Ellison S. Onizuka: A Remembrance.* Honolulu: Mutual Publishing/ Signature Publishing, 1986.

Okimoto, Ken. *Exploring the Hāmākua Coast: A Pictorial Guide to the Plantation Era.* Honolulu: Watermark Publishing, 2002.

Piercy, LaRue W. *Big Island History Makers.* Honolulu: Mutual Publishing, 1990.

Puakō Historical Society. *Puakō: An Affectionate History.* Vancouver, B.C.: Creative Connections Publishing, 2000.

Pukui, Mary Kawena, et al. *Place Names of Hawai'i.* Honolulu: University of Hawai'i Press, 1974.

Sahlins, Marshall. *How "Natives" think: About Captain Cook, For Example.* Chicago: University of Chicago Press, 1995.

Schmitt, Robert C. *Historical Statistics of Hawaii.* Honolulu: The University Press of Hawai'i, 1977.

Schweitzer, Sophia V. *Kohala 'Āina: A History of North Kohala.* Honolulu: Mutual Publishing, 2003.

Stannard, David E. *Before the Horror: The Population of Hawai'i on the Eve of Western Contact.* Honolulu: University of Hawai'i Press. 1989.

Takaki, Ronald. *Pau Hana: Plantation Life and Labor in Hawaii.* Honolulu: University of Hawai'i Press, 1983.

Thurston, Lucy G. *Life and Times, of Mrs. Lucy G. Thurston.* Honolulu: The Friend, 1934.

Twain, Mark. *Mark Twain's Letters From Hawaii,* edited by A. Grove Day. Honolulu: University Press of Hawaii, 1966.

Vaughan, Palani. *Na Leo i ka Makani: Voices on the Wind.* Honolulu: Mutual Publishing, 1987.

Wells, Edwin Dwight. *Memoirs of Henry Obookiah and Supplement.* Los Angeles: Reprinted from 1818 original by D.B. Eberhart, 1956.

Whitney Henry M. *The Hawaiian Guide Book for Travelers.* Honolulu: H.M. Whitney, 1875.

Wilcox, Carol. *Sugar Water: Hawaii's Plantation Ditches.* Honolulu: University of Hawai'i Press, 1996.

Website Resources:

Bakken, Earl. *Chronology of Kiholo and Pu'awa'awa'a.* http:// www.earlbakken.com/text. phtml?m=153.

Greene, Linda Wedel, et al. *A Cultural History of Three Traditional Hawaiian Sites on the West Coast of Hawai'i Island.* Denver Service Center: United States Department of the Interior National Park Service, 1993. http://www.cr.nps.gov/history/online _books/ kona/history.htm. U.S. Geological Survey Hawaiian Volcano Observatory. http:// hvo.wr.usgs.gov.

Steiger, Walter. *Origins of Astronomy in Hawai'i.* http://www.ifa. hawaii.edu.

Honolulu Advertiser: Koreans in Hawaii: 100 Years of Dreams, Accomplishments. Honolulu: December 2003. http://www.the.honoluluadvertiser.com/specials/ korean100/.

Hawaiian Homes Land specifics: http://state.hi.us/dhhl

CHRONOLOGY

(Text in bold indicates major Kingdom-, Territory-, and statewide events)

	1 million years ago The Big Island surfaces.
300 A.D.	Voyagers from the Marquesas in the South Pacific arrive.
ca. 1300s	Other voyagers settle, among them the priest Pa'ao and his chief Pili.
ca. 1753	Birth of Kamehameha, at Kokoiki near Mo'okini Heiau.
1779	Captain Cook anchors in Kealakekua Bay and is killed on February 14.
1790	John Young and Isaac Davis become Kamehameha's advisors.
1790	Kīlauea erupts and kills about four hundred people.
1791	Kamehameha gains supremacy over the Big Island.
1794	George Vancouver brings the first cattle to Kealakekua Bay.
1800–1801	Hualālai erupts.
1803	Richard Cleveland brings the first horses to Kawaihae.
1810	Kamehameha I has unified all islands under his rule.
1812	Kamehameha returns to the Big Island to live in Kailua.
1819	Death of Kamehameha in Kailua.
1819	Ka'ahumanu and Liholiho break the kapu; the old religion collapses.
1820	The *Thaddeus* with the first Protestant missionaries arrives in Kailua.
1823	William Ellis visits all districts of the Big Island.
Early 1800s	Merchants and whalers introduce foreign goods and cash.
1828	Samuel Ruggles plants coffee in South Kona.
1829	Joseph Goodrich builds the island's first sugar mill.
1830s	Spanish-Mexican vaqueros arrive to accelerate a ranching industry.
1840	The Catholic mission holds its first mass at Kailua.
1846	A grass hut at Kīlauea debuts as Hawai'i's first tourist hotel.
1847	John Palmer Parker starts Parker Ranch.
1848	The Mahele begins and introduces private land ownership.
1852	Chinese laborers, the first sugar immigrant group, start to arrive.
1859	Mauna Loa erupts.
1866	Mark Twain tours the Big Island.
1868	A 7.9 earthquake destroys large parts of Hilo, Puna, and Ka'ū.
1871	June 11 becomes the day to celebrate Kamehameha I and his legacy.
1876	Reciprocity Treaty ends American tariffs on sugar exports.
1879	William H. Purvis plants macadamia nuts in Hāmākua.
1877	Start of Portuguese immigration.
1881	Samuel G. Wilder starts work on the Big Island's first railroad.
1881	Mauna Loa erupts and threatens Hilo; Princess Ruth implores Pele.
1883	The statue of Kamehameha I comes to Kohala
1884	The Big Island counts more than thirty sugar plantations.
Early 1880s	Arrival of contract laborers from Scotland, Scandinavia, and Germany.
1885	Japanese immigration starts in earnest.
1893	Overthrow of Hawaiian monarchy.
1899	Benjamin F. Dillingham starts work on a railroad in Hilo.
1900	Start of Puerto Rican immigration.
1900	Hawai'i becomes a Territory of the United States
1903	Start of Korean immigration.
1906	Start of Filipino immigration.
1906	The Kohala Ditch opens.

1919	Hawaiian Homes Commission Act sets lands aside for Hawaiians.
1928	The Kona Inn opens in Kailua.
1929	Inter-Island Airways introduces inter-island commercial airplanes.
1939	Development for an airport at Hilo begins.
1941	Attack on Pearl Harbor and beginning of American involvement in World War II.
1946	A tsunami hits Laupāhoehoe and Hilo Bay and kills 120.
1946	First union contracts are signed and change old sugar ways.
1950	Mauna Loa erupts and erases a fishing village.
1953	Hilo opens a new airport terminal.
1959	Kīlauea erupts with lava fountains.
1959	Hawai'i gains statehood on March 11.
1959	Hawaiian International Billfish Tournament makes its debut.
1960	A tsunami hits Hilo Bay and kills sixty-one.
1963	The first Merrie Monarch Festival celebrates hula and Hawaiian culture.
1965	Mauna Kea Beach Hotel opens in Kohala.
1967	Commercial direct flights between the mainland and Hilo begin.
1970	University of Hawai'i installs Mauna Kea's first telescope.
1970	Keāhole Airport replaces the old Kona airport in Kailua-Kona.
1976	*Hokule'a* sails to Tahiti and accelerates the Hawaiian Renaissance.
1981	The Ironman Triathlon comes to Kailua.
1983	Kīlauea starts a continuing eruption at its east rift zone.
1983	United Airlines begins direct flights to Keāhole Airport.
1986	The Big Island mourns astronaut Ellison Onizuka, who was lost on the space shuttle *Challenger*.
1984	Mauna Loa erupts and threatens Hilo.
1987	Hilo ceases its Mainland flights.
1992	Puna Geothermal Venture starts commercial operations.
1993	Bill Clinton signs a Bill of Apology to Native Hawaiians.
1995	Maiden voyage of the *Makali'i*, a double-hulled voyaging canoe.
1996	Sugar operations on The Big Island end with final closure in Ka'ū.
1996	Kona begins direct flights connecting to Japan.
1990s	The Big island enters a real estate boom.
2000	Total population of the Big Island reaches 148,677.
2005	A record-breaking year for Hawai'i's visitor industry brings over 1.5 million people to the Big Island.
2006	A magnitude 6.7 earthquake, its epicenter in Kona, jolts Big Islanders out of bed on the morning of October 15. A second earthquake, magnitude 6.0, strikes seven minutes later.
2011	A tsunami spawned by an 8.9 magnitude earthquake in Japan hits all Hawai'i's shorelines, causing no fatalities but strongly impacting the Big Island's Kona Coast.
2014	Hurricane Iselle makes landfall on the Big Island of Hawai'i as the strongest tropical cyclone in recorded history.
2014	Lava flowing from a vent near Pāhoa threatens the town, causing businesses to close and students to switch schools, while threatening the area's main highway. In early 2015, the flow's front ceases to advance and stops posing an immediate threat.
2015	Activists block construction of Mauna Kea's 14th telescope, seeking greater cultural and environmental protection for the mountain.

INDEX

CONTRIBUTING PHOTOGRAPHERS AND ARTISTS

The images in *Big Island Journey* are by ship artists, daguerreotypists, nineteenth-century cameramen, and modern-day photographers and illustrators. The faces, places, and events of yesteryear that have made this work possible appear in their illustrations and photographs. The following have contributed visual material.

Photographers / Artists: Herb Kāne • Kucera Design Ski Kwiatkowski • Jack and Mary Ann Lynch Boone Morrison • Douglas Peebles • Franco Salmoiraghi • David Weiss • Richard Otaki

Archives: Baker-Van Dyke Collection • Bishop Museum • Hawai'i State Archives • Hawaiian Mission Children's Society • Hawaiian Historical Society • Kona Historical Society • Library of Congress • Lyman House Memorial Museum • NASA • Pacific War Memorial Association • Don Severson Collection • State Library of New South Wales

Families and Individuals: Cabatu Family • Ishii Family • Nakahara Family • Otaki Family • Sugino Family • Yugawa Family • Noel Black • Alex Higdon • Hal Yamamoto

MAJOR CONTRIBUTORS

Bennett Hymer's passion for vintage photographs has led him to either produce or co-author several "old picture" books including *Hawaiian Yesterdays, Hawaiian Journey, Hawai'i Looking Back, Waikiki Yesteryear,* and *Voices on the Wind.* He is currently the head of Mutual Publishing.

Herb Kawainui Kane is an artist-historian and author with special interest in Hawai'i and the South Pacific. He was raised in Waipi'o Valley and Hilo, Hawai'i, and Wisconsin. He holds a masters degree from the Art Institute of Chicago and the University of Chicago. He currently resides in rural South Kona on the island of Hawai'i. His books include *Pele, Goddess of Hawaii's Volcanoes; Voyagers* which includes 140 of his works in color; and *Ancient Hawai'i.* His research on Polynesian canoes and voyaging led to his participation as general designer and builder of the sailing canoe *Hōkūle'a,* which he served as its first captain.

Kucera Design is a prominent, award-winning graphic design and multimedia company based on the island of Hawai'i. Clark and Wendy Kucera's endeavors encompass a broad range of subject matter with an affinity for cultural events and nature in its purest form. Over twenty-years, they have captured the Big Island in a photojournalistic style.

Mary Ann (Bruchac) Lynch, noted American photographer, writer, filmmaker, and curator, began her photography and film career in Honolulu in the 1970s. She has received many honors and awards, published, and been a guest artist at colleges and universities from New York to the far Pacific. Her work appears in the collections of the Center for Creative Photography, the Hawai'i State Art Museum, and the International Center for Photography (ICP). She lives in upstate New York with her husband Jack.

Boone Morrison is an architect, photographer, film maker, teacher, and arts entrepreneur. His work is represented in many public, institutional, and private collections. In 1986,

Summit Press published his book *Images of the Hula.* Since 1971 he has maintained his home and studio in Volcano Village on the Big Island, where he continues to photograph. He is now working to bring his Miloli'i images and stories to publication.

Richard Otaki owned and operated Ace Photo Studio on Waiānuenue Avenue in Hilo from 1946 to 1984. Prior to Ace Photo Studio, he was a photographer with the Army while stationed at Fort Shafter. Over thirty-eight years, he has taken thousands of photographs of daily life in Hilo town, including family portraits, weddings, funerals, graduation and school yearbook pictures, and historic events such as the volcanic eruptions and the 1946 and 1960 tsunamis. He now raises orchids in his home in Hilo.

Franco Salmoiraghi came to Hawai'i in 1968 to teach photography at the University of Hawai'i-Mānoa Art Department. He lived on the Big Island for nearly twelve years and continues to visit there to photograph. His work is published in local and international books and magazines. Documentary photography is his main interest, and he has explored historical places and worked on many extensive documentary projects, including the island of Kaho'olawe; Waipi'o Valley; and the waning sugar industry—"The Last Days of Sugar in Hawai'i." His intent is to photograph people and the landscape with reverence and dignity, clearly and directly, so that their essence and spirit are illuminated.

Sophia V. Schweitzer lives and works in North Kohala on Hawai'i Island. Born and raised in the Netherlands, she developed a deep interest in the unsettling history of the Hawaiian Islands when she arrived here in 1988. In 2004, her book in collaboration with Michael S. Gomes, *Kohala 'Āina, a History of North Kohala,* won a Kahili for the Literary Arts and was chosen Best-of-Show in the statewide Keep-It-Hawai'i awards. As a freelance writer, she focuses on energy and environment. (www.sophiavschweitzer.com)